MY BLUE DEVIL HAS WINGS

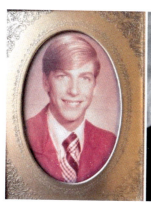  

DEDICATION

For my husband, Bob, who is always there for me and our children. He supported and encouraged me to be a facilitator for GriefShare and other ministries at Saint Ambrose Parish.

For Brent and Brittany, who lost a brother and then faced many challenges after their dad's stroke. For always being willing to lend a hand and take care of their dad; for being supportive, uplifting and encouraging when life turns upside down.

For my family, friends, Saint Ambrose Parish, Brunswick community, and surrounding cities that have come together to support us through this difficult time in our life.

For Blake, who always brought so much joy and laughter into my life. I will always treasure his bear hugs, jokes and his BIG personality, as well as his smile that lights up every room. Until we meet again in God's loving arms...

For all the loved ones that have gone before us; Blake Bartchak, Jeff Chaya, Kevin Fox, Lexi Poerner, Uncle Jimmy, Grandma Boots, Papa, Debby and Grammy.

ACKNOWLEDGEMENT

The reason I am writing this book is because God has helped me through the tragedies in my life and He has given me hope. Here is my story.

God inspired me and gave me the courage to write this book. The force behind this book was my beautiful son, Blake, with his BIG personality, and his love for life. His smile and his laughter lit up the room. His spirit and ability to be fully present each day inspired me to share my story.

I don't know how I would have made it through this journey without God and the love and support of family, friends, Brunswick community, surrounding cities, and Saint Ambrose Parish. I also want to thank all the individuals that had the opportunity to walk side by side with me on this journey when I was a facilitator with GriefShare, and when I was a Stephen Minister. Thank you for opening your heart and sharing your story of your loved one. God brought us together to walk side by side and not alone.

I want to thank my daughter, Brittany, for always encouraging me to write my story. After being a guest speaker at Brunswick High School at a Fellowship Christian Athletes (FCA) meeting, Brittany told me that I should finish writing my book. She said I could reach more people and help others through their grief.

I want to thank Audiobook Publishing Services for taking the time to listen to my story, and for believing that I had a story to share. During this process they guided me to bring my story alive with Audiobooks. They also were highly informative about how to market my book and how to get my story out to others that are grieving and going through challenges.

I want to thank Jake Ambrose for taking the time to pull all of Blake's football highlights together in a short time for Audiobook Publishing Services. Sending a copy to our family was priceless.

I want to thank Barb Ortiz for helping me edit my story. We walked together on this journey after the loss of her beautiful daughter, and a few years later, the loss of her husband. We are two mothers that have leaned on each other and have grown closer to God through our losses. I know that God brought us together to bring this book alive and to help others that are grieving a loved one. What I have learned from being a grief facilitator is that we all have a story to share, and when you walk with others and share your heart, you grow closer to God. I cannot thank Barb enough for walking with me on this journey and for helping me bring the story of my son, Blake alive through "My Blue Devil has Wings."

I want to thank my friend, Karen M. Howell for reading my story. It was through her difficult questions that I realized I needed to go back and share my feelings of grief. I kept those feelings hidden because I was afraid to expose that grief; I didn't want others to think that I didn't have faith. It was during this time that I felt all the grief tucked away deep in my soul that I was able to write about my feelings and emotions through the story. I want to thank Karen for reading my story and letting me know I had to face my grief instead of going around it.

TABLE OF CONTENTS

DEDICATION 3

ACKNOWLEDGEMENT 4

INTRODUCTION 8

PART I 9

CHAPTER 1: MY BLUE DEVIL HAS WINGS 9

CHAPTER 2: IT'S NOT GOOD-BYE IT'S SEE YOU LATER . 19

CHAPTER 3: A COMMUNITY COMING TOGETHER 41

CHAPTER 4: FIRST BIRTHDAY IN HEAVEN 48

CHAPTER 5: SENIOR YEAR FOOTBALL SEASON
WITHOUT BLAKE 53

CHAPTER 6: FIRST HOLIDAY WITH BLAKE IN HEAVEN 57

CHAPTER 7: CHRISTMAS MIRACLE 60

CHAPTER 8: UNFORGETTABLE MIRACLES 78

CHAPTER 9: THE YEAR ANNIVERSARY 83

PART II 93

CHAPTER 10: MORE TRAGEDY 93

CHAPTER 11: HEALING 110

CHAPTER 12: BLESSINGS IN DISGUISE 119

CHAPTER 13: GIFTS 126

CHAPTER 14: SIGNS 130

CHAPTER 15: PRAYER 143

CHAPTER 16: GOD'S LIGHT 167

CHAPTER 17: DOES GOD PREPARE YOU FOR THE
TOUGH DAYS TO COME? 175

CHAPTER 18: SURRENDERING OVER TO GOD 186

CHAPTER 19: CHOICES 188

CHAPTER 20: FEAR..193

CHAPTER 21: FAITH & HOPE..............................200

CHAPTER 22: SUFFERING 207

CHAPTER 23: TRUST 210

CHAPTER 24: JOY 213

CHAPTER 25: PURPOSE 217

CHAPTER 26: WHAT IS LOVE? 220

CHAPTER 27: BELIEVE....................................... 232

CHAPTER 28: IN THE ARMS OF HIS HEAVENLY
FATHER.. 246

APPENDIX 1 256

APPENDIX 2... 258

APPENDIX 3.. 259

APPENDIX 4... 260

APPENDIX 5... 261

APPENDIX 6... 262

REFERENCES... 263

SCRIPTURE REFERENCES.............................. 266

REVIEWS 267

INTRODUCTION

As I reflect on my life, I realize that I have gone through three tragedies. God has affected me differently each time.

When my Uncle Jimmy passed away from suicide, I was in the 7th grade. I felt angry and alone - I was very mad at God.

When my son Blake passed away in a car accident, I felt God was with me - I had trust in God.

When my husband Bob had a stroke and almost died, I had to accept what was happening and give it all over to God. I prayed, "Not my will, but your will be done."

We all have choices in life, and we decide on how we handle each situation as it comes into our lives.

John 3:16 NIV
"For God so loved the world that he gave his one and only Son, that whoever believes in him shall not perish but have eternal life."

1 Thessalonians 5:16-18 NIV
"Rejoice always, pray continually, give thanks in all circumstances. for this is God's will for you in Christ Jesus."

Romans 5:3-5 ESV
"Not only that, but we rejoice in our sufferings, knowing that suffering produces endurance, and endurance produces character and character produces hope, and hope does not put us to shame, because God's love has been poured into our hearts through the Holy Spirit who has been given to us."

****

Note: Some of the names in this book have been changed to respect the privacy of certain individuals.

PART I

CHAPTER 1:
MY BLUE DEVIL HAS WINGS

It was June 3, 2012, and Blake was lying on the couch watching *Saving Private Ryan* [1] as Brittany and I were leaving to go to Brittany's dance recital. Bob was at a night at the races as he worked for a fundraiser company on Friday and Saturday nights.

That evening, I helped in the back because I had watched her perform the night before. Brittany dances at Dancexcel. Every year, we go out to dinner with all the dance moms and our daughters, but for some reason, this year everything fell through. Brittany and I decided to just go home. When we pulled into the driveway, we saw Blake and his friends in the front yard goofing around. Brittany called her dad because Blake had friends over. The rule was you could have guy friends over, but girls were not allowed over if we were gone for the night. This night, we were both gone. Sisterly love; always trying to get her older brother in trouble. She reported, "Hey Dad, do you know what your son Blake is doing?" "Yes, I do, Brittany, he is at home, why?" "Do you know that girls are over?" "Yes, I do, Brittany." Brittany looked at me with shrugged shoulders and said, "Blake's not in trouble, but he should be."

Brittany and I went into the house to make some dinner. We were starving. It was late, it was about 10:00 at night, and it was a very long night, so we decided to make grilled cheese. This is one of Blake's favorite meals that he prepares. He always makes it the best as he adds so much cheese.

As we sat down to eat, Brittany and I reminisced about the evening. Then, suddenly, Blake started banging on the back window. I jumped up so high that I almost fell out of my seat! With a great big smile, larger than life, he laughed, pointed his finger at me with his silly Blake grin, and said, "I gotcha." I started laughing because he always had a way to "*get* me." I opened the screen door and asked, "So what are you guys doing?" "We are going to walk Jeff home." Jeff and Kevin had graduation the next day, and they needed to get to bed. I agreed, "Okay, see you soon, and be careful."

It was almost midnight, and Blake wasn't home yet. This is not like him. He always made curfews. I went upstairs to tell Bob. "Oh, Terri, it's not even midnight. I'm sure he will be home soon. After all, he was just walking Jeff home, and that was only an hour ago," Bob said. Time went by, and at 12:30 a.m. Bob texted Blake, with no answer. At 12:45, he texted him again, and no answer. At 1:00 a.m., he had Brent text him, but no answer. Bob was getting pissed off. He texted him again. "Blake, if you don't pick up your phone, your phone is mine." Still no answer. So, shortly after 1:00 a.m., Bob went out to look for him.

Brent called the Chayas, and Jeff wasn't home either. I was pacing back and forth. I couldn't even breathe. What is wrong? This is not like him. Why isn't he texting us back? I just kept pacing from the kitchen to the dining room and to the front room, going in circles from room to room. I would look out the front room window, then I would walk into the dining room, and look out that window. I just kept watching the porch light flicker. No sign of Blake anywhere. Come on, Blake, just come up the driveway. Please, God, just have him come up that driveway.

I would look out at each window as I passed by. Come on, Blake, where are you? I just want to hear our garage door opening and Blake coming through the back door. Pacing back and forth through the house, crying, I was barely able to breathe. I whispered lightly to myself, where are you, Blake? Please just come home.

I started pacing again, and I went back into the kitchen. I turned on the back light, hoping to see him. I opened the screen door and looked out again. I wanted to scream, "Blake, where are you? It's time to come home, and it's after 1:30 a.m." No sign of Blake anywhere. Where is he? Where could he be?

Bob came home about 1:45 a.m. "I looked everywhere for him, and I could not find him." We both went upstairs. I lay in bed clutching to my covers, hoping he would walk through the door. Bob was pacing back and forth in our bedroom, texting him repeatedly. We were both worried, my heart was racing. I knew this wasn't good. I could feel the tension in my whole body, and I was shaken to the core. Bob was starting to get mad as he was pacing back and forth in our bedroom, he was starting to lose it. I was also starting to lose control and kept praying God just be with him. Just have him come home and be with us. Bob continued pacing and he was starting to swear. The tension was growing. When I looked at Bob, I saw a fear come over him. I kept telling him, "It's going to be okay." "Terri, this is not okay. Something is wrong. I feel something is terribly wrong."

We heard a car coming down the street. Bob murmured, "Terri, I don't think this is good." Before he could even say the words out loud, I ran down the hallway and flew down the stairs. With six stairs left, I just jumped to the

10

hallway of our house and opened the front door. A police car was pulling up. I stepped onto the patio, skipped the steps, and ran for the driveway. The police officers were getting out of their cars. I ran to them, and I frantically asked, "Do you have Blake? Where is my son? He is such a great kid, and he has never been in trouble before." The officer said, "Is your husband home?" I answered, "Yes." "Well, let's go inside."

Bob was standing in the hallway with the front door open. I will never forget the look in his eyes. Bob looked scared and distraught, and his eyes were filling with tears. He knew something wasn't right, and so did I. Both officers came into the house. They both took off their hats and stood at attention, with their hats behind their backs. At that moment, I felt like I was the mother of a child who lost her son in the war. Then one officer said to us, "Your son, Blake, was in a very bad car accident this evening in Columbia Station on Boston Road." I asked, "Is he at the hospital?" Bob questioned, "Where is he, and can we see him?" The officer replied, "I am so sorry to tell you this, but your son Blake passed away this evening."

I couldn't believe this was happening. I just saw him. He then informed us that Blake had his seat belt on, and he was the passenger in the car. Again, he reiterated, "I am very sorry for your loss." "We believe that your son died instantly from the impact of the car. Jeff Chaya was driving the car. He also had his seat belt on, and he also passed away in the car accident." As he was talking, I just couldn't comprehend what he was saying. The words were coming out, but I just didn't want to believe them.

Brent came walking down the stairs and he heard what the officer had just told us. He kept pacing from the kitchen to the dining room, walking in circles around and around. Brent kept repeating, "This is my brother and my best friend, this can't be. I just saw him a few hours ago, this just can't be." The officer continued telling us what had happened. Lexi Poerner was also in the car. She had passed away, and she was seated in the middle of the back seat next to Kevin. Kevin Fox was thrown out of the car and was life-flighted and taken to Metro Hospital. There was one survivor, that was Julia Romito, and she was taken to a local hospital.

They began telling us all the details. "They were going over railroad tracks on Boston Road at a fast speed, the car hit a ditch and a tree, and the car turned over." I was trying to comprehend everything he was telling us, as I was fighting back tears. I looked over at Bob and his eyes were filled with tears, as he was trying to keep it all together. I couldn't take my eyes off Brent sobbing and repeating, "I can't believe I just lost my brother and best friend."

Brent and Blake did everything together. They were best friends; I loved seeing them always together. I kept my eyes on Brent and prayed to God, "Please, please be there for Brent. Brent is going to need you desperately because Blake is everything to him."

I asked the officer if I could see Blake and what we should do next. He informed me, "We identified your son. He had his license on him, so there is no need to go see him. I would stay right here with your family." He then asked, "Is there anyone we can call for you?" My heart was beating so hard, I didn't have the heart to tell my mom and dad. When I was in 7th grade, my Uncle Jimmy passed away. He was my mom's brother. I didn't want her to go through this all over again, losing someone she loved.

So, I decided to call my sister first, and the phone just kept ringing and ringing. She was not picking up. I desperately needed to talk to my sister. She means everything to me, and she "gets me." She would know what to say; she would listen and let me cry.

I wanted to hear my sister's voice, to tell me it was going to be okay, and to take away all the pain that I was feeling. I had a huge lump in my throat. My heart felt like someone took a melon scoop and took a huge part of my heart away. This is my son; he is a part of me. What am I going to do without Blake?

The officers were still standing in the hallway. They asked again if we needed anything. I answered that I am going to call my family. I stated, "On days like today, you probably hate your job. My husband and I want to thank you for coming over and being with us this evening."

I then decided to call my mom, and she answered about six rings in. She was in a sound sleep. "Hello, Terri, why are you calling so late? Is something wrong?" I think calling that late at night gave it away; she guessed right. Something *was* wrong. "Yes, mom, I don't even know how to tell you this, but Blake passed away this evening." "What - what happened?" I mumbled, "Blake was in a car accident. Can you and Dad come over so we can be together?" I told her everything that the officer told us. She said, "Your father and I will be right over."

My mom kept trying to call my sister Traci, my brother-in-law Todd, and my nephews, Troy and Tyler. Finally, Tyler picked up his phone. My mom said, "Tyler, I hate calling this late, but can you hand your phone over to your father?" My mom told Todd that a horrible car accident had happened, and Blake didn't make it. Todd had to wake up his wife (my sister) and tell her that her nephew had passed away that evening.

12

Traci called me right away. Her voice was exactly what I needed. I told her everything that had happened, and we cried together. She said, "Todd and I will be right over." I looked over at Bob. He was sitting on the couch, sobbing with his hands over his face. I went over to him, and we cried in each other's arms. I wanted him to hold me and take away the pain. I looked up at the staircase, and I saw my daughter, Brittany, walking down half asleep, rubbing her eyes. In her little voice, she asked what was happening. I told her to come on down, and she sat on my lap. I just kept hugging her and crying, as I was trying to get the words out to tell her that her older brother, Blake, had just died in a car accident. She muttered, "Not Blake, I cannot believe this is happening. We just saw him outside with all his friends."

We were all sitting on the couch, holding on to each other, and crying. I looked over at a picture I had on the table. It was a picture of my Grandma Boots and Papa Jim on my wedding day. My grandma was sitting on my grandfather's lap, just as I was sitting on Bob's lap. I kept staring at the picture. That was a day that was filled with love and laughter. At that moment, I realized that I wasn't alone. My grandmother had lost her son; she taught me so many lessons throughout her life, and now I, too, had lost my son.

I remember this one day when I was at her apartment and she was sitting in my grandfather's recliner. She looked so small in that recliner as she held onto her little blue book. It was the *Mothers' Manual.*[2] She was holding onto it like her life depended on it. She said, "Terri, I have this beautiful poem, and I want you to have it." It was folded up and placed in front of her little blue book. She told me, "I have it memorized, so I want you to have it. Your Uncle Jimmy loved you so very much. You were the little sister he always wanted." Even though I was only his niece, I knew I had a special place in his heart.

I went upstairs and I opened her jewelry box that I had been given. I was very blessed to receive this after she passed away. I found her beautiful poem folded up, as it was lying right on top. It had a picture of my Uncle Jimmy from when he was a young boy stapled in the upper right-hand corner. I remember reaching out for this poem many times in my life, when I was going through struggles. I told myself, "If my grandmother can go through life without her son, I can go through this struggle." Here I was on the night my son passed away, and I had a piece of my grandmother with something she clung onto when she was struggling over the loss of her son.

I'll Lend You A Child
by Edgar Guest

"I'll lend you for a little time a child of mine," He said.
"For you to love - while he lives
And mourn for when he's dead.

It may be six or seven years
Or twenty-two or three,
But will you, till I call him back,
Take care of him for me?

He'll bring his smiles to gladden you,
And should this stay be brief?
You'll have his lovely memories as solace for your grief.

I cannot promise he will stay,
Since all from earth return,
But there are lessons taught down there
I want this child to learn.

I've looked this world over
In search for teachers' true,
And from the throngs that crowd
Life's lanes, I have selected you.

Now will you give him all your love,
Nor count the labor vain,
Nor hate Me when I come to call to
Take him back again?"

I fancied that I heard them say,
"Dear Lord, thy will be done,
For all the joy Thy child shall bring,

The risk of grief we'll run.
We'll shelter him with tenderness,
We'll love him while we may,
And for the happiness we've known
Forever grateful, stay.

But should the angels call for him
Much sooner than we've planned,

We'll brave the bitter grief that comes
And try to understand."

I held Brittany in my arms, tears rolling down my face, and Brittany looking up at me. I shared with her the words my grandmother shared with me when she told me about Uncle Jimmy; I just changed it to reflect Blake. This is the day that God wanted to be with Blake and to bring him home with Him. God loved Blake so much that he called him home. I know that this is very hard for us to understand and to let him go. Our family has been very blessed to have had Blake in our lives. He brought us so much joy and laughter. He teased you sometimes, because he loved you. Blake is not gone; he will be with us always.

The doorbell rang. It was my sister Traci and her husband Todd. They came into the living room, and we cried and hugged each other. We couldn't believe that this was happening. One by one, our family members were coming in: Bob's parents, his sister Debby and her husband Joe, his sister Jean and her husband John, and his brother Rick. Joe and John sat next to me; they are both firemen. They told me that the media may want to present a story of them drinking and driving. You know that drinking was not involved because Brent was just with them, and they were not drinking. The car is going to look like an accordion and be very mangled and smashed; however, for us to get the passengers out of the car, we have to pull all the metal back so we can get them out. When you see pictures on TV, just remember what we have to do to pull them out.

We all sat in the living room trying to wrap our heads around what happened to Blake and his friends. My mom and dad finally arrived. I asked my mom what took them so long. My mom said that they went to the accident scene on Boston Road, but they couldn't really see anything. It was blocked off. The police officer there told her that she should be with her daughter and her family. We all sat in the living room crying and holding onto each other.

When everyone left and my family went to bed, I couldn't sleep. I just kept tossing and turning, so I decided to get up. I just stood in the dining room crying. I went over to my favorite picture of Jesus, called the *Prince of Peace*. I received it as a Christmas gift from my parents last year after reading *Heaven Is for Real*.[3] I always find such peace when I look into Jesus' eyes. For some reason, my light would not go on in the room. I could not see the warmth of Jesus' face. I wanted to look into those beautiful green eyes and know, by looking at this picture, that Blake was with Him. I would feel comfort knowing he was with Jesus.

15

I roamed all through the house. "God, what do you want me to do?" I couldn't stop crying. All I wanted was to see the face of Jesus, but the light would not go on. I then decided to sit in the kitchen. I looked outside my patio window and remembered the last time I saw Blake when he knocked on the window and scared me, and I almost fell off my chair. He pointed his little finger at me and said, "I got you," and his smile was so big.

I know God knew Blake was going to die that night. God wanted me to see his smiling face through a glass window. As I was looking out that same window, I sobbed. I asked God, "How am I going to get through this?" I cried for a while, and then I heard something inside of me say Go get Blake's Bible. So, I went upstairs to look for his Bible. My mom and dad gave this to him for Christmas in 2009. Every year, my parents give something for the grandkids that is religious to celebrate the true meaning of Christmas.

The cover of the Bible was a football cover. It even felt like a football with leather bumps so you can grip it. As I ran my hand over the Bible, I could picture Blake holding onto his football. He just loved the game and everything about it, especially being surrounded by all his friends. Football was everything to Blake. I remember when he graduated from elementary school, all the kids were talking about how they couldn't wait for high school so they could play under the lights at Brunswick Stadium and have all the crowd cheering them on. He talked about that all the time.

As I sat in his room on the edge of his bed, I looked up at a life-size fathead (vinyl wall graphic) of him, which we just bought for Christmas this past year, after he scored the first and only touchdown of his life. He made a pick-six the last game of his junior year, with only a few seconds left on the clock. Little did we know that this would be the last play of his life.

Blake scored that touchdown against Medina High School, one of our biggest rivalries. Because my sister's kids go to Medina, my whole family was at the game. I didn't have a camera or a video camera, but one of the parents captured his catch as he ran down the field for the touchdown.

I looked up at the picture of him with that huge grin on his face and the football in his arm. I was so glad he had that one moment to shine. As a defensive player, he was always blocking his defenders; his purpose was not to get a touchdown. Here at this moment, he was the one to score!

Blake had no idea that this would be his last play of his life. As I looked into his eyes behind his football mask, I began to wonder. I realized that next year, the year he had been waiting for his whole life, he would be in heaven. God wanted Blake to play for the Angels and to be on His team instead of playing for the Brunswick Blue Devils. We all have dreams, and this was his dream.

I kept rubbing my hands over the cover of the Bible and feeling the touch of the football. Here I was holding onto the Bible as I looked up, and I saw my son holding onto a football. I was going to need God's words to help me through this and help me to understand. I looked down at the cover of the Bible and it read *"Official Witness Ultra Grip - New Found Life (NFL), Romans 6:4"* - I actually never read the verse for Romans 6:4 NIV, so I looked it up - "We were therefore buried with him through baptism into death in order that, just as Christ was raised from the dead through the glory of the Father, we too may live a new life." I reflected on this. God led me to Blake's Bible; this was the night he passed away. This verse was all about death. His new life, the life he has right now, is a new life - a new life with God in heaven.

I walked downstairs with the Bible in my hand and sat at the kitchen table. I just stared out into the night. Looking out at the same window where I last saw Blake smiling at me, I looked down at the Bible and thought to myself, "Where do I even begin. I don't even know the Bible that well." So, I took the Bible, and I just let it fall open on the table. It opened to Matthew Chapter 10 around verse 36. Okay, I thought Matthew was Blake's middle name, and he loved football. When you think of the number ten, you think of the Big 10, and 36 was Blake's football number. This was where God led me.

"Do not think that I have come to bring peace upon the earth. I have come to bring not peace but the sword, for I have come to set a mother against his father, a daughter against her mother, and a daughter-in-law against her mother-in-law, and one's enemies will be those of his household. Whoever loves father or mother more than me is not worthy of me, and whoever loves son or daughter more than me is not worthy of me, and whoever does not take up his cross and follow me is not worthy of me. Whoever finds his life will lose it and whoever loses his life for my sake will find it."

I thought to myself, God, these are very powerful words coming from you. I have to love you over the son that I just lost. I know everything about Blake. I can't even imagine a day without him in my life. I knew one thing, that I could not do this journey alone. I now wanted to know everything about God and about heaven because Blake was no longer in this life; he had been called home to be with his Heavenly Father.

I closed my Bible and went into the living room. I sat on the couch and kept thinking of Blake in heaven and what it would be like. Suddenly, I noticed a ray of light shining in the front window. It was around four o'clock in the morning, and pitch-black out. "Where is this light coming from?" I thought. It was so bright. I went over to the window and looked outside. The ray of light went straight up to the heavens! If only I could walk up that ray of light and see Blake. At that moment, I heard music playing in my head, and it was *This Little Light of Mine - I'm Going to Let it Shine*.[4] I remember singing that song with Blake when I helped teach his second-grade religion class. I can picture Blake dancing around and smiling really big. He had a way of always making me laugh.

Then I heard, *"Be Not Afraid - I go before you always, come, follow me, and I will give you rest*.[5] That song was played at my Uncle Jimmy's funeral. That song would make me very angry and sad, but hearing it this time, I felt at peace. Maybe my Uncle Jimmy is with Blake right now, and he is showing him all around heaven. It kept playing softly in my head. I felt as if God was holding me. I felt so calm and relaxed in His arms. I just took it all in.

Then I heard His voice telling me that I had to celebrate Blake's life. Your son was filled with so much joy and happiness, and he needs to be celebrated. "How do I do that?" I asked. "The time will come, and you will know."

CHAPTER 2:
IT'S NOT GOOD-BYE
IT'S SEE YOU LATER

The next morning, all our neighbors showed up on our doorstep. They saw the news on Facebook. Word travels fast. They hugged us and cried with us. Some of the neighbors that showed up were Lisa, Dale, Debbie, Chrissy, Tom, Viv, and Michelle. Mark, one of my neighbors, hugged me so tightly and told me, "I am here for you." He whispered to me, "My brother passed away, and it was tough on all of us." He was choked up, so he could barely get the words out. I needed that hug at that moment; to know that I was not alone, and that he could feel my pain.

This was graduation day for Jeff and Kevin, and all the Brunswick High School (BHS) students. Most of them probably heard the news that two of their classmates passed away last night. Some of them would probably hear about it when they arrived at commencement. My heart was aching for all those students, and for the parents of Jeff and Kevin. I heard both Jeff and Kevin had a rose and a commencement program on their chairs for the graduation ceremony.

When my parents arrived that morning, I told my mom that I wanted to celebrate Blake's death. She said, "How are you going to do that?" I mentioned, "I'm not sure yet, but last night I heard God's voice. He told me that the time will come, and that I will know. So, currently, I have no idea, Mom."

Around noon, Danny and his mom (who is also my good friend, Dianna) came over to see us. Danny was one of Blake's best friends from grade school through high school. They played baseball and football together over the years, and they were teammates on the Brunswick High School football team. Dianna commented that she was sitting at church with her younger son, Zach, when she received several text messages from Danny, who was working at the time. The messages were saying that Blake was in a car accident with other students from Brunswick, and he passed away. She told me that she just stared at her phone in disbelief. She had to go to the lobby of the church to call Danny. Zach came out and asked what was wrong, and she told Zach what happened. They cried together and decided to leave the church. She dropped off Zach, picked up Danny at work, and they both came over to our house. When they came to the door, we just clung to each other and cried. We could not believe that Blake passed away. We reminisced about our sons growing up together. We even carpooled to PSR religion classes for a couple of years. So many memories flashed in my head.

19

At that time, Father Bob arrived from our church, Saint Ambrose. Father Bob talked to us and gave us so much comfort as he shared how Blake and the other Brunswick students are in God's loving arms. He went over to Bob to comfort him and also talked with Brent and Brittany. Our family felt so blessed that our friends and Father Bob came over.

Mrs. Wheeler, one of the principals at BHS, came over with a beautiful blue vase with a dozen white roses and a white ribbon tied to the vase. It was so stunning. She also had Blake's football jersey. When I saw that, I wanted to cry. She has two boys around the same age as my two boys. She said she didn't even know what to say. I noted, "That is the perfect thing to say." She told me Blake always made her laugh, and that it wouldn't be the same without him walking through the halls at Brunswick High. I just kept looking at Blake's jersey. I remembered last night, God telling me that I needed to celebrate Blake. This is how I could do it, I thought. So, at that moment, I said," I know what you can do for our family, you can get the word out that I want everyone to come as who they are. I don't want anyone to dress up. They can come in their athletic wear; they can wear their jerseys or sports jackets, whatever they would like." She commented that she did not think the Superintendent would go for that idea. "Well, if he doesn't agree, he can wear a suit, you and I both know that is how Blake would want it." Blake loved being comfortable. He would want them to come to see him for the last time, wearing and supporting BHS.

She put the word out. The students and some teachers met up at the high school. Brent went up that evening and met up with all of Blake's friends and classmates. They shared stories and did a whole lot of crying. They passed out blue ribbons and white and blue balloons. They also made many signs to place around the city. They all signed Blake and Jeff's football helmets, and they signed a rugby ball for Kevin. They also signed the huge banner that football, basketball, and other sporting events run through before each game.

Our family felt all the love and support from our community and the surrounding communities, especially from Strongsville and Medina, who are our biggest rivals on the football field. The clock tower in the center of our city had a sign that said, "Forever in Our Hearts," and under the clock, a big blue ribbon. The community digital message board read, "The Brunswick Community mourns the loss of our students." One by one, it would flash each individual child separately – "Jeffrey Chaya, Blake Bartchak, Kevin Fox, Lexi Poerner, and prayers for Julia Romito." The Brunswick High School - Home of the Blue Devils sign posted – "Our thoughts and prayers are with the families of" and listed all the names. One resident placed a huge blue and white ribbon made out of wood with a "B" in the center of the ribbon on their lawn. We, as well as the Chaya Family, live in The Fairways Development. The Fairways placed two huge blue ribbons on both sides of the entrance sign. Signs were all over Brunswick. You would drive down the streets, and you would see blue ribbons tied to so many trees. Our family truly felt loved, and our community joined us in our pain and suffering.

I grew up in this small, little town. We moved to Brunswick when I was five years old and started kindergarten. Brunswick is everything to me. I cheered for Brunswick and was on the same field Blake played on. I felt so much love as I drove past many signs. I headed to the Hallmark store down the street. I was looking for something I could hold onto at the wake and the funeral. As I looked around, something caught my eye. It was a very small coin with a cross on it. The packaging read:

The Cross in my Pocket

"I carry a cross in my pocket, a simple reminder to me of the fact that I am a Christian, no matter where I may be. This little cross is not magic, nor is it a good luck charm. It isn't meant to protect me from physical harm. It's not for identification for all the world to see. It's simply an understanding between my savior and me. When I put my hand in my pocket to bring out a coin or key, the cross is there to remind me of the price he paid for me. It reminds me, too, to be thankful for my blessings day by day and strive to serve him better in all that I do and say. It's also a daily reminder of peace and comfort to share with all who know my master and give themselves to his care. So, I carry a cross in my pocket, reminding no one but me that Jesus Christ is Lord of my life if only I'll let him be."

First thing when I got in the car, I opened it up. I rubbed my hands over the cross, and I noticed small beads going down the cross and going across. I laid the coin in the palm of my hand, and I stared down at the cross. Jesus paid the price, and he laid it all down for us. As I sat in my car, I thought of Blake in the presence of God. I wondered what heaven is like. I thought and I wondered if he was with my grandparents and my Uncle Jimmy. I wondered if he was with Jeff and Lexi and if they were meeting so many other kids.

As I stared down at the cross, I rubbed my finger over the beads on the cross. I flipped the coin over and laid the cross down in the palm of my hand. I pressed the coin down in the middle of my palm. I could feel the cross digging into my palm. I couldn't even imagine the nails that went through Jesus' palm of His hand. The pain that I was feeling cut me like a knife and was so overbearing. I felt a dig at my heart that was so deep; it felt as if someone had taken out half my heart. I felt so empty and lonely inside.

I laid the coin in my hand, crunched my fist together, lay my head down on the steering wheel, and just cried. The tug at my heart was so deep, and the lump in my throat was so intense, I had trouble breathing. I couldn't stop crying. I opened my hand slowly and looked at the cross. He's not alone. He is home with our Savior. I took the coin in my hand and looked at the cross. I rubbed my hand over the coin, and I noticed writing on the back. On the back of the coin, it read, "Do not be afraid, I am with you always." Those words are the exact words that I needed to hear. Do not be afraid, I am with you always. God is with me, and God is with Blake. God is the connection between both of us. I felt a sense of relief and peace. Blake is not alone. I know where he is. He is with God.

That evening, Sunday, June 3rd, Saint Ambrose Parish gathered the community for a Prayer Vigil in loving memory of Blake, Jeff, and Lexi. All three of them were parishioners at Saint Ambrose Parish. Prayers were going out to Kevin, who was in critical condition and fighting for his life at MetroHealth Medical Center, and prayers were going out to Julia Romito, who survived the accident. Kevin ultimately succumbed to his injuries. The church was filled with family, friends, students, and teachers. I felt so loved and not alone as I looked back and saw the whole church was filled, and people were standing against the walls. People were even flowing outside of the church. I saw so many people that I knew, and it was comforting knowing they were here to support all of us.

Father Bob Stec led us all in prayer. "Today is one of those days that defy words. It is because they loved so greatly, they have found their way to be with God. They have loved so greatly that our church is literally bursting here this evening." Father Bob presented a candle to our whole family, the Chaya Family, and the Poerner Family. He wrapped Lisa Poerner, Paula Chaya, and me in prayer shawls. Blue ribbons and five candles were burning at the altar. Students, one by one, left cards there with written memories and then lit candles of their own.

Bob and I found out after the vigil that many of the students and the community were gathered near the railroad tracks after they heard about the car accident. They built a memorial of flowers and teddy bears alongside the road. The tree that they hit was covered with messages and blue ribbons. A petition to fix the railroad tracks on Boston Road in Columbia Station sits in the hollow of a tree next to the site.

The next couple of days were so tough getting ready for the wake and funeral. Our family came over, making posters and gathering pictures. Tom, from Saint Ambrose, came over with his laptop. He was the Music Director at Saint Ambrose. Helen, the Music Ministry/Parish Life/Wedding Coordinator, also came with Tom. They helped my mom and me pick out scripture readings and songs for the funeral mass.

One of Brittany's dance dads from Dancexcel, Ron, offered to put a video together of Blake's life for the funeral. He truly helped us out, and he captured Blake's personality perfectly.

We had so many people coming over, dropping off cases of water, food, and bringing over flowers. We would cry and share stories together.

The community continued placing ribbons all over the city. Royal blue wristbands were made and written in white. There were angel wings on both sides of the initials of each child - KF * JC * LP * BB *. Each child also had their own individual wristband. Blake's wristband was royal blue and written in white; it said, "Blake" with a football in the middle before "Bartchak." The "B" in Bartchak had the Brunswick Logo, with a cross on each side of the words R.I.P.

Miranda Flowers, who just graduated from Brunswick High School that year, along with Jeff and Kevin, designed T-shirts. "Blue Devils on Earth, Angels up above" with a cross in the middle, and it had angel wings behind the cross. On the back of the shirt, it read, "Rest in Peace, J. Chaya, K. Fox, L. Poerner, B. Bartchak". At the bottom of the shirt, "Forever in our Hearts 6-3-12" with angel wings between their names. She had these made at the Bullseye Activewear and Promotions Workshop.

On the morning of June 6th, our whole family went over to my cousin Dawn's for breakfast. This was before we all headed over to Saint Ambrose for Blake's wake. She invited the entire family, including all my aunts, uncles, cousins, and the whole side of my husband's family. My cousin, Bonnie, had shirts made that were royal blue with white lettering in an arch that read, "Our Devil Has Wings," and in the center was the Brunswick "B" Logo and angel wings on both sides. The back said "BARTCHACK" with the number "36." My brother-in-law Rick, came up to me and he said your cousin Bonnie spelled our last name wrong. She added an extra "C" in BartchaCk. I mentioned that I noticed it also. Bonnie came up to me later and stated, "Terri, I feel so horrible that I misspelled your last name." I noted, "Bonnie, what you did for our family is beautiful, and I will treasure this shirt forever. Just look at it like this, that the "C" was added because Christ is with us. He will always have our back. He is carrying the "C" in BartchaCk. God will be holding all of us. Especially at a time like this, we will all need Him to help us each and every day."

23

When we entered the church that afternoon around 1:00 p.m., I saw a window frame box of a Brunswick Blue Devils Jersey in the lobby of Saint Ambrose. It read: "We remember Blake Bartchak Edwards Middle School 2006- 2009." All the teachers at the middle school signed it. Blake had so many wonderful memories of Middle School. He made so many great friends that his best friends remained through High School. When I saw the jersey, I started to cry.

I remembered his favorite memory of Middle school at the end of 8th grade, his trip to Washington. When he came home, he was talking a mile a minute and telling me that he got the whole bus to sing *Don't Stop Believin'*.[6] He said, "Mom, I had a blast in Washington! I met so many kids from Willets Middle School (the other middle school in Brunswick). I can't wait to start high school next year."

So many memories were flowing through me. We started bringing in all the pictures and lining them up at the church for the wake. Blake was laid out at the left side of the altar, with Jeff laid out at the right side of the altar. We had a closed casket, and so did Jeff. I wanted to remember Blake the last time I saw him having fun with all his friends and smiling.

Right above his casket was a gorgeous spray of white roses with a beautiful blue ribbon with "Family" written above the flowers. Over to the left side and at the head of his casket, we enlarged his one and only touchdown picture, and the last play of his life. It was a picture of Blake holding onto the football and running in for a touchdown. It looks like he is running straight to heaven and will be playing for the Angels.

It was time and people started coming in. My family was with me up at the front of the altar. I held onto the cross and placed the cross with the bumps in the palm of my hand. I could feel it and know that God was with me. Bob was holding my other hand, and he started to cry. I whispered to him, "We have each other, and we can do this together." Brent and Brittany were next to Bob. My parents and Bob's parents were also with us. My sister Traci was always at my side, asking if I needed anything.

So many people were coming through the line. I heard so many wonderful and some very funny stories of Blake, and each one was funnier than the next. One girl that I will never forget shared with me how she knew Blake. She said, "I'm only a freshman and I met Blake the first week of school. I was very depressed that day and was looking down. He came up to me and said, 'Hey, why are you so sad. This is High School, the best years of your life. I want to see you smile.' Every day after that, he would look for me in the halls, and he would be smiling so big and looking for my smile. He

24

brightened up my day, each day. I just wanted you and your husband to know how much your son helped me through my freshman year." I was so glad she shared her story with Bob and me.

I looked up at the crucifix that was hanging above the altar. I held tightly onto the cross in the palm of my hand. I thanked God for coming to me the night Blake died, and for guiding me to celebrate Blake's life. I'm so glad that everyone who was coming through the line was dressed in Brunswick Blue attire or dressed comfortably. If I clung to myself and my pain, I would have missed all these beautiful stories of Blake.

Another lady came up to me and shared a very interesting story about Blake. Blake worked at Buehler's grocery store. She said she was at Buehler's looking for the perfect potato. She saw Blake in the back, and she asked him if he could help her find the perfect potato. One without any spuds growing out of it, and it can't have any brown spots or bruises. They were both looking, and they couldn't find one. Blake went in the back, and he came out with this big crate of potatoes. They both were looking through them, and finally, she found one, and she exclaimed, "I found the perfect potato!" She said it was used for a project at Saint Ambrose of a resurrected Jesus. She sent me a picture of it, and here it is.

So many people who shopped at Buehler's shared many stories of Blake. One mother said she has a son with special needs. Blake would lift his spirits up and make him laugh. Her son would always beg her to take him to

25

Buehler's so he could see Blake. Blake would then always help her take her groceries to the car and help her son get in his car seat.

One of the cashiers told me that Blake was always cracking jokes and would always make everyone laugh. He just never had a bad day. Every day was good for him.

Then two men came in and they said they were the Buehlers. I couldn't believe it when they said they were from Buehler's and that their family owned the grocery store! I asked "Did you know Blake?" They said they never met Blake, but they heard so much about him, and they wanted to meet his parents. They said that his work ethic was outstanding and that he was always going above and beyond. When he saw wrappers or garbage on the floor or in the carts, he would pick it up and throw it away. He made the customers feel welcomed and made them laugh. He was always picking up shifts and working as many hours as he could. I thanked them so much for coming and sharing that with us.

I also had something to share with both of them. On Blake's first day, he came running down the stairs in his forest green polo shirt with his Buehler's name tag and his khaki pants. He cried out, "Mom, this is not going to work." "What's not going to work, Blake?" "These pants. They are wrinkled." "Blake, they are not wrinkled. You look great." "No, mom. They have to be perfect. I am representing Buehler's." "You are right, Blake; you are representing Buehler's. I will go and iron your pants." They both laughed and said they were glad we shared that story with them. I still can't believe the owners would take the time to come and see Blake. I thought that most people would remember Blake from playing football; however, after hearing so many beautiful stories from employees and customers from Buehler's about how Blake was so much more, I learned I was wrong. I appreciated that so many people shared those stories with us.

One of my neighbors from when I was growing up in Brunswick hugged me tightly and kept crying. She babysat me when I was younger, and then she taught me lots of cheers. She also helped me make the Brunswick cheerleading team in high school. She kept holding onto the necklace she was wearing and rolling the blue crystal bead in her fingers. Suddenly, she took off her necklace and placed it on me. She said you need to have this necklace. We both have three children. It will represent your whole family. She said the big blue crystal bead in the middle is Blake. I realized he is also my middle child, and the two smaller white crystal beads above it on both sides will be Brent and Brittany. The two smaller blue beads above that will be you and Bob. When you look at this necklace, hold the blue crystal bead in your fingers and know that Blake is always with you, and you will always have three children. Robin and her family, from the first day of Blake's accident, were special angels for about two weeks. We would get a knock at the front door, and they would leave a basket full of breakfast food and some fruit with a bottle of juice, with a beautiful note signed, "Love the O's." We looked forward to getting those delicious morning treats to start off our day during this difficult time.

The Brunswick football players came through the line. They shared so many funny stories about Blake. One of the football moms gave me a football pin with angel wings above the football. She placed it right on my shirt. I was wearing the shirt that Bonnie had made for all of us. We all had them on. We were all a sea of blue. Everyone who was coming along the line was wearing the shirts that were made to represent all the kids. "Blue Devils on Earth, Angels up Above," or they were wearing T-shirts or sweatshirts that represented BHS. One after another, so many stories were shared by students, neighbors, family, and friends.

I looked up, and a bunch of Strongsville Football players came up to pay their respect. They had their green jerseys on with a tie, and they told us how sorry they were for the loss of Blake. We always enjoyed playing against Brunswick, and we remember him from all the years of playing football. Each one gave us a hug. At that moment, I knew that Blake was smiling from heaven, knowing that even the Strongsville team came to see him.

My cousin's wife, Chrissy, came over to me and said, "Come with me." She took me over to the side of Saint Ambrose and surprised me by having all my co-workers at PricewaterhouseCoopers (PwC) together. I worked downtown, and my co-workers were from all over the Cleveland area. I was so glad Chrissy gathered all of them and had them all in one place. It was great hugging them and receiving so much support, and it came at a time when I needed a break.

I went back in and greeted so many more people. I kept holding onto my cross in my pocket and rubbing my fingers over the cross. When I felt overwhelmed, I placed the cross in the palm of my hand and pressed down to feel the cross etched in my palm. I knew that I was not alone. God was with me, and Blake was watching over me. I looked over at Bob, who became choked up so many times and was trying hard to hold it in. Brent went out of line a few times to be with friends, and so did Brittany when she saw her dance-friends or friends from school. I looked over a few times and saw one of Bob's best friends, Scott Haborak, better known as "Habo", sitting in the pew with his beautiful wife Diane. They were some of the first ones to arrive, and they stayed the whole time, sitting in the pew, supporting us.

I looked up and noticed that the line was so long. I didn't know how we would get a chance to see everyone. I glanced at the time, and it was 7:30 p.m., and I knew that it ended at 8. I looked at Bob and mentioned, "The line is so long, and I want to thank everyone for coming." So, Bob and I got out of the line, and we decided to start from the beginning of the line and go through and talk with each person quickly. We wished to thank them so much for coming and supporting our family after the loss of Blake. We went through the whole line in the church. When we looked outside, it stretched all the way around the whole church, down to the parking lot. I told Bob this line is as long as the lines at Cedar Point. We both know how much Blake loved Cedar Point and that he would wait forever in line to ride the rides. He truly gave us a ride to remember. I was just remembering that Blake was at Cedar Point the night before he died. Blake truly lived a fun-filled life.

It was almost 8:00 p.m., Father Bob and other Saint Ambrose staff members were trying to gather everyone into the church for a Candlelight Prayer Vigil.

Bob and I, and our whole family, sat in the first 4 or 5 rows of the church. The opening song that they played was *I Can Only Imagine* by MercyMe. [7]

> I can only imagine what it will be like when I walk by your side. I can only imagine what my eyes would see when Your face is before me. I can only imagine.
>
> Surrounded by Your glory, what will my heart feel? Will I dance for You, Jesus, or in awe of You be still? Will I stand in your presence or to my knees, will I fall?
>
> Will I Sing Hallelujah? Will I be able to speak at all? I can only imagine. I can only imagine.
>
> I can only imagine when that day comes, and I find myself standing in the Son. I can only imagine when all I will do is forever, forever worship you
>
> I can only imagine.

As that song was being played, my heart was drawn to the crucifix. The words are so etched on my heart that I could imagine Blake, Jeff, Kevin, and Lexi together with God. I can't even imagine seeing God face to face with open arms and holding our children. I can picture Lexi dancing freely in the heavens, and Blake smiling so big with so much joy and a carefree spirit. I can imagine them in the heavens, as tears are rolling down my face, how

28

proud I am of those four beautiful angels that are in the presence of our Heavenly Father.

Father Bob, our Pastor at Saint Ambrose, led us all in prayer and gave us words of encouragement that these four beautiful angels are with our Heavenly Father in heaven. We will see them again one day.

Scripture Reading:
2 Corinthians 5:1, 6-10 NABRE

A reading from the second letter of Paul to the Corinthians.

"For we know that if our earthly dwelling, a tent, should be destroyed, we have a building from God, a dwelling not made with hands, eternal in heaven.

So, we are always courageous, although we know that while we are at home in the body, we are away from the Lord, for we walk by faith, not by sight. Yet we are courageous, and we would rather leave the body and go home to the Lord. Therefore, we aspire to please him, whether we are at home or away. For we must all appear before the judgment seat of Christ, so that each one may receive recompense, according to what he did in the body, whether good or evil."

The Word of the Lord.

Candles were passed out to everyone. When Father Bob lit the first candle, he said, "God is the light of the world, and He is with us always." They turned down the lights in the parish, and the church lit up with the glow from each candle as they were lit from the first candle. They sang the *Brunswick Alma Mater*.

Brunswick High School Alma Mater

In memory of the years gone by,
We sing Our Praise to thee.
Our loyalty to Brunswick High
She'll live eternally.
And when these days are finally gone
and friends are far from sight,
our hearts will all resound in cheer
for the Brunswick Blue and White

Closing Song:

Brunswick High School Fight Song

Fight the team across the field, show them that Brunswick's here.
Set the stands reverberating with a mighty cheer,
Rah - Rah - Rah!!
Hit them hard and see how they fall.
Never let that team get the ball.
Fight! Fight! With all your might
cause, we're winning this game tonight!
Fight!

Everyone in the church sang the *Brunswick Fight Song*.

My friend from work, Jyll, and her boyfriend, Stan, came to the wake. Stan is part of the Rat Pack Tribute Band. He sang *Sweet Caroline* [8] for Blake. Blake always loved that song, "Sweet Caroline – Bump, Bump, Bump." He loved those "bump, bumps!" I truly needed to hear that song. It always brings me so much joy. Blake would play that song so loud throughout the house. I know he is smiling down on us this evening and bopping his head to the "bump, bump, bumps."

The whole church was lifted up that evening. Our family felt so much love from our Brunswick community.

Tomorrow is the day we would all say goodbye to Blake. He would always tell me, "It's not goodbye, mom, it's see you later." So, as I attend his wake tonight, I will have to remember the words my son always told me, that it is never goodbye, it is see you later. Someday soon, I will see you again.

That morning, we woke up very early to attend Jeff's funeral mass. His mass was before Blake's at 9:30 a.m. at Saint Ambrose. The church was filled. It was a memorable ceremony. After the mass, they brought many of the Brunswick students over in school buses and took them to Resurrection Cemetery. When we arrived, I noticed that Jeff was buried right next to where we were going to be burying Blake. They were best friends growing up in The Fairways, teammates on the football field, as well as co-workers at Buehler's. Now they will be together forever and laid out to rest next to each other at Resurrection.

It was our turn for the funeral mass on the same day. As we were heading back to Saint Ambrose, we drove from the cemetery, and we passed our development. I just started crying. How am I going to do this? Blake lives here. We have so many memories. I can't let him go. Tears were flowing down my face. I reached into my pocket and grabbed my cross. God, please give me the strength to get through this day.

When we arrived at Saint Ambrose, we all met in the Chapel. Our family sat in the front pew. I just kept staring at his casket. We had Blake dressed in his white Brunswick football jersey #36. I laid his blue #36 jersey on his bed at home. We all signed his casket. One by one, everyone was signing it. It was time to carry the casket to the back of the church. His pallbearers all lined up around his casket. This included Rick Bartchak his uncle; Ted Gerencser, my brother, his uncle, and Godfather; Troy and Tyler, Blake's cousins; Brad Darlington, his best friend since middle school; Danny Stepp and Kyle Michalik, grade school friends (they played baseball and football all through the years); Kyle Howe and Chris Manning, friends from High School; and Landon Foerst, Brent and Blake's good friend for many years. I was so proud of the men who were standing before me, ready to carry Blake's casket. Father Bob said a prayer over all of us, and then it was time to walk Blake down the aisle. I just stared down at the casket. I had a very hard time holding it all in, as tears rolled down my cheeks. I held onto the cross in the palm of my hand. I pressed it down with my thumb, so the cross was etched in my palm. It gave me strength that Jesus was with me on this walk that was led by the pallbearers.

The choir of Saint Ambrose sang, *Be not Afraid*. I felt a calmness come over me, remembering God being with me the night Blake passed away and hearing that song play in my heart. Our whole family, and extended family, walked down the aisle right behind them. I looked up at the crucifix hanging above the altar. What came to me is that I have a God who loves me, and He would die for me. I am so blessed that He came to me that night and told me to celebrate Blake, because he brought all of us so much JOY. I walked slowly down the aisle with Bob holding my hand and Brent and Brittany by my side. I was so glad that I wore my Brunswick Mom's jersey that I wore to every one of Blake's football games. I placed that little football pin with the angel on my jersey. I can celebrate today. This is the day Blake is reunited with his Heavenly Father.

I can picture Blake grinning from heaven when he saw the church packed with family and friends! They were all dressed in blue and white. Go BIG Blue! At that moment, I always remembered Blake saying, "Go BIG or Go HOME." Well, Blake, this church is filled with so much LOVE, and you are home and in the arms of your Father.

As I walked down the aisle with my son being carried up to the altar, below the crucifix hanging above the altar, I saw Father Carlin. He is the priest who has been with our family through so many tough times. Standing next to him were Bishop Mark Leonard Bartchak (he is related to Bob's family), Abbot Gary G. Hoover, and Deacon Tom Sheridan.

When we reached the front of the altar, our family sat down in the first couple of rows. Father Bob led us all in prayer and pointed out that this church was filled with so much love at the loss of Blake.

My Brother-in-Law, Todd started off with a letter that was written to our family from Blake's Middle School's football and wrestling coach, Rick Buchner – "Mr. B". He brought this letter over the day after Blake died in a car accident. He had tears in his eyes. He said, "Your son truly made an impact on my life. He is definitely going to be missed by many."

Mr. B's Letter:

> Bob, Terri, Brent, and Brittany,
>
> I wanted to put something down on paper because I know I would not be able to talk to you all without breaking down. I am so deeply saddened by the loss of Blake. I can't imagine the loss you have suffered.
>
> It is not very often that I become attached to a family like I have yours. I have known all of you for eight years now, from the time that Brent walked into my 6th-grade class. I have seen your children grow and mature into outstanding individuals. That is a credit to you, Bob, and Terri. The heart and soul you have poured into your children is commendable.
>
> I am writing this letter to let you know the special place that Blake holds in my heart. It is not often that a student walks into my room and captures my attention. I was actively involved in watching Blake grow up through middle school. I spent 6th grade, two wrestling seasons, and an amazing 8th-grade football season with Blake. My three years with Blake are some of my most memorable. He had the uncanny ability to make me smile or laugh, no matter the situation or mood. I can still hear him, "Mr. B, Mr. B, Mr. B." He always wanted to please me, entertain me, and make me smile.
>
> That never stopped once he left Edwards. I ran into him at least once a week in Buehler's. He would always turn my short trip into a long one. He would talk my ear off. I will miss those moments and that bond that I had with him. He will always have a special place in my heart.

I wish there were more that I could say or do. I know the outpouring of support you guys have received has been amazing. I truly want you all to know that I am here for your family anytime!!!!

I pray that during this horrible time, you know Blake made a difference. He made my life a better one and touched my heart like I had never realized, as he did with many others. Please give each other a big hug from me. Thank you for the opportunity to have had the honor of getting to know Brent, Blake, and Brittany. I will miss him.

"May God watch over us while we are apart from one another".

Rick Buchner "Mr. B"

As tears dripped down my face, I looked up at the crucifix. I am so glad Blake made a beautiful impact on others. He honestly lived a life full of laughter and smiles.

Opening Prayer and First Reading - Ecclesiastes 3:1-12 NIV - Read by my nephew, (Blake's cousin) Dominic Verzi

A Time for Everything

"There is a time for everything, and a season for every activity under the heavens; a time to be born and a time to die, a time to plant and a time to uproot, a time to kill and a time to heal, the time to tear down and a time to build, a time to weep and a time to laugh, a time to mourn and a time to dance, a time to scatter stones and a time to gather them, a time to embrace and a time to refrain from embracing, a time to search and a time to give up, a time to keep and a time to throw away, a time to tear and a time to mend, a time to be silent and a time to speak, a time to love and a time to hate, a time for war and a time for peace. What do workers gain from their toil? I have seen the burden God has laid on the human race. He has made everything beautiful in its time. He has also set eternity in the human heart; yet no one can fathom what God has done from beginning to end. I know that there is nothing better for people than to be happy and to do good while they live."

The mass went on. I somehow continued staring at the crucifix above the altar.

The homily was led by Father Carlin, who has been part of our family since I was in second grade at Saint Ambrose. He has helped our family through

33

the loss of my Uncle Jimmy and both of my grandparents. He was also our Pastor at Saint Charles Parish when we lived in Parma and were newly married. During the homily, he talked about my Uncle Jimmy and how God was with us always through the valleys of life. He talked about our family belonging to Saint Charles Parish and that he baptized Blake. Father Bob also talked during the homily and brought up Blake, as well as all four teens, who were loved by so many. This was why the community is coming together during this difficult time.

When it was time to bring the gifts up to the altar, Father Bob made this exceptionally memorable for our family. We had Blake's Godparents, Jean and Ted, and my brother-in-law, Rick, bring up the gifts. My brother Ted, who also played football for BHS, brought up Blake's letterman's jacket, which represented Blake being brought up to the altar. My sister-in-law, Jean, brought up the wine, and my brother-in-law, Rick, brought up the bread.

When Father Bob consecrated the bread and wine into the Body and Blood of Jesus, I took in every word. I looked up at the crucifix, thinking of how much Jesus loves us that he would die for us. Each word was etched on my heart. When Bob and I went up to receive the Body and Blood of Jesus, I took in every detail of the crucifix, thinking about Blake in the arms of God. The Eucharist meant so much more to me after losing my son.

As I went back to my seat, I kneeled. I was mesmerized by the crucifix, reflecting on Blake being in heaven. I thought about the day Jesus died, and how Mary would have felt letting Him go. My heart was filled with so many emotions, as all our family, friends, and the Brunswick community came up to the altar to receive the Eucharist. As they walked by our family, we received many hugs and handshakes. With each embrace, I would have a memory that would come to mind that I will cherish forever.

Remarks of Remembrance read by Mark Simonitis:

> When I received the tragic news early Sunday morning, my heart was crushed. I prayed that the name on the Internet Posting was wrong. This couldn't be real.
>
> You hear of these tragedies happening on the news far too often, but it was always somewhere else, in some other town, not here, not to my friends.

Terri and Bob, there is nothing anyone can say or do that will make this all better. We cannot begin to understand how you feel or convey how sorry we all are for your loss.

It's hard to believe that over eight years have passed since we moved into The Fairways Development. And it wasn't long after we moved in that we met the Bartchak family.

My memories of Blake are those of a chubby, little, freckled-faced kid whose smile was so big that it forced his eyes closed. Well, the chubbiness left him, and he grew into a strong young adult, but that smile never changed.

Blake was so full of life and energy, and it was as contagious as his smile. Blake had such a passion for football and for life.

Through these past few days, the Bartchak family has been exposed to so many people that were impacted by Blake's life. New realization of how much he was loved and how much he meant to so many.

Over the years, I got to know the Bartchak family, neighborhood Christmas parties, and Cinco de Mayo celebrations would bring our families together.

These parties usually found Bob and me quoting lines from many of the classic movies like *Animal House,*[9] *Stripes,*[10] *Caddyshack*[11] and *Blazing Saddles*[12].

Well, Bob, I am going to reference a quote from a movie that we have never mentioned at any party. It is also from a classic movie, *The Wizard of Oz*[13].

When the Tin Man asked for a heart, the wizard responded to him:

A heart is not measured by how much you love, but by how much you are loved by others.

- A quick look around this church
- The attendance at the prayer service on Sunday
- A walk through our development
- The sea of people at the Wake yesterday
- Or a drive down 303 with all the ribbons flashing blue and white.

35

And you can easily see how big Blake's heart was and how much he was loved.

I was told that Strongsville High School (our football rival) was a sea of blue this week. Let that sink in for a minute. Can you imagine Blake watching from Heaven and seeing Strongsville wearing *blue* all week?

The outpouring of love and compassion from family, friends, and the community has been nothing short of amazing. The love that has been shown for Blake and the Bartchak family is beyond anything I have ever seen.

The Bartchak family would like to say special thanks to:

- The Brunswick City Schools
- PwC
- Pat Catan's
- Taste of Excellence
- Buehler's
- Saint Ambrose Parish
- City of Brunswick and all the businesses in the area that have supported us during this tough time
- All the love and support from the Brunswick Community
- Father Bob has been a blessing to the Bartchak's and this community in this time of need. We thank you for your compassion and love, Father Bob.
- We need to celebrate the wonderful memories we have of Blake.

We all have plans for ourselves and our children, but tomorrow is promised to nobody. We think ahead to how we are going to do this, that, or the other thing. It's nice to dream and hope, but we are no more in control of our lives than we are of stopping the sun from rising tomorrow.

God has a plan for all of us. We may not understand how and why He does the things he does, but we have to trust in His actions. It is impossible for us to see the big picture and how each one of us was created to help execute His plan. We don't have the Playbook. He does.

Blake's role in this life was complete. Mission accomplished.

God called for Number 36, sent in the play, and Blake executed it to perfection.

It is my prayer for all of us that we keep the faith and find strength in Christ, knowing that He is in control and that His love for all of us is beyond measure.

It is my prayer that we all turn to God in good times and bad. To celebrate the highs with God and to find peace with Him in the valleys.

I am not sure what heaven looks like, but if Blake has his way, the new official colors of Heaven are now blue and white.

God, please grant us the peace and calm that only you can bring. Go Big Blue! Play on Number #36.

May God comfort us all in this time of need and hold us in the palm of His hand.

I looked back, and the church was covered in blue! I saw so many families, friends, and BHS students. I had a huge lump in my throat, the tears just rolled down my cheek as they sang, *When It's All Been Said and Done*[14]

> When it's all been said and done,
> There is just one thing that matters:
> Did I do my best to live for the Truth?
> Did I live my life for You?
> When it's all been said and done
> All my treasures will mean nothing.
> Only what I have done
> For Love's Rewards
> Will stand the test of time.
> Lord, your mercy is so great
> That You look beyond our weakness,
> And find purest gold in miry clay,
> Turning sinners into saints.
> I will always sing Your praise
> Here on earth and in heaven after,
> For You've shown me Heaven's my true Home,
> When it's all been said and done,
> You're my life when life is gone.

One last prayer over Blake, and then it was time to say goodbye.

One by one, the people were leaving, and the pews were emptying. Again, I stared at the cross as the Saint Ambrose choir sang *How Great Thou Art*.[15] I looked from the crucifix to the casket as more tears slowly dripped from my eyes.

We climbed into the car. All the cars and buses from BHS were lined up to follow each other to Resurrection Cemetery. The streets were lined with people waving from the street. People were standing outside their company holding signs and waving. When we passed the fire station, even they were standing outside the firehouse and waving. We slowly passed The Fairways, our development, and our neighbors were standing outside, waving and holding white and blue balloons. The tears started again when I saw all our neighbors.

White and blue flags, as well as the Brunswick "B" logo flag, were all lined up at the front entrance of Resurrection Cemetery. When the hearse pulled up with Blake's casket, Brent, his big brother and best friend, led his cousins Troy and Tyler, Uncles Rick and Ted and his best friends Brad, better known as Chip, Danny, both Kyle's - Howe and Michalik, Landon, Chris and Eric, with the rest of the Football team behind them, carried Blake's casket through the Brunswick Football banner for one last time. The banner was signed by all the students the day after he passed away with football teammate Jeff, Lexi, and Kevin. They placed his casket right next to where Jeff was laid down this morning. I noticed a flower arrangement in the shape of a blue jersey with the number 36 on it. I smiled so big when I saw that flower arrangement.

We all gathered around the casket. Bob was right by my side, holding my hand. I then looked over at Brittany, and I noticed that she was holding onto Blake's football helmet, swinging it back and forth slowly, as she and her cousin Tara were crying. My heart was aching for her and our whole family. Our life was forever changed. I hope she will be okay. I hope we all will be okay. I looked all around and felt so blessed to be surrounded by so many wonderful family members and friends. Even my very close friend Sue came all the way from Texas to be with us, which meant so much to me. I saw Brent clustered with the football team and so many BHS students. Our whole community was gathered to be with us. I felt very overwhelmed and loved by so many people. Blue and white carnation flowers were being distributed for everyone to lay a flower on Blake's casket. Father Bob Wenz officiated with the last and final prayer for Blake. One by one, each person laid a flower on Blake's casket along with their final goodbyes. I heard bagpipes playing in the background by our neighbor, Tom McLaughlin, better known as Tommy Mac, and Andy, a childhood lifeguard who was the lifeguard in our neighborhood.

One of Blake's best friends, Allison Fisher, handed me a beautiful red rose. I have always loved roses. My mom named me after Saint Therese, also known as "The Little Flower." Allison said a woman at the church gave her this rose. Blake came to her in her dream and wanted his mother to have this rose, so this rose is from Blake. I looked at the rose closer, it was the most perfect red rose. I gave Allison a huge hug and told her this rose was picked from the heavens above. "You have no idea how much this rose means to me!" I laid that single, red rose on top of Blake's casket, among all the white and blue flowers. As I laid this perfect rose on his casket, the football players gathered around Blake. Chip played his guitar, and Eric sang *Good Riddance* [16] by Green Day. I know Blake was smiling from heaven, as he always told me, "It's never goodbye, it's see you later." I can't wait to see you again in heaven, my Little Blue Devil.

CHAPTER 3:
A COMMUNITY COMING TOGETHER

Brunswick Strong

We drove back up to Saint Ambrose for the funeral luncheon. The gym was filled with family, friends, many of Blake's football friends, and students from Brunswick. I was very thankful to Pat Catans and other local businesses around Brunswick for donating food and beverages to help our family during this time.

When I finally arrived home, I went upstairs to change. On my floor was a blue spiral notebook that I wrote in when I felt alone, scared or distant from God. It was opened to a particular page. A time when I was struggling with my faith and was angry at God. How did this binder end up next to my bed?

I looked down at the words on the page and started crying. "I am not alone. God is with me." I had written those words years previously when I questioned God's existence and the presence of heaven. It was then that God revealed Himself to me, and I experienced a profound love that I had never experienced before.

I had to get ready for Lexi's wake. It was at Jardine's Funeral Home in Strongsville. The line was very long; however, when we arrived, they let us right in. It took us a long time to get to Lisa, Jim, and Savannah, Lexi's sister, but when we did, Lisa and I just hugged each other. We didn't want to let go. We both said we couldn't believe this was happening.

Lexi's gorgeous pink prom dress was hanging up, and it had beautiful crystals going up the front of her dress, and which looked like angel wings. I know Lexi bought a pink dress for her junior year because she wanted to save her favorite color, purple, for her senior year. I felt so empty inside. Lexi was a junior, and she still had her senior prom. My heart ached for the Poerner family to be going through this just like us. Our two families will both be missing out on all those senior moments, the year that our children waited so long for. Blake always talked about going to prom, getting a limo, and having all his friends come over to take pictures. In a moment's time, it was taken away. Now neither of us will be able to celebrate those moments with our children.

The next morning was Lexi's funeral mass, and we were heading back up to Saint Ambrose Parish. Bob and I sat in the back of the church. As I was sitting, I saw the sunlight coming into the church, with the little dust particles coming down and landing on each person. It gave me a different perspective. It was angel dust touching each person in the church. God's love was everywhere.

The mass was moving along. During the communion reflection song, *Ave Maria* [17] was sung, and it was perfect. I kept looking at Lisa, and then to the crucifix. My eyes were filled with tears, knowing the pain of losing a child myself. As I looked at the crucifix, I saw a pair of hands softly cradling the Poerner Family. Those hands were strong, but oh, so gentle. God has all four of our children in the palms of His hands. The tears swelled up and overflowed down my face as I listened to *Ave Maria*.

After mass, I talked to Abbot Gary, and I told him what I saw. "I saw the hands of God holding up Lexi's family." He told me that he saw a beautiful girl with long flowing hair dancing in a meadow full of beautiful flowers. How amazing! I can't even imagine how beautiful heaven would be.

We then headed to Resurrection Cemetery. After the service, I walked over to where Blake and Jeff were laid to rest. The blue and white flower arrangement shaped in a jersey with the #36 stood right next to the pile of dirt that mounted up. We were talking about Lexi with the Chayas. She was only 16 years old; her birthday is August 2nd, the same day as my birthday. I said, "Wow, Blake will never forget my birthday, because it's the same day as Lexi's, and I'm sure she will be dancing in the heavens." As I said that, the jersey flower arrangement swayed back and forth and brushed against my elbow. I could hear Blake laughing, saying, "Mom, do you think I could ever forget your birthday?" I knew from that day forward, I would always be celebrating my birthday and thinking about Blake, Lexi, Kevin, and Jeff.

That evening, we headed to Kevin's wake. Kevin was a true hero. He made the selfless gift of donating his organs, saving the lives of others and improving the quality of life of many. We drove to the wake with the Chayas. I was sitting in the back seat of the car, and on the radio, I saw the name Blake go by on the radio screen. I'm sure the songwriter was Blake someone, but seeing his name made me smile. What a beautiful sign from above. I know that if I keep my eyes open, I will receive little gifts from above.

When we arrived, we saw the Poerners, and we stood in line with them. Lisa was sharing some memories of Lexi. She told me that in her family room, she saw a video case on the floor, and the movie was *Charlie St. Cloud*. [18] She said that Blake and Lexi were just watching this movie together the week before they died. I stated, "That is crazy. That movie is about a younger brother who passed away in a car accident. Zac Efron, the older brother, would go into the woods and have conversations with his brother. I wonder if our children could have conversations with us."

After sharing our hearts and talking about how tough this week was, we reached Sherri, Jim, Colleen, and Sean. We all just hugged each other and cried. We couldn't believe this horrible reality around us.

The next afternoon was Kevin's mass, and it was a lovely service. The church was filled with so much love from family, friends, and Brunswick students. Just like it was for all four of these children. We felt total love from the Brunswick community, and it helped carry us through this very tough week.

When I arrived back home, my body crashed. I felt so overwhelmed with grief from not only the loss of my own son, but also the loss of the other three children. I knew that from this day forward, my life would be forever changed and that it would be different. I would always have a place in my heart for Blake, but now I have to learn to live without him in my life.

In the days that followed, the Brunswick community came together, as did our families. My cousin, Bonnie Romano, helped get a community initiative started with so many others, especially Dave Harley and Kim Bublik.

The Brunswick community was devastated after the loss of my son, Jeff, Kevin, and Lexi on June 3rd. Three days later, a community meeting was held to brainstorm what could be done to help the community and those affected, both now and in the event of another tragedy occurring. From that meeting, a charitable organization called The Brunswick Blue Pride Foundation was created with an ongoing mission of family support, advocacy, and scholarships for Brunswick High School Students.

On Monday, June 11th, from 11 a.m. to 2 p.m., Panini's, a local restaurant, sponsored a Memorial Fundraiser to help raise money for the families that lost their children. They offered a selection of meals for free to all customers in exchange for donations. They even had tents set up across the street for to-go boxes with sandwiches and chips. (Four years later, when Brittany was almost sixteen, she worked at Panini's. She wanted to work at a place where the community helped us during a very difficult time in our lives.) Dairy Queen donated proceeds of their sales, as well as Pizza Hut and other local businesses, all to show their support. All of us were very thankful to Panini's and the Brunswick community for all their support.

On Wednesday, June 13th, at the Brunswick High School football field, they had a Memorial Balloon launch. The field was filled with so much love and support from the community. Buehler's grocery store, where Blake and Jeff both worked, donated blue and white balloons. The bell choir at Saint Ambrose made a rosary out of balloons. They released the first set of balloons, which was in the shape of a rosary, with a cross on the end, followed by blue and white balloons that were launched into the heavens. Our families felt all the love and support from our community.

On July 1st, they had a fundraiser at Brunswick High School to raise money for the Brunswick Blue Pride Foundation. We listened to the Brunswick Marching Band and watched the Cheerleaders. They had a Chinese Auction, side boards, a 50/50 raffle, a dunk tank, obstacle courses, plenty of blow-ups to help with skill training for a variety of sports, concession stands, and more. The money raised would be used to support local families in the event of future tragedies and to create scholarships and advocacy programs for BHS students.

On July 19th, the community came together and created an incredible memorial at Brunswick Lake. Eric Engelke and Jim MacLellan of Engelke Construction Solutions, along with Mark Svozil of Davey Tree, brought the vision to life. There were donations from twenty-six area businesses, as well as members of Boy Scout Troop 518 from Saint Mark Lutheran Church, who constructed the picnic tables located under the pergola. Also, a 35-foot oak tree surrounded by four spruce trees serves as a lasting tribute to the way the Brunswick community came together during a difficult time. Brunswick Mayor Gary Werner cut the ribbon to the New Brunswick Lake Memorial along with Sean Fox, my son Brent, and daughter Brittany, Dominic Verzi, my nephew, Allie and Amanda Chaya, Lisa Poerner, and Colleen Fox.

Architectural Justice designed beautiful plaque memorials that were mounted on stone pillars under the pergola for Blake, Jeff, Lexi, and Kevin, with a picture of each one, and a saying under the picture. They also have an elegant plaque that reads "Blue Devils on Earth, Angels up Above" with the logo they used for the shirts, with a cross and angel wings behind the cross. Written underneath it states, "This marks a time when an entire community came together. May this special place be a source of comfort and reflection to honor and remember all our loved ones who passed before their time. Eternally in our hearts … The Community of Brunswick." Each pillar has a plaque, one for each of the four teens killed in the accident.

44

When Blake passed, I received a card with the meaning of the name, Blake.

The meaning of the name Blake - (Harmony) - Every good gift and every perfect gift is from above and coming down from the Father of Light - James 1:17.

Every time I think of this and his name, I always think of the Father of Light. When Blake entered the room, he shone with so much joy. He was my little shining star. Even though Blake died at a very young age, he will be remembered by the brightness of his light. He brought us so much joy.

Football meant everything to Blake, and in his junior year at the beginning of the season, Blake was injured. He didn't want to tell us. Blake was determined to play out his junior year injured. At the end of the season, he came to us and said that something was wrong, and he was in pain. We took him to the Cleveland Clinic, and sure enough, Blake had a stress fracture, and he was on crutches.

When Blake passed away, we received a beautiful card from his doctor. This is what it said:

> It is with heartfelt sympathy that I send this message. I have three boys of my own, and I cannot even begin to imagine the pain that you are going through right now. I have thought a lot about Blake these past few days. Even though I only knew him for a brief period of time, I could tell that he was not only a tough kid for playing an entire season with a stress fracture, but also a very kind, funny, and thoughtful kid. He had a wonderful smile. It was great to see him in the Clinic. Your family has been constantly in my thoughts and prayers.
>
> May you have comfort in knowing he is walking with Jesus.

I received another letter from Blake's coach –

> I just wanted to write your family a letter and express my condolences on the loss of Blake. I cannot begin to imagine how hard it would be for all of you during this difficult time. As you know, Blake was a great person and someone that I thank God I had the opportunity to coach. It has been difficult this summer not having him around, but I know he is with us all. He was always so positive and a very hard worker, no matter what he did. He led by example, and I feel that is what makes a special football player and person. I always pushed the linebackers very hard, and he always responded by giving it his all, even playing through a stress fracture for most of last season. I know he left a lasting impression on all of his teammates as well. They are working so hard and want to make Blake proud of them throughout this season. This was the best we have practiced since I have been here this summer. I know that there are great leaders on this team who want to make you guys proud.
>
> I will always carry Blake with me for the rest of my life. He is a special person, and I will never forget him or your family. Please know that if anyone ever needs anything at all, do not hesitate to

contact me. We are going to have a great season this year, and I know that your family and Blake will be there every step of the way. God Bless, and thank you for showing me how to stay strong through the hardest adversity possible.

Coach Gibbons

On July 29th, the community came together and had their First Annual Angels in the Outfield Baseball game - Senior Babe Coaches vs. Players Memorial Competition. It was so much fun cheering on both teams. So many of the coaches who played were coaches who coached Blake through the years. Many of the players played with him on the baseball field and on the football field. What a great event that brought many wonderful childhood memories to life again. When I saw the Ursems, I remember countless fun memories. Coach Ursem would always call Blake, "Clutch." Blake scored many home runs when he played on his team.

CHAPTER 4:
FIRST BIRTHDAY IN HEAVEN

I remember Blake's first birthday in heaven. The week before, leading up to his birthday, was very painful. All the anticipation and the feeling of him not being with us was unbearable. I felt lost and alone. That week, I felt God was nowhere to be found. I could not feel Him holding me and lifting me up. That week, I kept thinking about Grandma Boots and the strength that she had when her son passed away. I remember her sitting in her recliner, clutching her little blue book. I wish I had that little blue book. She hung onto every word as her tears touched the cover of that book. I remember her telling me that the Blessed Mother was able to get her through her toughest days because she could understand the pain after experiencing the loss of Jesus when He died on the cross. "The Blessed Mother is the only one who can relate to all the pain that I am feeling," she told me.

Well, that day finally came, it was August 27th, and it seems like yesterday Blake was born into this world. He would have been 18 years old. I remember sitting on the floor in his bedroom and looking up at his life-size fathead when he got his one and only touchdown. I could see his eyes through the helmet. I wonder what heaven is like. If he were alive, I wonder what he would be doing on his birthday before his senior year. I can't do this to myself and think of what he would be doing. The pain was overwhelming.

As I sat in the middle of his room, I looked over at his white plastic storage drawers. I have not had the courage yet to go through his personal things. I contemplated opening it up and going through it. Then all of a sudden, I found myself going through it. He had a bunch of his high school spiral notebooks on top, and then I came across something he wrote in 8th grade, Blake's Autobiography Project, with a picture of him in 8th Grade wearing a Brunswick football shirt. Underneath his picture, he wrote, "Don't judge a man until you walk a mile in his shoes," 2008-2009.

Work in Progress - April 15, 2009

> We are all a work in progress. As an eighth-grade student, I have grown in many ways. At the beginning of my 8th-grade year, I struggled with my attitude, but now I am open-minded about doing things. My self-confidence has soared since the beginning of this year. One of my most prestigious accomplishments is my work ethic; nothing is ever done without completion. I wouldn't change one step I took to get where I am today.

At the beginning of this year, I would look at work or a problem and fret that it looked too hard, and I put negative thoughts in my head without even trying to start the problem. I would fear the thought of being wrong. It was a very notable aspect of me. Teachers and students saw it whenever I was called upon. It wasn't until the start of the third quarter that my math teacher pulled me aside and told me I have to start thinking positively, otherwise known as PMA (Positive Mental Attitude). Once I put the thought in my head of positivity, I never looked back. Now I am a very involved and hard-working student. This also puts the idea of believing in myself into play.

Self-confidence always struck me as something hard to grasp or take in. Growing up, you never want to say the wrong thing or look stupid. No one likes to be embarrassed or ashamed. For the beginning portion of this year, I was the same way. I hid behind the curtain and lay low in the classroom. Then it struck me, what do I care what other people think of me? Everyone is so afraid to fail; they will never grasp the expression that you won't get anything unless you ask questions. Once I took that to heart, I became a more active student in the classroom and I am happier in my schooling institution. I can now look and think about how I didn't have faith in myself. It's so easy to talk and trust my work and believe I got it right now.

I was always one to do my homework; doing it wasn't the issue, my work ethic was. I would do the work without taking in what I was learning just to get it done. Suddenly, I found out this was a very ineffective strategy. Test scores went down, and grades dropped. I knew I had to change my ways. My first thought was to get help. That went on for a month or two, but the scores stayed the same. I knew my work strategies needed improvement, so I slowed down on my homework and did extra work to ensure that I knew what I was doing right. This work ethic indeed turned out to be effective.

This eighth-grade school year is one to remember, with so many significant improvements and good times. I understand that my positive mental attitude, great self-confidence, and strong work ethic will not only help me through the next four years of my life in high school but will follow me up into the real world, where I will have great attributes that will lead me to a very promising and successful life.

As I look back on Blake's life, I realize that Blake had an enormous change in eighth grade, and he became a leader. He grew into himself and into his confidence. The teachers in our lives truly make a difference and shape who we are.

(Influential Person Letter)
On 3/31/09 - Lebron James

Dear Lebron James,

I am writing this letter to thank you for having such a positive influence on me. I, myself, and many other people nationwide, look up to you and praise you for what you have done. You started with nothing, barely obtaining a home to stay at, but you endured and have become a global icon. People like me idolize you for this. It shows there is hope out there to become what you want! The road to success isn't an easy one, but a person like you made it look easy. All the temptations to break and you never did, it made you a stronger person, which one day I also aspire to do one day.

Your Fan,
Blake

Who Am I?
Descriptive Essay

People have different opinions of what they think of me. My parents think I'm very ambitious to make a little cash at any time. My teachers, well, they think I'm a bit chatty, do all my work, and don't do half bad, but I seem to have to stop chatting with friends in between lessons. My friends have mixed feelings about me. Some think I'm very sweet and kind because I'm there for them when they're down. Some of my friends believe I'm kind of annoying. They think I'm annoying because I laugh at a lot of things that they believe aren't funny.

I believe I'm a courageous person. I'm courageous because I'm very brave. I stand up for what I believe in, and I'm a leader, not a follower. Courage shows you're strong when the going gets tough. I think I fit that definition of courage.

I am who I am. If I could, I wouldn't change one thing about me, well, maybe my height, but that's all. I believe I am a strong person who has good judgment and knows what's right and what's wrong.

I feel my friends, family, and teachers like me for who I am, not for what they want me to be.

"I am" Poem

I am ambitious and smart
I wonder when I will be called "Dad."
I hear the wind blowing in my ear when I'm running.
I see the night pushing the day sky past the horizon.
I want to be successful so I can be a role model for my friends and family.
I am ambitious and smart.

I pretend that one day I will be a superstar for millions to see.
I feel the sun beating down on my back.
I touch success every day I go to school.
I worry I won't live up to the expectations I have for myself.
I cry at the thought of losing a family member.
I am ambitious and smart.

I understand life has its ups and downs.
I say what I mean.
I dream of being something great.
I try to make people proud.
I hope to be a great father figure to my children.
I am ambitious and smart.

By Blake Bartchak

As I read this, I could not stop crying. Blake wanted to be a dad - He wondered when he would be called a dad. Then he mentioned it later in his poem - I hope to be a great father figure to my children. I know that Blake would have made an amazing dad, because he was always holding all the babies in our family. He would spend hours with them and make them laugh. I know he would have loved to be their coach and to guide them on this journey of life. He would have made one heck of a father, as well as an incredible husband. I miss him so much.

At his young age, he understood that life has its ups and downs, and he would cry at the thought of losing a family member. In Blake's short life, he never lost a close family member. All of his grandparents were still alive. Here we all are - we lost him, and we are all crying over his loss.

In his poem, he wrote, "I worry I won't live up to the expectation that I have for myself." Like mother, like son. My biggest worry is the same. I am

51

always worried that I won't live up to the expectations that I have for myself.

In his poem, he also stated, "I try to make people proud." He always made us very proud. Throughout this poem, he wrote, "I am ambitious and smart." As I read this poem over and over, I realized that for such a young person, he understood what was important in life. He was wise beyond his years, for most children his age, it is all about them. In his poem, I see his character; what he wanted for his future, which was to be a dad and to be a role model for his children, for family and friends. He truly made a difference to all of us in his short life here on earth.

God led me to this autobiography on his birthday. To remind me that he was, and still is, my beautiful son. He might not be with me, but he is always in my heart.

That evening, we started off with a mass in the chapel at Saint Ambrose, surrounded by family and friends. Then we went up to Resurrection Cemetery. All my family came up to celebrate Blake; the Chaya, the Poerner, and the Fox Families all came up. All of us knew what it felt like to lose a child. Some of Blake's friends also came up to be with us. We had blue and white cupcakes with the number 36 on them to represent his football number. We all gathered in a circle, and we sang *Happy Birthday* to Blake and lifted a bunch of blue and white balloons to the heavens.

When everyone left, my mom handed me a gift bag. When I looked at the bag, I said to my mom, I hope this is Grandma Boot's little blue book, *Mothers' Manual* by A. Francis Coomes S.J. She exclaimed, "How did you know?" I said, "I didn't know, I was just praying about it all week, as I didn't know if anyone still had it." I was praying I had her little book, so I could pray the same prayers she prayed when her son passed away. When I opened it up, it was exactly how I remembered it. It faded over time, and the cover had a stain from all the tears that she cried. The book was falling apart, and the pages were loose, but it was the perfect gift to receive today, because those pages were dear to my grandmother's heart. They were pages she read repeatedly. Now I have the same book that I can read over and over to help me through the loss of my son, Blake.

CHAPTER 5:
SENIOR YEAR FOOTBALL SEASON WITHOUT BLAKE

It was August 31st, and the first home game at Brunswick High School. The first game was on August 24th at Padua High School, and we won that game 42-7. All I could think of was that this was to be Blake's senior year, the year he had been waiting for his whole life. He always talked about how he couldn't wait to play under the lights with all his friends and be cheered on by all the Brunswick fans.

The team gathered in the locker room before the game, and as they formed their lines to go out onto the field. There was a banner above the door that said, "As Our Angels watch over us". It had Blake's football picture on the left with his name under it, and Jeff's football picture on the right with his name under it. In between them is the Brunswick Logo with Angel wings. Written down below, it said, "Play like a Blue Devil Today!" Each player hit the banner as they walked out of the locker room and onto the field. They still have the banner up today in the locker room, and before they go out to take the field, each player hits the banner.

The football team asked us if we wanted to flip the coin at the beginning of the game. We said we would be honored.

Bob and I, and Brittany sat on Brunswick's home side bench. Brent led the team with Team Captains Brad, Blake's best friend since middle school, and Eric. Both held up Blake's helmet in the air. Brad is holding it on one side, and Eric is holding it on the other. They proudly walked through the Brunswick Banner. I know Blake is watching from above, and he will always be a Brunswick Blue Devil and an angel up above.

As they walked through the banner with the whole Brunswick football team behind them, the stadium was silent. Then they all stood straight in a line. They held their football helmets in front of them and looked up at the American flag as they sang the National Anthem. As I looked over at Brent and the whole football team, I had tears rolling down my face, thinking I wish Blake were here with his teammates. After they sang the *National Anthem*, Brunswick played the *Brunswick Fight Song*, and we were ready to start the game.

The referees came over and said it was time to toss the coin. We all locked arms with the team captains. We walked slowly to the middle of the field with our Brunswick "B" logo in the center of it all. We joined up with the team Captains of Lake Catholic Cougars; they were on one side, and we were all standing on the other. Brent, Eric, and Brad placed their arms around each other as they tossed the coin. Let the game begin. We won that game 38-10! I know Blake had the best seat in the house and was playing right by their side.

On October 19th, it was Senior Parents' Night. A night that Bob and I could not wait to walk through the Brunswick Blue Devil Tunnel with Blake at our side. Brad and Eric led the team, and they proudly held Blake's Helmet up in the air with his #36 shown on the back of his helmet. Brad held one side of his helmet, and Eric held the other side, as they went through the big Brunswick Blue Devil tunnel. They said, "You are gone, but not forgotten."

Bob and I stood side by side on the home side bleachers with Brent and Brittany in front of us. I had a huge lump in my throat, along with tears rolling down my cheeks. This was his year, the year he talked about since he was a little boy. He couldn't wait to play for Brunswick High School and play under the lights. We couldn't wait to celebrate with him and walk by his side through the Brunswick Blue Devil Tunnel.

This was the same field that I walked down in my senior year, with my parents at my side when I was a cheerleader for Brunswick High. Now, at this moment, when we were supposed to walk by Blake's side with him on both of our arms, we were watching Brad, Blake's best friend, and Eric holding up his helmet. As I look into the dark night with the bright lights shining over the field, I know our beautiful Brunswick Blue Devil is always watching over us. He is now our beautiful Angel in Heaven. I know he has the best seat in the house, as he is cheering on all his Blue Devil Teammates.

This day was a very tough day for both Bob and me. I know this was a day that Bob could not wait to walk with his son on senior night, to experience that moment together, as one football player to another. Bob played football for Holy Name High School. He always told me those were the best of times, being part of a team and being with his classmates.

Then it was time for the game to start. The team gathered to go through the Brunswick Blue Devil Tunnel and then went through the Brunswick Blue Devil Banner. The banner that everyone signed when all four of the teens died in the car accident. The same banner that Blake's casket went through when he died. To me, the banner represents a community coming together during a very difficult time. Blake always said, "Go Big or Go Home," and that evening we won 31-19.

At the end of the year, they had a banquet, and they gave us Blake's Senior Banner along with a memory book. Each senior received a book that was about them. When I turned to Senior Parents' Night, October 19th, 2012, this is what it said.

Senior Parents' Night
October 19th, 2012

Blake Bartchak - In memory of our fellow teammate and friend.

Our celebration walk of our senior year could not be made without you.
You are gone but not forgotten.
Our friend through the years

That year, they dedicated the season to Blake.

They had a wonderful season:

August 24th	Padua Franciscan	Win - 42-7
August 31	Lake Catholic	Win - 38-10
September 7	Austintown-Fitch	Loss - 35-7
September 14	Hudson	Win - 26-22
September 28	Mentor	Loss 21-49
October 5	Twinsburg	Loss 26-14
October 12	Strongsville	Win 27-16
October 19	Solon	Win 31-19
October 26	Medina	Win 21-0

I noticed that at the end of the season, we won 6 games and lost 3 – Blake died on 6-3, and his number was 36.

CHAPTER 6:
FIRST HOLIDAY WITH BLAKE IN HEAVEN

First Thanksgiving with Blake in Heaven - Angels and Rainbows

It was November 22nd, and our first Thanksgiving without Blake. At 1:00 p.m., we met up with the Chaya and Poerner Families to be with our kids. It was still very difficult to believe that they were gone, and not with us. It was so nice that we all had each other to lean on.

Later, we went over to Jean's house, Bob's sister, for Thanksgiving dinner. When we arrived at her house, Brent sat down on the stairs leading upstairs. Brent and Blake always sat on those steps at her house. When we were all talking, I noticed a big, circular rainbow right next to Brent. I know Blake was present and wanted to sit next to Brent. When we sat down for Thanksgiving dinner, right before we said our Thanksgiving prayer, a rainbow appeared right behind the angel on top of Jean's curio cabinet. The rainbow spread across the angel's wings, and it was so bright on her ceiling. Jean told me this is the first year she decided to bring out her angel early. She usually puts it out for Christmas.

Our Thanksgiving Miracle. Blake was with us.

On December 18th, I received a call in the morning from Mickie, whose son Zak worked at Buehler's with Blake. I met Mickie in my bereavement class and found out her dad died on Blake's birthday. She was struggling with the loss of her dad. He died of Alzheimer's the same way my grandmother passed away. I talked to her on the phone a few weeks ago and made her realize that she lost him slowly. Her mom was having surgery. She prayed to her dad and to Blake that her mom's surgery would go well. A couple of days later, she had a dream about Blake. I asked Mickie if she would type a message about how she remembered her dream about Blake. This is what she sent over to me.

On Monday, December 10th, when I was sleeping, I had a dream, and your son, Blake, came to me in my dream. He asked me to get blue angel ornaments for you and the moms of those in the accident. I did not see Blake in my dream. As I think about it, I only recall hearing his voice asking me to do this for him and the other kids. He was speaking to everyone.

I awoke the morning of December 11th (which was my parents' 68th wedding anniversary), and all day I kept having the thought of "blue angel ornaments" popping into my head. The next day, December 12th, I went online and started searching eBay and Amazon for blue angel ornaments. I scrolled through page after page looking at hundreds of blue angel ornaments, not knowing exactly what I was looking for. Just then, I was following the voice from my dream, asking me to look for and get blue angel ornaments. I found one that seemed to be "the one" and remembered where it was and kept looking, but went back because the feeling it had kept telling me that the blue angel ornament was "the one" I was supposed to get for everyone. Once I clicked on it and saw it up close, I loved it. It was a Swarovski crystal ornament (my mother has a collection of Swarovski snowflake crystal ornaments, and so do I), and I was already familiar with the brand name. The blue was beautiful! It reminded me of my daddy's wonderful blue eyes, and I knew that was it, and that I had to have one for myself too. I immediately placed the order on Amazon.com. The box arrived on Saturday, December 15th, at my doorstep.

I called Terri on Monday, December 17th, and we met on Tuesday, December 18th, at Starbucks, where I gave her the ornament that I knew was a gift from Blake; and all the kids to their moms for Christmas, as well as a gift to me too from my Daddy. I was so glad it was the "right one," and I followed my instinct to act on my dream from Blake. After talking with Terri that evening and finding out that she played in my home as a kid growing up on the next street, I knew our paths in life were meant to cross.

Merry Christmas from your Blue Angels in Heaven!

Love,
Mickie

When I met up with Mickie at Starbucks, she told me all about her dream, and she gave me wonderful angel ornaments for all the moms. I told her that it looked like God's loving arms are protecting the angel inside. I could not thank her enough for sharing this with me and for buying all of us these beautiful angel ornaments. I felt so blessed that I received a gift from Blake from heaven above. I especially felt blessed that Mickie followed her voice and listened to her calling. I will treasure this ornament forever.

CHAPTER 7:
CHRISTMAS MIRACLE

We made it through Thanksgiving, and Christmas was around the corner. Each day it was so tough to just get up and move. My husband was really struggling. He wanted to go to Florida the week before Thanksgiving and come back around January 5th. I told him that Blake loved Christmas, and he was the one who always helped me decorate the house and put the manger up each year. I knew that Blake would want us here in Brunswick to be with family and friends. He said he just wanted to escape. I know that we all grieve differently, and I had to respect the way Bob was grieving. He spent so much time being with Blake at the cemetery. I go two to three times a week, but I know he is with me all the time. Blake is always part of me.

I asked Bob if I could decorate the house for Christmas and change all our red and green to Brunswick blue and white. He commented that it was fine, but I know he really didn't want to do anything. I felt in my heart that I really wanted Blake to be part of this Christmas and every Christmas. My mom helped me. She made beautiful blue and white wreaths for all the windows, and a stunning blue and white wreath for the front door with an angel ornament to one side. I decorated my staircase with blue and white ribbons with little white snowflakes. I decorated our family Christmas tree with all our Christmas ornaments through the years. I had another Christmas tree for our front window. I decorated that tree with pictures of Blake through the years, added angel wings, and cross ornaments throughout the tree.

My mom and dad surprised me one evening. They decorated the four pine trees by the fire pit that we built that summer in memory of Blake. We have two trees on one side and two trees on the other side of the firepit. The first tree was all white lights, the 2nd tree was all royal blue lights, and then on the other side, the 3rd tree was all white lights, and the 4th tree was all royal blue lights. I looked at the trees and started crying. I knew Blake was smiling from heaven when he saw these beautiful blue and white lights - Go Big Blue!!! What a beautiful gift from my parents to surprise me with blue and white Christmas lights by Blake's fire pit.

This year, Saint Ambrose Parish decided to dedicate memorial trees to those who lost loved ones. They placed four trees going up the main entrance for Blake, Jeff, Lexi, and Kevin. They placed a sign with their name on it by each tree. The whole campus was filled with decorated trees of their loved ones who had passed, and their names on the sign. Blake's tree was filled with pictures of him through the years and football ornaments. On top of the tree, I decided instead of placing a star on top, I would place a little white football helmet. I decorated it to look like his Brunswick football helmet. Jeff's tree was also decorated in blue and white with football ornaments and pictures of him. Lexi's tree was all decorated with purple ornaments, with beautiful pictures of her through the years. Kevin's tree was red for his love of hockey, and he had pictures of himself through the years with lots of hockey ornaments, as well as Christmas tree ornaments.

They started the evening off with the Saint Ambrose Choir singing in the church. We were then led out of the church by Father Bob. When we all gathered around the front of the church, they turned on a switch, and the whole campus lit up with all the decorated Christmas Trees. Our family and friends gathered around Blake's tree, and we talked all night with the Chaya, Poerner, and Fox families. We walked around, looked at all the decorated Christmas trees, and talked to others who had lost loved ones. We were all lifted up with abundant love, understanding, and peace that filled our hearts. At this moment, everyone understood how hard this Christmas was going to be after the loss of someone they loved. They continued this at Saint Ambrose for a few years after.

The Girl Scout Troop 90502 had a Candlelight Vigil and Caroling at the Brunswick Lake Memorial for all our loved ones who had passed. They also invited other families that lost loved ones in the past year. We all stood under the pergola and the surrounding area, as we listened to Christmas music that was playing. When they developed this area at Brunswick Lake, they also added music that plays all the time. The Girl Scout Troop passed out little white candles. Their parents lit their daughters' candles, and in turn, they lit each one of ours. The light was being passed around one by one, and soon each candle was lit. They also handed out pamphlets with all the songs, so we all joined in singing. The first song they sang was *Mary Did You Know?*[19] As I watched all the girls singing with their mothers watching over them as they were singing, I couldn't help but stop myself from crying, as my son was no longer with me. I am a mother, and I can feel Mary's pain as each line of the song is sung. Everyone joined in, but the voice of young children truly tugged at my heart.

> "Mary, did you know that your baby boy will one day walk on water? Mary, did you know that your baby boy will save our sons and daughters? Did you know that your baby boy has come to make you new? This child that you've delivered will soon deliver you."

I reminisced that it seemed like Blake was just born into this world, and not long ago, I was holding him in my arms. The tears were just rolling down my cheek.

"Mary, did you know that your baby boy will give sight to a blind man? Mary, did you know that your baby boy will calm a storm with His hand? Did you know that your baby boy has walked where angels trod?"

As I looked up to the sky, my son and all these families around me, all our loved ones were surrounded by God and all the angels.

"And when you kiss your little baby, you've kissed the face of God?"

I can't even imagine the look on Blake's face when he met God face-to-face and received a kiss from his Father up above. I remember kissing his little cheeks and rubbing my hand over his beautiful head, as if it were just yesterday.

"Mary, did you know? The blind will see, the deaf will hear, and the dead will live again, the lame will leap, the dumb will speak the praises of the Lamb. Mary, did you know that your baby boy is Lord of all creations? Mary, did you know that your baby boy will one day rule the nations? Did you know that your baby boy is heaven's perfect Lamb? Is this sleeping child you're holding the Great I Am?"

As the tears continued to fall, I felt so blessed that I was the mother of Blake. I was able to hold him and be his mom for seventeen fruitful years. Now, he is in the arms of his Heavenly Father. I could feel the love that Mary had for her son as she watched her son grow up. Mary herself had to endure so much raising her sweet son, and then had to let him go. Going forward, I will turn to Mary, as she is a mother who had to let her child go and to be with God. My grandmother taught me the prayers of the Blessed Mother. I watched her hold onto her little blue book as she prayed many times, never knowing that I would someday do the same. Losing a child is the hardest thing I have ever had to do.

The next song they sang was *Silent Night* [20,] and this song brought more tears to me. This song is part of our family traditions. Every Christmas Eve, we sing *Happy Birthday* to Jesus. Whoever gets the M&M in their cake places baby Jesus in the manger. I will always remember the look on Blake's smiling face when he was eating his cake, and he saw the M&M. He held the M&M so high! He yelled, "Look what I have, I have the M&M." That smile was so contagious, and it melted my heart. His excitement lit up the room, and he was so excited that he would get to place baby Jesus in the manger. We read the Bible verse when Baby Jesus was born and then sang *Silent Night*, as Blake placed Baby Jesus in the manger. So many amazing memories were flowing through my mind as I watched all these beautiful young girls sing their hearts out to *Silent Night*.

The last song they sang was, *The Little Drummer Boy* [21] Blake always smiled so big when that song was played. I can see him with his silly grin, shaking his head back and forth, and drumming in the air when the "*Pa rum pum pum pum, rum pum pum pum, rum pum pum pum*" played. I looked around at everyone under the pergola, and each person's face was lit up from the candlelight. What a very special night this was with all of us gathered for this coming Christmas. They were all singing with joyous hearts. You can certainly tell they were smiling under all their winter clothing with scarves and mittens on, holding their candle in one hand, and holding tightly onto the pamphlet with their other hand. They were singing as loud as they could. After they sang all the songs, they passed out cookies for all of us to enjoy. What a memorable day, they truly brought Christmas joy into our hearts that evening.

A few days later, I received a card in the mail from my Aunt Terri. She wrote me a letter, and she returned a Christmas card to me, which our family gave to her family the Christmas of 1997.

> Dear Bob and Terri,
>
> Recently, while cleaning out a cabinet, I came across a file I hadn't looked at for several years. In it were a few random items and this card. Terri, I imagine you will remember when you made these for everyone with Brent and Blake. Those little handprints inside made me smile (remembering) how much fun you had creating such masterpieces!
>
> I was unsure if you had any copies, but I thought I would forward ours to you. I gauged Brent to be around 5 and Blake around 3ish?
>
> Those little hands of Brent and Blake's have touched so many hearts throughout their lives. Thank you for allowing us the opportunity to watch those little boys grow up to be such fine and loved individuals. Blake has to be smiling down from heaven, seeing what beautiful, fun-loving impressions he made on so many lives. I will forever remember these impressions of their hands and the smiles that would have been on their faces!
>
> Love,
> Aunt Terri

I gave each family member a homemade Christmas card in 1997. In the center of the card was a big triangle painted green in the shape of a Christmas Tree with painted red, circled ornaments throughout the tree. It had a brown tree trunk. When you opened up the card, it had Brent's handprint in green paint with his name underneath, which he wrote, and Blake's handprint in red paint with his name, which he wrote with some help from me. In the center was written 1997.

I cried when I received this Christmas card in the mail. I can remember sitting at the kitchen table in our little house in Parma, working on all those homemade Christmas cards. It seemed like yesterday when they were so small.

It was the week before Christmas, and we always celebrate Christmas with my side of the family, with my parents, my sister's family, and my brother. This year, we decided to have it at my sister's house. In the past, we always went to my parents to celebrate Christmas, but we wanted to change it up this year. We were all sitting in my sister's sunroom with their beautiful family Christmas tree adorned with lots of ornaments from throughout their children's lives.

Many presents were given, and I thought we were all done. Then, a few minutes later, my mom and dad came into the room holding a very large present and handed it over to Bob and me. I looked at my parents. They said, "This is for you". I thanked them. Bob and I looked at each other and we couldn't imagine what it was. We opened the present together. It was the most beautiful and heartfelt present I have ever received. It was a portrait of Blake sitting on the bleachers holding a football with the biggest smile on his face. Mrs. Klingel, a retired teacher at Brunswick High School, made this for my parents to give to us. My mom remembered me saying that I would never have a senior picture of Blake. Well, she gave us the best Christmas present ever. I received my senior portrait of Blake! It was unbelievable how she captured his smile and his personality in this picture. I don't know how she did it, but she did. Another thing was that somehow, he looked a little more mature than his junior year school picture. The way he was sitting on the bleachers and holding the football captured his free spirit.

Coincidentally, as a perfect example of how God has a plan for everything in his own timing. The week before, God let me see the artist who drew Blake's portrait. It was at a book signing event at a cute little cupcake shop in Medina Square. This is where my cousin Bonnie's husband, Joe Romano, was autographing books, as well as drawing characters for young children to have. Joe did all the illustrations for a health book. Mrs. Klingel gave him some drawing lessons and some techniques. She wanted to be there to support him. We just happened to be at the book signing at the very same time. I am so glad that I had the opportunity to meet her. Every time I look at that portrait it reminds me of our first Christmas with Blake in Heaven, and the artist behind the portrait, who was the art teacher when I attended Brunswick High School.

Christmas was coming soon, and Bob was very down. He really just wanted to go to Florida. My heart was aching for him and for our whole family. I kept praying that God would be near and would comfort him and our family.

On Saturday morning, December 22nd, I received a text message from Jen Kirkpatrick, a neighbor down the street. Her husband, Rich, has been in the hospital since Monday. He was at the Cleveland Clinic and had emergency heart surgery. She said Rich is taking a bad turn, and his breathing tube was removed on Friday. They had to place it back on Saturday. Jen also said she was praying to Blake to be by Rich's side, and to close the gates of heaven because she wasn't ready to let him go. She asked me if I could give her any prayers or anything that she could hold onto. In a gift bag, I dropped off my favorite devotional book, *Jesus Calling* [22] by Sarah Young, a copy of the *Mothers' Manual* - Prayers of the Blessed Mother that was my Grandma Boots, and I marked the page for a sick husband. I also placed a wallet picture of Blake in his junior year, along with Blake's candle that I received on All Souls Day at Saint Ambrose, with his name on the candle. I told Jen that I had placed everything in the cooler that they had set up on their front porch. Later that day, I received a text from Jen. It was Saturday, December 22nd at 6:07 p.m. This was her text message to me: "So, the last two hours have been touch-and-go with Rich. The minute we lit Blake's candle, we received the word he was stable again - Thank you! God is amazing." I heard that her sister picked up the gift bag from her house and was driving to the hospital. Jen told her, "You have to stop somewhere and light Blake's candle." She did.

Not too long after Jen received the text message with the picture of Blake's lit candle, the doctor came out to the waiting room and told her, "I have no idea what happened, but I think your husband is going to pull through." Jen said, "I know what happened, we lit Blake's candle."

Jen kept us all "in the loop," and sent us text messages on Rich's condition. This news brought hope to Bob and I. The thought of Blake's candle helping Rich pull through gave us faith that Blake was watching over us and interceding for us.

Bob and I both prayed and we lit a candle for Rich; this was helping us get through Christmas. It was taking our minds off of the loss of Blake and we were praying to God and Blake for a miracle.

Christmas was here and our family went to Christmas Eve mass. It was so beautiful, and the church was packed. Before the mass, they reenacted the story of Mary and Joseph, with baby Jesus being born in the stable. All the kids looked adorable, dressed up in their costumes. During the mass beautiful songs were sung. Bells were passed out when you walked into the church. All the little kids were ringing their bells throughout the mass. Every time I heard the bells ring; I would look up at the crucifix and think, "Every time a bell rings an angel gets their wings." I know that this Christmas, Blake will have the most amazing Christmas, being with Jesus.

After Christmas Eve mass at 4:00 p.m., Bob went to the cemetery because Brent told him that Grandma Rini and Papa Jerry had a battery-operated Christmas Tree at the cemetery. When he was at the cemetery praying, he saw a bunch of lights going into the heavens. He went over to where it was. It was my friend, Bonnie, and their family, sending lanterns up to heaven for their son Chris, who died at age 36. Bonnie and I have become good friends since both of our sons died that past summer. Bonnie gave two lanterns to Bob for our family to send off in memory of Blake. A true gift from God that Bob was at the cemetery at the exact same time. I believe God brought this miracle to us because Bonnie and I have leaned on each other that year. I went to see Blake at the cemetery in the morning. I wanted to spend time alone, just the two of us.

When Bob came home, we packed up our car to go to my parents for our celebration. We are always the first ones to arrive. My sister and her family always go over to Todd's family first to celebrate, and arrive later. The house started filling up with all my aunts and uncles, all my cousins, and their kids. All the kids were very little, and they were filled with excitement knowing Santa was coming soon. That would start with all the wonderful traditions that we have been doing since I was a little girl.

My sister and her family arrived. The house was filled with lots of conversations and delicious food. My mom was going around and passing out glasses of Kahlua filled with vanilla ice cream, milk, and chocolate syrup. They tasted like milkshakes. I went into the kitchen to help her pass them out, and I noticed that the bottle of Kahlua was established in 1936. I looked at the bottle again, and then I started to cry. We have been toasting with Kahlua for many years, and I never noticed this before. As I looked at the bottle ESTD 1936, I started to smile as tears rolled down my cheeks. That is Blake's football number. This is my favorite drink, the only drink that I really like, and it's Blake's number. As we all gathered in the living room, my mom said Let's lift our glasses and toast Blake, Grandma Boots, Papa Jim, and Uncle Jimmy. As we lifted our glasses, I felt so much love and joy in the room. I knew that Blake was up in heaven with all our relatives who had gone before him.

It was time for all the Christmas traditions to begin. Every year, we have some type of Christmas piñata. This year, my mom, known as Grandma Rini to all the kids, bought a football piñata in memory of Blake. All the kids had a turn trying to break the piñata. Sometimes, Brittany doesn't have a turn because powerhouse Garrett goes before her. This year, Brittany actually had a turn. When Brittany placed the blind fold over her eyes, she noticed there was something written in the inside of the blind fold. It read "Unique 36 06/12" another sign from God above. The number 36 from Blake's jersey and the month/year he died was 06/12. I'm so glad Blake was with us on Christmas. He always loved all the traditions on Christmas Eve. After the piñata breaks, Blake always placed half of the broken piñata on his head so we could take a picture. When the football broke and the candy spilled out, Brittany placed half of the broken piñata on her head just like Blake used to do. Now Brittany takes that role each year and places it on her head.

After we cleaned up everything from the piñata, we gathered all the kids around the table downstairs and sang *Happy Birthday* to baby Jesus. Each year we have a cake that is decorated with an advent wreath, and we place an M&M in the cake. Whoever finds the M&M gets to place baby Jesus in the manger. This year it was my cousin Carrie's son, Garrett. How beautiful that Garrett is the one to place baby Jesus in the manger. Blake is now up in heaven with my Uncle Jimmy, and this is Uncle Jimmy's grandson. My cousin Carrie is my Uncle Jimmy's daughter. Uncle Jimmy made this wonderful manger that we place baby Jesus in every year. He made this manger right before he passed away. I also have one of the mangers that he made, a few years before my Grandma Boots passed away, she gave me hers. She told me I know that your Uncle Jimmy would have liked you to have this, he loved you very much. We read the passage in the Bible of when Jesus was born and then Garrett placed baby Jesus in the manger while we sang *Silent Night*.

As I looked over at Bob on the couch, I see a tear rolling down his cheek. I can feel his pain as our son is missing from the group of kids gathered around the manger this Christmas season. I went over to the little gifts that I made to pass out this Christmas Eve. They are little red stockings with Blake's junior year school picture in the middle with a felt football sticker in the left-hand corner of his picture, and above on the white part of the red stocking, Blake's name was written in royal blue glitter. Each stocking was filled with a copy of Grandma Boots' *Mothers' Manual* that she held so close to her side when her son passed away. I wanted everyone to have a little piece of Blake, and a little piece of Grandma Boots who started all these beautiful traditions, when I was a little girl. I placed the following on the inside cover of the book.

"I hope you enjoy this prayer book as much as I have enjoyed receiving it."

My Mom found Grandma Boots' prayer book and gave it to me this summer on Blake's Birthday.

I know this is a gift from above. Grandma Boots loved and prayed to the Blessed Mother. Every Tuesday before noon, she would say ten *Hail Marys* and she always said that something wonderful would happen. I will always remember her love for the Blessed Mother.

When she passed away my Grandma Boots had ten grandchildren. We were her pallbearers at her funeral. At her grave site we all stood in a circle and held hands as we prayed ten *Hail Marys* before noon on a Tuesday. I remember coming home from the funeral, and I received a basket full of goodies. They were a bunch of memories that reminded me of her. The grapefruit reminded me of how she cut it up in little triangles. She poured sugar all over the top to make them sweet. In the basket was also a packet of M&M's, she always had some M&M's in her pocket. She would ask, "Do you know what I have in my pocket?" But the one thing that really stood out was wrapped in a package, and it was mint brownies. Our family always had these mint brownies at parties and get-togethers. I remember Grandma Boots saying these are our heritage brownies; they are Irish brownies. A little piece of her was in this precious basket that I received the day of her funeral.

I remember crying on the couch, remembering her always telling me that if you pray ten *Hail Marys* on a Tuesday something beautiful will happen. Well Grandma, it is Tuesday, and we prayed ten *Hail Marys*. You are in the arms of your Heavenly Father and joined together with your beautiful son.

I also typed up this meaningful poem. Behind the words was a picture of the Wisemen on a hill looking over Bethlehem. I gave one copy to each person, and we read it all together as we cried.

I'm Spending Christmas with Jesus Christ this Year

Written by Wanda Bencke

I see the countless Christmas trees,
Around the world below.
With tiny lights, like heaven's stars,
Reflecting on the snow.
The sight is so spectacular,
Please wipe away that tear.
For I'm spending Christmas,
With Jesus Christ this year.
I hear the many Christmas songs,
That people hold so dear.
But the sounds of music can't compare,
with the Christmas Choir up here.
For I have no words to tell you,
The Joy their voices bring.
For it is beyond description,
To hear the angels, sing.
I can't tell you of the splendor,
Or the peace here in this place.
Can you just imagine Christmas?
With our Savior, face to face?
I'll ask Him to light your spirit,
As I tell Him of your love.

69

So then pray one for another,
As I lift your eyes above.
Please let your hearts be joyful,
And let your spirit sing.
For I'm Spending Christmas in Heaven,
And I'm walking with the King.

I looked over at Bob, Brent and Brittany, and everyone gathered in the living room, and felt blessed. God blessed me with the most beautiful family.

At the end of the night, Bob said come outside, I have a special gift I want to share. We all gathered around my parent's front yard as Bob and Todd lit the lantern that was given to him at the cemetery. It took a while for the flame to light up and fill up the lantern. When it finally did, the lantern floated in the sky slowly and swayed back and forth. Then it was going straight for the house across the street. We all became very scared that the lantern would hit the house and start the house on fire. I know Blake, the jokester, was laughing at this, and I wonder if somehow, he could make this happen just to make us all laugh. Then suddenly, the wind came and blew it away from the house. Our whole family watched as it was floating higher and higher in the sky and into the heavens, it looked like the Star of Bethlehem. Little by little, the light was getting dimmer and dimmer, and then it was gone. The light had disappeared into the night and into the heavens to be with Blake.

The next day, when we woke up, it was Christmas day. I felt so empty inside. I loved it when the kids would pile in our room, and say, "Santa was here, wake up". When they were little, Brent and Blake shared a room, and they would be up all night talking about what Santa was going to bring them this year. As they grew older, they had their own rooms but on Christmas Eve they would sleep together. At that moment, I wish I could go back in time. A time when we were all together, and a time when Blake was with us.

Today, the four of us headed downstairs. It was a different feeling, a feeling I will never forget. Again, I had the biggest lump in my throat. I truly wanted to melt and cry, but I knew that I had to bring Christmas and the Christmas spirit to our family. That is what Blake would have wanted.

Blake was the one that always became excited for Christmas. He always helped me decorate the house and he loved putting out the manager every year. It was hard decorating this year without his help, but I know he was watching from above. As we opened all the Christmas gifts we were all trying to be happy, but it was hard. We all felt the loss of Blake. He was the one that brought so much joy and excitement to the holidays with his big personality, his huge smile, and laughter.

After cleaning up from opening all the gifts, Brittany helped me set the table. She said this Christmas didn't seem like Christmas. "I miss Blake so much." I said, "I know, we all miss Blake. Christmas is always going to be hard for us, but Blake is always with us." I went upstairs and decided to bring down Blake's candle to add to our centerpiece. "Blake's light will shine with us always, especially on Christmas."

The doorbell rang, and the house was filling up one by one. We all gathered in the kitchen and Papa brought over the shrimp. It was always a Christmas tradition on Bob's side of the family. Papa fed us well. Papa's famous line was eat up and when you were so full, he would say eat some more until you were ready to burst. You never went home hungry when Big Don was in the house. We all sat around the kitchen table and at the kitchen island, eating appetizers as the roast was cooking in the oven.

Well, it was time and the roast were ready. Everyone that knows me knows that I am a terrible cook. Each year they take a picture of me getting the roast out of the oven like I was slaving over it all day. I knew Blake was laughing from heaven when he saw me getting the roast out of the oven. He always would crack jokes about it.

As we all gathered around the table, I lit Blake's candle so he would be with us. John started us off in prayer, he talked about Blake being in heaven, and that he would always be with us. We shared so many beautiful stories. After dinner we went into the family room and opened gifts. We could all feel the loss of Blake, and his big personality that so often would light up the room.

The holidays were over, and our family survived them. It was Saturday morning, December 29th, and I was walking around the cemetery thanking God for all His many blessings, as well as for all the beautiful signs that I received. I felt God's presence, and I felt Blake so close to my heart.

As I was standing next to Blake's grave I reflected on this past Christmas. I was thinking about Rich and Jen and their two kids, wondering how he was feeling. Then a few minutes later I received a text message from Jen. Rich was out of ICU and was in a room. Thank you, God, for hearing our prayers. So many people were praying for their family.

On December 30th Jen came over to our house, to explain what Rich saw before he woke up. Rich saw Blake before he woke up! "Thank you, Blake, for this miracle." After that day, Bob kept repeating that Rich saw Blake in

71

heaven. Ever since that day, when Jen came over, Bob has been able to move forward. He was so excited that Rich saw Blake in heaven. I mentioned to Bob a couple of times right after Blake passed, that Blake is with God in heaven and he will be looking over us always. Bob kept saying, "How do you know?" I said, "Because we have faith, and we believe." He said, "The last time I saw Blake, we buried him in the ground." He wasn't sure if he would ever see him again. I reminded him that all those years of Catholic school and attending Holy Name High School they taught you that we will all meet again in heaven. He said, "I know what I was taught, but after Blake passed, I just lost faith. However, after hearing that Rich saw Blake in heaven, I believe." Sometimes seeing is believing, just like Thomas the disciple needed to see the hole in Jesus' hand to believe. Then he believed Jesus was risen.

A few days after Christmas, my sister Traci was at a Medina High School Basketball game with her friend Sue. Jen told me earlier that week that Rich's follow-up nurse is friends with my sister. What a small world and that just cannot be a coincidence. I asked Traci if she could find out anything more from Sue, which would be great. Sue said, "I can't say anything unless you ask me questions, and I can answer." So, Traci asked Sue a few questions.

Sue was sharing the miracles that happened to Rich, and how Rich saw Blake in heaven. When she was sharing what happened, Traci looked up at the scoreboard and it said 36 Home, 36 Away, 1:36 left in the 3rd Period and there were 4 fouls. Blake's jersey number, and he died on the 3rd and 4 teens passed away in the car. God works in amazing ways. This was truly our Christmas miracle when Jen told us that Rich saw Blake in heaven!

A few months later I received a card from Rich and Jen and they both shared what happened to Rich. I called this a "Christmas Miracle."

72

This was when Rich woke up after almost nine days in the hospital.

Rich's Story:

Rich said he was inside a house - he knew it was Cathy White's house, but it did not look like the inside of what he knows Cathy's house looks like. There was a large great room. It was a runoff from the living room into the dining area. There was a china hutch and it was brown and had solid drawers and doors. The top half had glass with plates and glasses inside. The glasses were light colored and there was yellow cream paint on the walls and cream carpet. The living room area had a step down and, at an angle off towards the door there was the dining room where people were sitting. The table was big and roundish. The hutch was behind Cathy. My Aunt and Uncle sat next to Cathy. From where Rich was sitting, he could see their three faces clearly. There were others at the table, but their backs were to Rich.

At the table were Aunt Donna P, Uncle Denny, Cathy White, and another person who Rich thought was not deceased. There may have been other people there, but Rich cannot call them out by name. There was no dinner, but it was a dinner party, and everyone was just sitting around having a conversation.

Rich was hanging off to the side - on the outskirts of the dining room conversation - he was a bit upset. Rich said it was like looking at the scene from TV with weird angles. Rich was with Jimmy P, Blake Bartchak, and Russ (Russ looked like Ron Burgundy from Anchorman. Rich never met Russ, but that is exactly who he looked like, and his wife Cathy confirmed that he did look like him).

The folks at the table were talking about it being okay to move on, but it was the real estate agent, maybe at an open house who was talking to the folks at the table. The conversation at the dinner table was about it being "okay to move on".

Rich could hear the conversation at the table. Then the scene would cut back to Rich with his clique and the angels said, "No it is not ok to move on - only for them" pointing at the table. Rich said it was conveyed to him like this - not direct words. Rich says he had the feeling he was not supposed to be in this conversation. The feeling

73

was that he was not right in this group. This was not his conversation any longer. He was being told to leave the clique.

Then Rich was outside in a garage. He was in a high-chair type of chair, and he fit in the high-chair but could not move in the high-chair. He was with his Grandma Morrow. She did not say anything and was just sitting there. She was just "there", and that was Rich's Dining Story.

Jen's Version of When Rich Woke Up:

Rich woke up on December 26th after an almost nine-day journey of sedation, paralytics and less than a 5% chance of living through his ordeal.

One moment during our alone time in the ICU Rich said to me "Did we go to a dinner party at Cathy White's house?"

"No, Rich, you have been sedated for the last week and a half." Rich continues in his tired and almost asleep manner, "No we were there with your Aunt and Uncle, Jimmy and Cathy and others. They told me it was okay to move on." My heart sank. "No, Rich, it is not okay to move on, Rich. Rich!" I screamed in my head. But I was calm and said, "I don't get it." We had not been to a dinner party that week at all, so I was confused. Rich said, "No, Jen not me … them". The conversation was over, and he fell asleep. My heart was still in my stomach. What does that all mean? Them, who? I dismissed the conversation as not being able to understand and thought he was still under some drugs that remained in his body.

A day or so later, Rich revisited the story with me. He went into further detail telling me that the dinner party was with Joe and Cathy, my aunt and uncle and others. In addition, Rich added further detail about there being "cliques". Rich was not with me in the same clique. He felt as if he was floating with a different clique. My aunt's brother was with him, and I asked Rich why he said it was okay to move on. Rich said they told me it was not okay to move on with them, the people in my clique. "Who told you that?" I asked him. Rich said – "the people in my clique." "Who was with you?" I wanted to know.

The third conversation I had was with my brother. Rich was telling the story from the beginning. He said we were at a dinner party at

Cathy White's house. Cathy and Joe, my Aunt Donna and Uncle Dennis and others were at a dinner party. Rich was in a different clique and the cliques did not interact. The clique that Rich was in felt as if they were floating around not quite at the dinner party but there. Rich was hanging out with Jimmy P (aunts' brother), Russ (Cathy's husband) and Blake Bartchak. I asked, "Blake was there?" Rich said, "Yes, I have been saying that. Did I not tell you that before?" All three in his clique kept telling him that he was not allowed to move on. Not allowed to hang with them and he had to go outside. The way that I understood what he was saying was that these angels told him he could not go with them, and he had to come back to me and the kids!

When Jen shared what Rich saw, and after receiving these letters in the mail, we believe Rich saw Blake in heaven along with Jimmy P and Russ who have all passed away. The three of them told Rich it is not your time; go back and be with your family.

On June 2nd, 2013, Sue wrote me a letter, one day shy of Blake's one-year anniversary of the accident.

Dear Terri,

I'm writing to you to let you know that I still think of you often and pray for you a lot. I know this is a difficult time for you and I pray God will give you the strength to get through it. I wanted to share a story with you that I know you've heard but thought it might comfort you at this time of year, on Blake's one-year anniversary.

It started out as a regular busy day for me at work. I was going through my list of patients and was grateful I had a young 40 something guy on my schedule. Then I went through his record and thought my God this guy is like a walking miracle; I can't believe he survived. He literally died and had to be revived. I walked in the room to see him and asked if he remembered anything about being revived. He looked at me and said, "Yes, I remember everything." He told me he was at a beautiful dinner party and everything was white. He was with people he knew, and he didn't want to leave. I asked who he was with, and he told me he was with people who had passed on and he mentioned their names and one of them was Blake! It was so unexpected, so unbelievable, so amazing to hear. I hear these stories many times from parties, but this one really hit home. He went on to say that he didn't want to leave. It was the most beautiful place he'd ever seen. White, peaceful and he was having fun. He said then they told him he couldn't hang out with them anymore. He asked why and they said he had to go he had to go back. He saw heaven and Blake was there! I believe it and I know you do too! I hope that helps you.

There is another part to the story though. I saw the patient for follow-up visits for several weeks on a weekly basis. The last day I saw him he looked great, and we parted ways. He seemed grateful to be alive and doing well. I can't help but think that maybe he really wanted to be back at that beautiful dinner party at the table with Blake, having a wonderful time… at the Lord's Table. Anyway, the patient left the exam room, and I was charting on him when all of a sudden, the emergency call light went off in that room! No one was in the room! The doctors came running, other nurses came running, only there wasn't a patient in the room! We tried to shut it off and couldn't until finally it stopped. Everyone was saying "that's weird". I couldn't help but think that it was Blake playing a little trick, making us laugh. That's never happened before and it hasn't happened again, but I took it as a sign! I hope this letter lifts your spirits with the thought that Blake is in heaven; someone who died and was brought back to life actually saw him there. It wasn't a dream; the guy died, went to heaven, saw Blake, came back, and lived to talk about it. Believe it! This is truly a miracle.

With Love,
Sue

Bob had a very difficult time after Blake died and sat at the cemetery all the time. I had to call Bob's boss in September and ask him if he could call Bob to say he missed him at work and really needed him back. His boss was reluctant at first; I convinced him to do it. His boss took Bob out to dinner. When he came home, he said, "They missed me and would love to see me back in the office." Bob informed me he was going back to work on Monday. He needed that purpose again.

The near-death experience did not happen for no reason. It changed Bob because he was similar to doubting Thomas from the Bible. Aren't we all like doubting Thomas? We have to see that our loved ones are okay, and they are with God. The unknown is so difficult. We miss our loved ones and want to make sure they are in a safe place. This gave our family comfort knowing Rich saw Blake, it gave our family peace.

If you would like to see the YouTube interview - Man says he saw Brunswick Teen in Near-Death Experience[23]
- https://youtu.be/bVPnWGogL30

CHAPTER 8:
UNFORGETTABLE MIRACLES

My First Easter without Blake

It was Sunday, March 31st, and our first Easter with Blake in Heaven. All week I was nostalgic and crying. It was a tough week, as I missed Blake so much. Our family went to Easter Mass. I couldn't take my eyes off the crucifix. I kept thinking Jesus sacrificed for all of us and that he would die for me. I felt so empty inside and lost without my son by my side. Then I looked up again and I let that soak into my soul, that Jesus would lay down His life and He would die for me. I realized that I would sacrifice my life, and I would do anything for Blake, for Bob, Brent, and Brittany. That is what true love is. The love that God has for us, He shows us through His one and only son. As I reflect on this Easter morning, I was drawn to the crucifix; on how much God loves us, and that He would sacrifice His one and only son for me and for you. God understands my pain. At that moment, I felt love like never before. God raised His son up in all His Glory, to share with us that He was resurrected, and we will see our loved ones again in the Glory of God our Father.

My First's Mother's Day without Blake

It was May 22, 2013, and my first Mother's Day with Blake in Heaven. I was in West Virginia for Emily Dowler's wedding. She was Brittany's dance teacher. I went down with Beth and her daughter Casey, Carolyn and her daughter Rachel, Brittany and me. It was a mother/daughter weekend. The next day was Mother's Day, and on our way home we decided to stop at a mall. We went into the Hallmark store, and I was looking all around. I always look at all the spiritual items, especially after the loss of Blake. A young man who was attending Walsh College came over to me. He was shopping for something spiritual for his grandmother. I told him how lucky his grandmother was to have him as a grandson. He shared that she has taught him so much about religion, and that he also wanted to buy something for his mom. I started to cry, and he hugged me. I told him all about Blake. He prayed over me, and he said Blake sounded like he was an amazing kid. His name was Ryan. Ryan suggested that he could be my son for the day. I told him, "You don't know how much your prayers and generosity mean to me. I know God sent you to me for the day, because I needed a hug." Thank you, God, for your many blessings and for sending someone.

Prom Night

It was May 24, 2013, and it was prom night for Brunswick High School. Blake talked about his senior year the very day he started his freshman year in High School. He always talked about playing football and he also talked about prom night. He wanted everyone to come over to our house, take pictures, and get a big limo bus with all his best friends.

The morning of what would have been Blake and Lexi's prom Lisa Poerner bought Blake a boutonniere. It was blue and white with a dragonfly and the tail had purple beads. Purple was Lexi's favorite color and the color dress she wanted to wear for prom. This day was going to be a very tough day for both of us, because Blake and Lexi were not with us. I bought Lexi, a purple corsage. I wanted to get Lisa a card, and I decided to go to Things Remembered. I was looking all around. I couldn't find anything. I was about to leave, and then I spotted, in the corner of my eye, the graduation stuff. I went over even though Blake and Lexi wouldn't be graduating. I found a silver picture case with a beautiful angel in a long dress. When you opened it up it had a place to put three pictures, and a heart to write something. Behind the heart there were words that said, "Strength, Hope, Love, and Courage." On the heart I engraved, "Lexi, you will always be our Prom Angel." I placed her prom picture with her beautiful pink dress in one frame, a beautiful picture with her angel wing necklace, and a very adorable senior year picture of her. Lexi was a class representative, and had her senior pictures done in her junior year, so her family was blessed to have them done early. When I rang it up the cost was $36.62? (Blake's football number 36). I know Blake and Lexi were with me, and they helped me pick this out for Lisa.

The week before, Sherri invited me to attend Kevin's Log Cabin dedication. They named a log cabin in memory of him at Coe Lake in Berea. Kevin had a list of fifty things he wanted to accomplish, and one of the things he mentioned was to have a house in the woods. So, this log cabin was dedicated to him. It is a learning center for kids in Berea and Sherri is a Teacher at Berea High School. Sherri received a dozen red roses. When I was helping her cleanup, a single rose with half of a stem fell out and landed on my shoe. Sherri said, "This rose is from Blake, you should have it." I continued to help Sherri clean up and I forgot the rose.

We went out to dinner that evening at Barbarino's with Lisa and Jim Poerner, Paula and Jerry Chaya, Sherri and Jim Fox and Bob and me. We all wanted to be together on prom night. It is where Lexi and Blake would have been if they were here. Jeff, Kevin and Lexi went to the prom last year. Blake never had the chance to go to prom, something he couldn't wait to experience with all his classmates.

That evening at dinner, Sherri handed me this gorgeous, half-opened, red rose. She said, "This is the rose from last week that you were supposed to take home." She then added, "I know this rose is from Blake because I had a vase full of a dozen roses and they all died, except for this one. This one lived, and the stem wasn't long enough to even touch the water. It looks like a boutonniere that you would wear to the prom. I know Blake was saving this rose for prom, and you were meant to have it." Thank you, God and Blake, for sending me a rose on Blake's prom night.

Earlier that afternoon I went to the Cathedral because we were able to leave work early. The Cathedral downtown has a beautiful statue of St. Therese in the back-left hand corner of the church, with rows of candles that you can light. I said some prayers, then I lit the candle. I went over three candles and six down to get my special 36. I kneeled in the pew, and I asked God to shine his glorious light on this beautiful day and to let me feel his presence. I said a prayer to St. Therese and then I noticed some prayer cards at the end of the pew, and I grabbed one.

My Novena Rose Prayer
Society of the Little Flower

O Little Therese of the Child
Jesus, please pick for me a rose
from the heavenly gardens and
send it to me as a message of love.
O Little Flower of Jesus, ask
God today to grant the favors I
now place with confidence in
your hands. . .
(Mention specific requests)
My request: God be with me always
and let me feel your presence.
Thank you for blessing me with Blake
Please send me a beautiful sign today as I miss him so much.
St. Therese, help me to always
believe as you did, in God's great
love for me, so that I might
imitate your "Little Way" each day.

Amen

Since I was a little girl, my mom always told me that she named me Therese after St. Therese of Lisieux: "Little Flower" because she always prayed to her. She also told me that she prayed to God, asking him for a sign to help her find the perfect husband. My dad showed up with a dozen roses. At the time my mom asked, are you sure God this is the one? He can be very goofy at times, and I am more serious. Well, he WAS the one. My mom married my wonderful father, Jerry Gerencser. He brings her so much laughter and joy. Every year on their anniversary he always brings her one perfect rose. My mom made a promise to God that she would name her first daughter after St. Therese for sending roses as a beautiful gift from above. As I knelt in prayer and read the novena over and over in my head, I felt God's presence and His love all around me.

Later that evening, as I looked down at the rose, I felt so much love from God that He would send me a beautiful rose from his heavenly garden. I feel very blessed that we all had each other to get through the pain of losing our child.

When we were leaving the restaurant, a police car was parked outside with the plate of 367. Thank you, God, another incredible sign. When I went to bed that evening, I thanked God for the beautiful gifts that I received that day. I can only imagine Blake, Lexi, Kevin and Jeff being all together, and just maybe they are having their own prom in the heavens.

It was May 31st, and I was getting very anxious with Blake's anniversary coming up, and Brittany's birthday tomorrow. We were driving to go to Brittany's recital, and it was pouring down rain. Suddenly, a beautiful rainbow appeared across SR 303. Thank you, God, for always sending us your promise to be with us, and for sending a rainbow on our path. That evening Brittany did a solo in memory of Blake to the song *Good Riddance* by Green Day. This song was played in the second-to-last episode of Seinfeld. Brent, Blake and Jeff loved Seinfeld and that is why Brittany picked that song. She took the words out and placed her own words of memories of him, things that she would miss about him in the future. Dancexcel surprised Brittany and hanging up in the air were beautiful white angel wings and in the center was a big #36 in royal blue. Brittany cried when she started her dance and saw it hanging above her. She knew that her brother was right beside her and looking down on her always. You can catch Brittany's number that she performed when she danced it at a competition at Hollywood Vibe It's Called Memories - Brittany Bartchak 2013 youtube.com.[24]

https://youtu.be/EsxyWfeHwuU

CHAPTER 9:
THE YEAR ANNIVERSARY

It was June 3, 2013, the one-year anniversary of the fatal accident. Bob and I went to breakfast with the Chayas and after breakfast we went to Buehler's to get blue and white carnations to place at Resurrection Cemetery. Our bill came to exactly $36.00.

Later that evening we went to mass at Saint Ambrose. Father Bob had a Mass of Remembrance. It was a memorable celebration of life. Father Bob lifted up all our families in prayer and shared some beautiful memories of the four angels who will always be watching over us. He made it very special, and he gave each family a candle with our child's name on it. They made extra ones to give out to the grandparents and to our family members.

We then went to the Resurrection Cemetery with all our family and friends. We all gathered and released white and blue balloons into the heavens. A group of football players came and Blake's best friends. One of his friends drew a picture of Blake with angel wings and gave it to me. I will cherish that picture always.

When I was lying in bed, I couldn't believe a year had passed by. I couldn't sleep. I could only think of how much I missed him, and what Blake would be doing now. What college he would have attended this coming year? I wonder what this new year would have brought to him.

I then realized that I couldn't do that to myself. I realized I did know where he was. He was with his Heavenly Father, but why do I keep torturing myself and asking those questions? Where would he be right now, if he was here on earth with me?

I came across a very good Bible verse this past year that helped me get through some very rough days.

Romans 5:3-4 NABRE – "Not only that, but we even boast of our afflictions, knowing that affliction produces endurance, and endurance, proven character, and proven character, hope, and hope does not disappoint, because the love of God has been poured out into our hearts through the Holy Spirit that has been given to us."

Our children that have passed have brought us so much joy and happiness, we will treasure them forever. Our loved ones are always with us. They are forever in our hearts.

I woke up and I reread the program they gave out at Mass that evening.

Mass of Remembrance
Saint Ambrose Parish

June 3, 2013

Blake Bartchak, Jeffrey Chaya, Kevin Fox and Lexi Poerner

The inside had the readings that were read and the songs that we sang. I turned it over to the back where a poem was written.

In our Hearts

We thought of you with love today.
But that is nothing new.
We thought about you yesterday.
And days before that too.
We think of you in silence.
We often speak your name.
Now all we have is memories.
And your picture in a frame.
Your memory is our keepsake.
With which we'll never part.
God has you in his keeping.
We have you in our hearts.

Author Unknown.

Underneath the poem they have each child's picture outlined in a white border.

I kept reading the poem over and over in my head. God has you in His keeping and I have you in my heart.

I went upstairs and tried to go to sleep, however, I continued missing having Blake here with all of us.

June 6, 2013, Saint Ambrose Grotto Dedication and Light Show - In memory of Blake, Jeffrey, Lexi & Kevin.

In remembrance of the four teens who lost their lives on June 3, 2012, Saint Ambrose unveiled a grotto in their memory. It will be a place where athletes, parishioners, as well as the entire community, can come for prayer and reflection. It was constructed over a two-week period with the help of several community businesses, including Brunswick's NLCI Land Management, Brunswick Auto Mart, Malone DesignScapes in Valley City, Marous Brothers Construction in Willoughby, and Cleveland - based Lake Erie Landscape.

More than 60 members of the Brunswick community, including the families of the four deceased students, all turned out for the dedication ceremony. This included Jim Tressel, former Ohio State University Football Coach. A quote from Jim Trussel appeared in *The Brunswick Post* [25] written by Melissa Martin –

"He hopes that the grotto, made possible through several donations of cash, materials, and labor will forever serve as a testament of the Saint Ambrose parish, (which is where three of the four students killed attended church,) and the Brunswick community as a whole, and the difference a community's love and support can make in a tragic situation such as this. When you're not the one that this happened to, you can't even fathom what you'd be thinking and what you'd be feeling. And to see the way this community has wrapped their arms around each other and the families, that is what is great about the part of the world we live in."

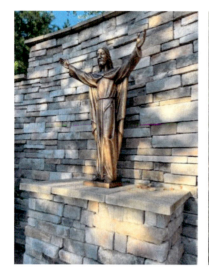

The Rev. Robert Stec, pastor of Saint Ambrose Church, said he hopes that the memorial, which is the second to be built in Brunswick over the past year, will help the community continue to move forward despite the loss of four of its own and continue to grow closer together.

"As we commend our Blue Devils to the Lord, this is a place where the angels will always be," Stec said during the dedication ceremony.

After Father Bob gave a speech, each family lit a candle in memory of their child.

Following the dedication, we all gathered, and we felt so much love from the whole Brunswick community.

That evening they kicked off the community's Summer Festival and the theme was GO BLUE!

Later in the evening, they had an amazing light show at 9:30 p.m. to celebrate the Eternal Light of Christ. They lit up the Water Tower and they played a song for each child. As the song was being played each child's name was written in white letters going down the Water Tower. They also had a huge white spotlight circling the area and shining on the Water Tower. When I saw Blake's name written down the water tower and heard his favorite song *Don't Stop Believin'* I smiled and danced. I knew that Blake was watching and grinning from heaven. He always said, "Go Big, or Go Home" and this light show was like nothing I had ever seen before.

At the end of the show, the four shafts of light beamed throughout the weekend to remind the community of the four friends who have gone home to the Lord and Julia Romito. We will always keep them in our prayers.

Later that evening the Brunswick water towers were lit up in blue and they did the most awesome laser show in remembrance of the kids. They played each of their favorite songs. Blake's song was "Don't Stop Believing". As they played his song, his name lit up on the one water tower. It was so unbelievable!!

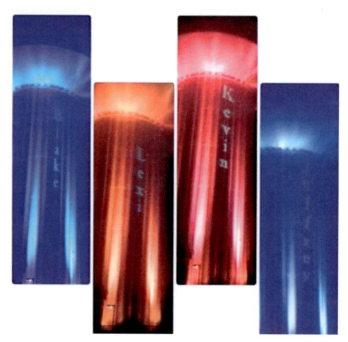

Cleveland.com - Sun News[26] by Sam Boyer:

Project Blue Line

Brunswick, Ohio - Wanted at least 5,000 people to set a world record.

That alone would be no mean feat, but add to that the goal of raising $40,000 for the Make a Wish and Brunswick Blue Pride foundations, and it's an ambitious project. Local organizers were determined to make it happen.

Project Blue Line is a collaborative effort of the Blue Pride Foundation, the City of Brunswick, Saint Ambrose Catholic Parish, and The One Thing, which is a student leadership program that includes students from Brunswick High School and many of the area's Catholic high schools. Patrick Meidenbauer founded The One Thing and is involved in the youth programs at St. Ambrose. He is coordinating the massive project with the help of Brunswick High School upperclassmen (Alyssa Emery, Rachel Deighton, Rachel Gaylord, Rosevine Azap, Lovette Azap, Morgan Schultz, Nicole Siliko and Abbey Kraft.)

Add to the mix, Cleveland Cavaliers basketball superstar Kyrie Irving, who visited Brunswick High School Students and staff on May 8, 2013, to support the effort. Irving wore a bracelet which honored the four young students from Brunswick who were killed in a car accident last year. He had remained in touch with local students. Irving signed several items that were auctioned as fundraisers for Project Blue Line.

In the past few years, there have been many young people who tragically lost their lives to suicide and car crashes. Brunswick was hit particularly hard. Many people had been searching for ways to show support for the families who had lost a loved one and to celebrate the lives of those who died. For these reasons, Project Blue Line was established.

This project encompassed three days. On May 16, it was a citywide Blue Out, where everyone was asked to wear blue. On May 17, if you wore blue, many local restaurants offered special promotions to those who mentioned Project Blue Line. Some of those restaurants include Chipotle, donated 50 percent of sales between 1 and 3 p.m.;

Sweet Frog, giving 5 percent of sales that day to the Blue Pride Foundation; and Yogurt City, offering 50 percent off to anyone wearing blue May 17 and 18.

The Big Day to set the world record was May 18.

At 3:30 p.m., the sign-in began and people obtained their number outside of Brunswick City Hall. You had to wear a blue shirt. Sign-in was until 4:15 p.m. Admission was free, but donations were accepted for the Make a Wish Foundation and the Brunswick Blue Pride Foundation.

Counting the video evidence of the record will be taken starting at 4:15 p.m. and will last about 15 minutes.

Snacks, drinks, and bakery would be available on a first-come first served basis (donations were still being accepted). There also were food trucks from around the area.

Everyone stood in line, starting on Boyer Road and working west of Pearl Road. All participants had to be signed up.

The celebration of the world record will be at the Brunswick Recreation Pavilion and lawns for about an hour after the world record event took place. There were a few items to be auctioned off including signed Kyrie Irving memorabilia, and a Sky Salon haircut. There was coloring and more activities too.

"So, get those blue shirts out, sign in, and line up," Patrick said.

On May 18th More than 1,800 people dressed in blue T-shirts lined up along Brunswick's Center Road to set a world record. More than $5,000 in donations was earned to benefit the Brunswick Blue Pride Foundation and the Make-A-Wish Foundation.

In *The Medina County Gazette*[27] on Monday, May 19, 2014, this was written by Nick Glunt:

Question: What's got 3,672 legs and may have set a record Sunday?

(I love seeing number 36 in 3,672.)

Answer: 1,836 people who stood along Center Road in Brunswick to form the longest line of people wearing blue T-shirts in remembrance of seven high school students who've died since June 2012.

The record-setting event was the brainchild of Patrick Meidenbauer, a St. Ignatius student and member of St. Ambrose Catholic Parish.

(I love it 1,836 - I see 36 again). Blake's favorite phrase, "GO BIG, OR GO HOME" – "Well Blake, your hometown set a record and had 1,836 people line up to break a record and raise money for a good cause."

thepostnewspapers.com

Irving shows support of Brunswick community...   Visit

thepostnewspapers.com

Irving shows support of Brunswick community...   Visit

May 17, 2013 - Brent addressed the senior class of BHS about driving safely with prom and graduation around the corner. His message to the senior class was to make good choices. He also mentioned, "A year ago I never thought this would be our family. Tonight, when you go home, hug your parents and your siblings because you never know when it will be your last day."

This was our new reality, this was our norm. I am so proud that Brent had the courage and strength to do this. This was his brother's graduating class, and he knew so many of the students in the Class of 2013.

Blue Pride Scholarships - Congratulations go out to Forrest Andrew, Allison Fischer, Nathan Hunter, Justin Miller and Erin Zaranec, who have been awarded scholarships by the Brunswick Blue Pride Foundation. This year Brunswick Blue Pride Foundation offered a $500 Scholarship to each of those five graduating students.

PART II

CHAPTER 10:
MORE TRAGEDY

Uncle Jimmy

My childhood was a fairytale. My parents gave our family a beautiful life because they poured out their love for each other on to us three kids. I am the oldest in the family and two years later I was blessed with a beautiful sister named Traci. Five years later after that, a younger brother Ted. When I was born my dad served in the Army in Vietnam, my mom went to work, and my Grandma Boots and Uncle Jimmy took care of me.

I grew up surrounded by grandparents who loved each other, and who poured out their love and devotion onto their ten grandchildren. On Sundays, our family would go to church. After church we would spend the whole day with my cousins at my grandparents' home. I remember playing with my cousins all day long. We would play school in the basement. Seeing that my sister and I were five years older than the rest of our cousins, we were the teachers, and they were the students. Then we would play outside. We played hopscotch, jump rope and games like tag, freeze tag, spud, red rover and all those outside games that kids played back then. I remember for at least two or three years; my grandparents made their backyard into an ice rink. We would spend hours together skating around the rink as our parents watched us. My favorite part was when I would lead, and my sister followed behind me, grabbed onto my hips and one by one my little cousins would join in. We would make this huge train and skate around the rink; whoever was the caboose would go flying around the rink. When one fell, we would all start to fall and then we would help pick each other up.

My grandparents made life fun. They taught us the value of spending time together. We always sat around in a huge circle and would talk forever. The noise level would grow louder and louder as we all snacked on food. In the center of the circle, all of us grandchildren gathered around this oblong, marble coffee table, and sat on the floor as we stuffed our faces with countless snacks. Often, after snacking all day, we would all gather together for a nice big family meal.

As we became older, my sister and I wanted to spend time with our aunts and uncles playing cards. We wanted to be at the grown-up table. I always sat right next to my Uncle Jimmy. He was my world. He was like an older brother to me.

I remember one Sunday, when we were all in the backyard at my grandparents' house, my Uncle Jimmy was swinging me all around. He grabbed my one foot and my one arm and swung me around like an airplane. I also remember him lying on his back with his legs up and I placed my stomach on his feet, and he was flying me around like an airplane. Unfortunately, I fell and landed on my elbow and heard a crack. I tried so hard not to cry. My Uncle kept looking at my arm and he tried to straighten it, as I tried not to cry. He could not straighten it. My Uncle Jimmy, my dad and my grandpa took me to the hospital. My grandpa was right; I broke my arm. I was in a cast almost the whole summer. My uncle felt so bad, and he bought me this adorable navy dress with red strawberries on it and an autograph stuffed dog. I had everyone sign the autograph dog because the cast I had could not be signed due to the texture of the cast.

We always celebrated Christmas Eve at my parent's house. My mom's whole side of the family would come over. I always loved being with all my cousins. I remember getting a knock at the door and it was Santa. He came in and sat down in the living room. He gave presents to all of us. When he handed me my present he looked into my eyes and when he smiled at me, I knew that it was my Uncle Jimmy. It was our little secret. He always made life so much fun.

One evening, close to Halloween, my Uncle Jimmy came over and we were eating snacks in the kitchen. Suddenly, the lights went out and it was pitch black. My parents were looking for the flashlight, but they couldn't find it. A big, tall monster figure was standing in our kitchen with a flashlight on his face, chasing us all around the house. My sister and I were so scared, we started crying. He took off his mask and behind the mask was my Uncle Jimmy. He told us that he turned off the electric box and wanted to scare us for Halloween. Well, he sure did scare us! He always had a way to bring fun and laughter into our lives.

As I became older, I remembered my uncle coming over and we would listen to music. I remember him bringing over these big black cassette tapes and he would place them into a cassette player. We would listen and jam to all these songs, but the song he played over and over was *Black Betty*.[28] When I hear that song on the radio, I think of my Uncle Jimmy.

I remember him sharing how much he loved his girlfriend. She had the same name as me. He said two of the most important people in his life were named

Terri. Terri is my nickname. He said, "I am going to marry her." I was so excited when he told me this.

They married and had two beautiful children. A boy and a girl. I babysat them all the time.

I will never forget when our family went on vacation with my Uncle Jimmy and his family. Money was tight, so we went camping in New York. Many things happened on that trip. I remember so much of it because when things go smoothly you tend to forget. On our way to New York our family piled into our family station wagon. I remember singing songs and listening to the radio, then we had a flat tire. It was pouring rain! My dad and Uncle Jimmy had to go out in the rain to fix that tire. We had all intentions that evening to sleep in our tents, but we ended up staying in a hotel room. We all crammed ourselves into one small room.

My baby cousin, Carrie, slept in her little baby carrier in the closet area. My sister, brother, and I, along with my cousin, slept in sleeping bags on the floor between the two beds. My parents were in one bed and Uncle Jimmy and Aunt Terri were in the other bed. We had chicken and coleslaw and ate out of ash trays that were cleaned, but I remember thinking that was pretty gross. But then, if we were going to do it, it would be okay. The next morning, we got up and went camping. My dad and my uncle were working on getting the tent up, while my sister and I played *Little House on the Prairie.*[29] We went down to the stream looking for tadpoles and frogs. We actually found a well and filled up our buckets with water. It never seemed to stop raining, but they finally did get the tent up. The next day we went on a long hike and my uncle taught my sister and I to tap our sticks together to keep the bears away. I remember my uncle scaring us as we thought a bear was on our tracks, but he was joking with us. He was always playing pranks on us. I cannot remember everything, but I do know we had another flat tire!

My favorite thing to do was to be with my uncle and aunt and spend time with their two children. When I was in middle school, I was bullied because I had a large nose. They would call me twins with another boy in school who was Italian and had dark black hair. I was Irish and had strawberry blonde hair. The only reason they told us that we were twins was because we both had large noses. I was very shy back then. I shared much of my pain with my uncle. He always told me to just ignore them and be strong. He advised, "Don't let them get you." He always listened to me and took away the pain that I was feeling. He had a way to turn a bad day into a joyful day.

October 25th, 1980, is the day I will never forget. One evening my mom received a phone call, and after she finished the call, she went upstairs to talk to my dad. When they came downstairs, they gathered my sister and I and my little brother and drove us over to my Aunt Jean's house. My aunt lived only five houses down from us. She told us that her, my dad, my aunt, and uncle would be gone for a little while, Traci and I needed to babysit for my three cousins. When they left, I told my sister this doesn't look good. I know something is going on, and they are not telling us. I saw my mom crying.

That evening was a very long night. Traci and I played Barbie dolls, house, restaurant and every game we could think of with our cousins. Finally, the side door in the garage opened. My mom, dad, aunt and uncle came in; my Aunt Terri and my grandparents were also with them. They were all crying. We had no idea what happened. My Aunt Terri took my sister and I upstairs to my aunt's bedroom where we sat on the bed. She looked at both of us. She said, "I am so sorry to tell you this, but your Uncle Jimmy passed away this evening." My heart sank to my feet, and I wanted to cry so hard. But I remember just trying to hold back my tears because my aunt had just lost her husband. She was so strong to tell us about our favorite uncle. We asked what happened and she started crying. We all started crying. She hugged me and brought me close to her side, saying how much Uncle Jimmy loved me. He loved both of you so very much. I will never forget all that pain I felt that evening, and how strong my beautiful Aunt Terri was that night.

It was time for the funeral and my sister and I were asked to babysit all the kids. I begged my mom to take Traci and me, as we wanted to say our last goodbyes. My mom told me that she had a conversation with my uncle a few weeks before and he told her if our parents (my grandparents) passed away, he didn't think Terri and Traci should go to the funeral. "They should remember them alive and happy." So, my mom took that as what my uncle would want. We stayed back and babysat.

I found out my uncle died by suicide. That was the hardest news that I ever heard at that time. Why, why would he take his own life? I could not understand. He was everything to me and to all of us. Why would he want to leave us?

I spent many days in my room crying and trying to figure out all the reasons why. I was so mad at God and the whole world. Why didn't God protect him from this? Why would Uncle Jimmy leave me? Why would he leave his wife and two kids? I will NEVER understand, I thought.

I heard many one-sided conversations as my mom talked to my aunt on the phone. I heard something happened to him when he was younger. To this day, I will never know exactly what happened.

I sat in my room and tried to process all that had happened. The pain grew stronger and stronger, and my heart felt so broken. I missed him, my favorite uncle in the whole wide world. The person that understood me; the person that took away all the bullies in my life. I saw myself drawing away from the world and I kept everything to myself. On the outside I looked like this happy and smiling child, but, on the inside, I was a broken mess. Many years went by, and I was still mad at God. I remember going to church every Sunday with my parents but just going through the motions.

My Relationship with God

As I look back, after Blake died, I realized that God prepared me for the death of my son, however, before Blake died, I had a different meaning of God. I thought God was untouchable and so far, away, but the day Blake died, God became real to me. Roughly seven months before Blake died, I was beginning to start a relationship with God. I was questioning my faith and wondering who God really is.

My Uncle Jimmy passed away from suicide when I was in 7th grade and I still attended church every Sunday morning. I said my daily prayers. I would recite the *Our Father* and the *Hail Mary* prayers and thanked God for my many blessings. I prayed for people in my life. I would pray for peace; for the leaders of our country and I prayed for the poor. That is how I talked to God. For many years deep down, I was mad that my uncle died. I have to admit when I was young, I always questioned why God didn't protect him.

Brittany, my daughter, asked me if she could attend her friend, Anna's church. Anna's church was a non-denominational church, and I said that we could go together. The service was about forgiveness. It really tugged at my heart. I was sitting listening intently. Deep down inside I was holding back my tears that were trying so desperately to run down my cheeks. Then, the tears just flowed down my face, and I couldn't breathe. I had so much pain and hurt in my heart. I kept asking, "Why God? Why did my uncle have to die?"

My heart was broken; I had anger building up so strongly that I was suffocating. After the service, Alex, the lead pastor, said, "If you want to be prayed over, please come and we will have various people around the church to pray over you." I went over to Alex, and he prayed over me. He asked, "Do you know God forgives you?" I replied, "Yes." He was very still and just prayed. He then said go and talk to God, ask Him to be with you. "How will He be with me?" I asked. He asked me, "How do you pray?" I said, "I pray the *Our Father*, and I thank Him for my many blessings." He said, "Yes, you can do that but also ask Him to come into your heart." "How do you do that?" He advised, "Go somewhere very quiet, maybe go to a park, or go for a walk in the woods, just be still and listen to God's voice." This was just a few months before Blake died, and years after my uncle had died.

That afternoon I decided to take his advice. I drove my car to North Park in Brunswick where it was very peaceful. I walked around for a very long time. I thought, "Okay God, I am here. Where are you?" The more I walked the more frustrated and angrier I became. "God, I showed up and I don't see you or hear you. Do you even exist? Where are you today?" It took a while as I tried to be still like Pastor Alex at Polaris Christian Church advised. He told me, "Just keep praying and God will be with you."

I pleaded with God, "If you are real, and want to have this relationship with me, please reveal yourself to me." I continued, "I am so annoyed with you! Why did my uncle have to die of suicide? Is he in hell or is he with you?" I cried, I screamed and I was so irritated and frustrated with God.

Then I heard His voice whisper so gently inside me, "Your uncle is with me." I took a step back and said, "What do you mean he is with you? My uncle died of suicide. I always thought if someone died of suicide they would not be in heaven."

For the first time I felt calm. I felt an inner peace and I could breathe again. That was all I have ever wanted; all these years I didn't know for sure. Each week I attended church, hoped and prayed that my uncle was in heaven. All these years in the back of my mind I was very angry with God. I prayed so many nights, "Are you real? Why do bad things happen? Why did my favorite person in the world have to die?"

God whispered, "You have so much anger inside of you. You have to hand your anger over to me because it was holding you back. You need to release your anger and give it to me so you can move forward."

At that moment, I breathed in slowly and breathed out slowly. I released all that anger I was holding onto for many years. I fell to the ground and cried. So many years of holding all that pain and anger inside of me. It felt so very good to release it and let it go; and let God hold me in the woods with the breeze brushing my skin.

In an inner voice, I heard God say, "Pick up your Bible." "God, you know that I don't know the Bible very well," I thought. I took my little finger and it went down and pointed to the book of Matthew. God led me to the Beatitudes. I had *The Message – The Bible in Contemporary Language*[30] with me at that time.

The verse said, "You're blessed when you feel you've lost what is most dear to you. Only then can you be embraced by the One most dear to you."

"Hmm, God this isn't funny that you led me to these words, I don't feel very blessed that my favorite uncle is no longer with me and is gone from my life. How can I possibly feel blessed?" I decided to go to the next verse because this verse was too much for me right then.

"You're blessed when you get your inside world, your mind, and heart put right. Then you can see God in the outside world."

I looked up at heaven and I thanked God for coming to me. I realized I was outside and this was the first time God became real to me. I thought, "Okay God, I am starting to see who you are. I will give that verse a chance."

I stayed at North Park for a long time and pondered on everything that I went through. I came to God with a tight fist screaming and crying. I had the courage to ask God, "Why did my uncle have to die?" God softly approached me and taught me how to forgive and how to let go. I held onto hurt and anger and God replaced it with love and joy. I held onto pain for such a long time. All the pain and anger placed a wedge between me and my Heavenly Father.

I felt an inner calmness and a love that was indescribable. I felt a love that I had never felt before. I wasn't afraid; I let go of something that held me back from getting close to God. For the first time I connected with my Heavenly Father and I understood who He was and how merciful He was. I realized I can talk to God with a fist, yelling with all my anger. I can also approach God with peace, joy, happiness and whatever emotions I had going on in my heart. I could invite God into my life, and into my world, and we could share every moment. That was the relationship Pastor Alex talked about that I did not understand.

This was a moment in my life when I realized God was more than just an imaginary figure in heaven, He was my Heavenly Father. He could hear my voice and I could hear His voice. That was what a relationship was all about. I did not even have to dress up. God will meet us where we are at.

I had a huge open wound that I clung onto for many years. I was the one not letting God into my heart. I kept God at a distance. When I cried out and yelled at Him, He drew me into His arms and He loved me.

I started reading His word in the Bible, and I started spending more quiet time to get to know Him. I truly felt a huge connection, and I could feel the Holy Spirit within me.

Then Blake died 7 months later. I believe if I didn't have the chance to get to know God, and how much He loves me, I would have never been able to handle the death of Blake. As I look back, I am so blessed that I was able to spend that one-on-one time with God. If I was still angry at God, I would not be able to feel Him in my heart.

Then another tragedy hit our family a few years after Blake passed away.

Bob - 2019

Bible Verse - Isaiah 38:7 NABRE - "This will be the sign for you from the LORD that the LORD will carry out the word he has spoken:"

The afternoon of the night Bob had his stroke, our neighbors, Tom and Viv, had Bob over to watch the Ohio State game. When he came home, he said he was exhausted and wanted to take a nap. As long as I have known Bob, he has never taken a nap in the middle of the afternoon. I questioned him, "Are you okay?" He answered, "I'm just exhausted." Bob has been running around taking care of both of his parents and taking them to their doctor's appointments. I know that both of his sisters were also calling him a lot that week with their schedules. I told him that it's a good idea to take a nap before we go out to dinner tonight. Well, that didn't happen. He became busy talking to his sister on the phone and then it was time for us to go.

When we arrived at Burntwood Tavern, he dropped his keys when he got out of the car. He then took about six or seven steps and dropped his keys again. I asked, "Are you sure you are, okay? That's not like you dropping your keys twice. Once maybe, but not twice." He said he was fine. Then he walked a few more steps and dropped his keys again. I said, "Let me hold your keys." However, he placed them in his pocket. We sat down at our table, as Jim and Lisa were already sitting down, and we immediately started talking. Soon after, Sherri and Jim arrived. Bob said, "I'll be right back. I have to go to the restroom."

We placed our orders, and our appetizers arrived. Bob didn't eat much. I even reminded him that I thought he was starving. He commented that he was waiting for his dinner to arrive. Again, he stated, "I'll be right back. I have to run to the restroom." At the time I didn't think much of it. When he sat down next to me and started talking, his whole mouth dropped. I couldn't make out anything he was saying. I cried out to Lisa, "I think Bob is having

100

a stroke." She replied, "I think you're right!" She immediately went to tell someone to call an ambulance.

Meanwhile, Bob stood up and started walking towards the front door and fell. Jim Fox went over to him and tried to pick him up but couldn't. Bob got up and then he fell again. Both Jims together were able to get him up and placed him on the chair until the ambulance came. I couldn't believe how fast they arrived. Before we knew it, they had Bob on a stretcher and in the back of the ambulance, as I sat in the front seat. They informed me they were going to take him to Akron General Hospital. I looked at the dashboard and we were in ambulance "36 - __ "I can't remember what came after the dash. I turned around and I told Bob, "You're not going to believe it, but we are in ambulance 36. Blake is with us."

When we arrived at the hospital, they took Bob straight back in the emergency room. Everything was happening so fast. So many nurses were working on him. They asked me if this just happened. I answered, "Yes, we were out to dinner, and he started having a stroke." They informed me that they are going to try and stop the stroke and perform a tPA. I asked what that was and they explained that it's an IV in the arm, it works by dissolving blood clots that block blood flow to the brain. After administering it, they brought in a small TV monitor, started talking with a doctor, and they kicked me out of the room. They told me after getting the results back, they had to reverse everything that they were doing because if they didn't, he would bleed out. I became very scared and started praying. My son Brent finally arrived, and we both sat outside of the room. That night was touch and go and all my family came, including my cousins and friends. They were in the waiting room. It was a very long night, and they didn't have a room for Bob for a very long time.

Finally, they had a room, and he was on the third floor in room six. I felt God was with us because he was on the third floor and room 6 - 3 / 6. "Blake is with you, Bob." I felt the presence of God in the room. They told us the doctor would be in first thing in the morning. "Tomorrow is going to be a very long day." They suggested, "Why don't you and your family go home and get some rest." So, we all decided to go home. My son Brent drove Brittany and me home. We could not believe this was happening to us.

It was so hard to go to bed. I was so worried about Bob. When I finally went to sleep, I kept having dreams of Jesus healing people, dream after dream. The first one was Lazurus at his tomb when Jesus brought him back to life. I just had a strong feeling that God was with Bob, and that He would pull him through this.

When we arrived early in the morning the next day, the physician's assistant told us it was not looking good. I asked him what his options were. He basically said he did not really have any options. I pleaded with him, "Well, can you just tell me what they were?" He informed me that Bob's stroke was very severe, and he will never really amount to anything. He will be on a feeding tube, be in diapers, and will not be able to walk or talk. I stated that when I looked into Bob's eyes, he was there.

I noted, "I see that you have a wedding ring on." He confirmed that he was married. I asked, "If this were your wife, what would you do?" He stated that they had this conversation, and she would not want to live like that. I informed him, "Well, my husband is a very simple man, loves to watch TV, sit with his dog, and I want to hear his options." He basically said that he is for the patient. "Well, this is my husband, and I want to do what is best for my husband." He said if we do not do anything, he will bleed out. Again, I exclaimed, "Well, I do not like that option. What is another option?"

Reluctantly, he informed that a surgery could be done. The neurosurgeon makes an incision in the scalp and removes a section of the skull bone, creating the bone flap. The neurosurgeon performs the necessary procedure, such as removing a tumor, repairing an aneurysm, or implanting a device. The bone flap is placed in a refrigerator, requiring another surgery to replace and secure it with plates, screws, or wires. I advised, "I want that option."

Over and over throughout the day, he was giving me reasons not to perform this procedure. Our family did a whole lot of crying. Brittany was with me when the doctor gave us all the news, and she was standing right by my side, as Brent was over to the side. We decided we needed a breather and stepped outside. The waiting room on that floor was packed, and we didn't want to be surrounded by people. We sat in the hallway. Brittany and I sat on the floor and sobbed. Brent was just pacing back and forth. Brittany placed her head in my lap, and I ran my fingers through her long hair. Then a young, new mother in a wheelchair wheeled by us holding her baby. Brittany started sobbing even harder. She looked at me and cried, "Dad has to be okay. I want him to walk me down the aisle someday. I want him to see my babies." I looked into her eyes, and I vowed, "Brittany, we are going to fight for your dad, and he will have the surgery procedure done." Then she said, "Mom, what am I going to do with my life? I just received my real estate license, and we were going to be a team." I promised, "Brittany, we will figure it out."

Late in the morning, so many of our family members arrived. All my aunts and uncles, my cousins and their husbands, even Traci's mother-in-law and father-in-law, Len and Carol came to the hospital later that day. We were all crying, but we were all together. We decided to get a bite to eat downstairs. My cousin Kelli reported, "Terri you're not going to believe this, but our bill came to $36." Another sign from God. I kept getting sign after sign. God was with us. We went back upstairs, and Deacon Gary and his wife Shari were sitting in the waiting room. They have been part of my life since I was in high school, when they started a youth group in their home. They both had been my spiritual guides my whole life.

Throughout that day, the physician's assistant came and talked to Brent, Brittany and me; then he brought in Bob's whole family, my parents, Traci and Todd. He told us he didn't think it was a good idea to have the surgery. Bob's sisters kept telling me, you have to keep my brother alive. I said that I am fighting. Later that day, my brothers-in-law approached me and asked what I was going to do. I advised that I really wanted Bob to have the surgery. Both Joe and John said they were not sure if that is a good idea. "We were both talking and if it were us, we wouldn't want to live like that," they said. I never really thought about what Bob would want.

Every time I went in to talk to Bob, he was hooked up to so many machines, but through his eyes he was talking to me. I could feel what he was feeling, and we were connecting.

When his boss, Mark and Deb arrived from RE/MAX, they were sitting in his room. I could truly feel what he was feeling. I could tell that he was very worried about Brittany because he didn't get to train her yet. I looked at Mark and I said, "Mark, I know that you and your team will teach Brittany the ropes with real estate." Mark answered, "Absolutely." The look in Bob's eyes was a look of calmness and relief. I could tell from that moment that this was truly a turning point in the right direction. I wanted to fight for him because he was here with us.

After they left, I went down to the chapel to pray and spent time alone with God. I kneeled at the foot of the cross, just cried and asked God to be with me. I felt His presence. I asked God what should I do. I pointed out that Bob was His son before he was my husband. I thought, God not my will, but your will be done. I am nervous to take care of him because I am not a nurse. However, I know you God will give me he strength to take care of him. Please God let me know what I should do. Then, in my inner soul, I heard Him say, "Watch what I can do." That was when I decided to have the surgery. It was not up to me; it was up to God. If he lives, I will take care of him. This will be my purpose, to take care of him. If he dies, he will be with his Heavenly Father and back with his son, Blake. I would take care of Brent and Brittany.

I went back upstairs, and the physician's assistant approached me again and said, "You have to decide." I informed him, "I did. I decided to have the surgery." He questioned, "Are you sure?" I said, "Absolutely."

I asked Deacon Gary and Shari to come in and pray over Bob. They had some holy water, and they placed it on Bob's forehead where the stroke happened, and they prayed over him. I felt so much comfort from both of them. Deacon Gary told me, "Terri if you have faith as small as a mustard seed, watch what God can do. He can move those mountains, and he will be with him through his surgery. You just have to have faith." I answered, "I do, I see light in his eyes. I believe that God can get him through this surgery."

The neurosurgeon and her team arrived and asked me if I understood everything. I replied, "Yes." "Do you understand that he can die on the table?" I answered, "Yes, I understand. I told her I have already accepted that he could die on the table."

I also told her what her physician assistant told our whole family, that he advised to let Bob bleed out. I insisted that I need to know all my options. He said that I really don't have any options, because this is not living, and he was here for the patient not for me. He looked at the patient's best interest. I said I still wanted to know my options. He finally informed me that they could perform bone flap surgery and remove some of his skull to take the pressure off his brain. I told him I want that option. He came to me so many times throughout the day to try to convince me not to have the surgery.

I asked the neurosurgeon, "Please, give my husband a chance. Only God knows what is best for my husband. I know my husband's stroke is very severe. You have been given an amazing gift to perform surgery. God will be with my husband and if he passes away, it is his time, but if he makes it through this surgery, he is meant to live. If you could perform this surgery for my husband, I know that God will be with you through it all. What is meant to be, I have already accepted."

After I said those words to her, she agreed, "Yes, I will perform the surgery for Bob." I was so excited she had said yes, because I knew I had a God that can move mountains.

My whole family went down to the chapel to pray. We all gathered in that little chapel in the hospital, and we filled it to capacity. My Cousin Dawn led us in prayer, and we prayed. Matthew 18:20 NABRE, "For where two or three are gathered together in my name, there am I in the midst of them." She read the full chapter. Then we read Matthew 17:20, "…If you have faith

104

the size of a mustard seed, you will say to this mountain, 'Move from here to there,' and it will move. Nothing will be impossible for you." When she was reading the passage, I felt warmth coming over me. I felt the presence of God among us. I could feel that Blake was also guiding us. I stood up and I told everyone that our family is very blessed that they were all with us. I know Blake is also among us and is praying for his dad.

We all sat quietly in the room while Bob was having surgery. After a while, we all decided to go back upstairs to wait. Joe and John took me over to the side and we talked for a while. They asked me how I was holding up. I said this is so tough, but I know God is with him. Whatever is meant to be, I will have to accept this new journey in my life. I know I will have all the support from this amazing group of family and friends.

The surgery was finally over, and one of the neurosurgeon's team members gave me a thumbs up. He whispered over to me that everything went very smoothly, and they didn't run into any complications.

God is so good. The power of prayer. I felt God's love pouring over me through this whole journey. I received so many signs from above that He blessed me while I was keeping my eyes focused on Him; and He led the way. I can't thank God enough for these beautiful signs because without them I might have given up hope. But with His love pouring over me and sending me these little gifts from above, God gave me the strength, because through Him all things were possible.

Another big blessing was a meal train that was set up for us a few days after Bob's stroke; everyone was signing up to bring meals. Our neighbors, friends and family brought us food almost every night of the week. We also received many get well and thinking-of-you cards with restaurant gift cards enclosed until Bob came home from the hospital. Our neighbor, Chrissy, loves to cook, she made us many meals when Bob came home, so Bob could enjoy them.

Right before Bob's stroke we were in the process of repainting and giving our house a little face lift. In our hallway and kitchen, we painted a few big squares of different colors of paint samples on our walls. We wanted to decide which paint color we liked best. One day, when we came home from the hospital, our friends, Chrissy, Debbie, Jack and Viv painted the hallway, kitchen, and up the stairs to our bedrooms. Scott and Chrissy hung ceiling fans in our rooms. I am forever grateful! Coming home after being at the hospital all day and seeing my house all painted and in order, truly made my day. When everything seemed crazy and out of control, our neighbors brought joy, happiness and order back into our life.

Bob spent some time at Cleveland Rehabilitation Hospital, Edwin Shaw. One day when I arrived at Edwin Shaw, I thanked all the nurses, physical therapists, occupational therapists and staff for all that they had done for Bob. They were able to teach Bob how to swallow and eat again, after taking him off the feeding tube. They also taught him how to sit up and walk with a cane. I am forever thankful and feel very blessed that Bob was able to stay there as long as he did. They became family to us and we are grateful.

When we brought Bob home, I ran into some challenges that I had to learn how to undertake. All the simple tasks that we take for granted, like bathing and going to the bathroom became somewhat demanding. I didn't realize that I would have to do all of this for him. At first it was challenging, but day by day, it became easier. His health improved and over time, Bob could do many things on his own.

The next challenge was to figure out how to work full-time and take care of Bob. I humbled myself and I realized that I could not do this on my own. I arranged, through Griswold Home Care, a person to take care of him in the morning from 9 to 1 p.m. I wish that I could have someone to help full-time, but I could not afford it. In addition, I had to ask family and friends for help. My friend Debbie, who lives a few houses down from us, offered to help. After her dad's stroke she took care of him for a few years, before he passed. Debbie was truly a gift from God, and she helped our family almost every day. She played Candy Land and various card games to get Bob to interact and to help him with his speech. She organized a schedule, as some days she could not make it. My cousin, Bonnie, came once a week, and she brought over some fun games that her kids had. Some of Bob's favorites were Don't Break the Ice and Hungry Hippo. My Aunt Jean came over a few times and she brought over a homemade game where she laminated various pictures of food, furniture, animals, shapes and colors. She would show Bob the card and he would try to say the word on the card. This game was a true asset for his speech. My Aunt Jean was a preschool teacher, and these games were very helpful for Bob.

Bob was getting used to his new schedule and living at home. Then the next challenge was outpatient physical therapy (PT), occupational therapy (OT), and speech. Therapy went well! In PT she was able to have him standing up, walking, going up practice stairs and so many other exercises and stretches that continued to help him grow stronger.

In OT, they had him moving his arm which was very difficult to do. Bob had to concentrate, look at his arm, and tell his arm to move. I was fascinated by how hard this task was for him. He would be exhausted from trying to get his arm to move. She also had him do various exercises with cups where he had to move the cup. She taught him how to put on clothes by wearing oversized outfits so he could dress himself. One task that was very difficult was teaching him how to put in his own contact lenses. I was very proud of him after he accomplished this for the first time. OT was very good for Bob, and it helped him to be more self-sufficient. He still needed some help, but OT truly helped him out tremendously.

In speech, because Bob had aphasia after his stroke, he has difficulty saying what he wants to say. It is all in his thoughts, but he cannot seem to get out the right word at times. When he was at Edwin Shaw, his speech therapist told me that his brain is like a file cabinet. He has all the words stored in his brain just like a fille cabinet has lots of folders. When the file cabinet tips over all the papers are all scattered over the floor. That is what aphasia is for Bob. He can see all the words in a category, for instance, but he cannot place the correct word at times. When he tells me to shut the door, he means to turn off the light. He knows what he wants to say, but he picks the wrong word.

The speech therapist at Medina Hospital had him practice reading sentences and she did various speech games and work papers to help him have conversations. This therapist helps Bob to ask for what he needs. I was very impressed with Bob's progress at Medina Hospital. He went for a couple of years, including during COVID.

One evening in December, we had a knock at the door. A bunch of people came over holding all these gifts. Brittany recognized them right away. It was "The Best Christmas Ever" group. Brittany had helped with this organization for a couple of years. She realized when they came knocking at our door that our family was picked that year. She had no idea this was coming. She didn't get involved that year because of Bob's stroke. Throughout the year they raise money, have golf outings, and other events to provide "The Best Christmas Ever" for families that were going through a difficult time.

They came in and they greeted us with many warm hugs. Everyone was so nice. When Michelle gave me a huge hug, she said your family was picked this year because of everything that your family had gone through. I started to cry. I was completely overwhelmed with how thoughtful this organization was. Michelle was Brent and Blake's fourth grade teacher, and both boys loved her. My cousin, Bonnie, went to high school with Michelle, and they are still friends today. Bonnie and her family were part of bringing us this amazing surprise. Michelle, her family and many others came over. I was so excited to see my friend Jeff and his family from Saint Ambrose, and all the others come over.

My mom, dad, and sister were over visiting, and they knew that this was happening tonight. They passed out so many gifts to Bob, Brittany, Brent, and me. They gave Bob and I an iPad to practice his speech with various speech apps. They gave Bob sweatshirts, sweatpants, socks, and so many other things. Brent received a baseball cap, sweatshirts, and clothes. Brittany received clothes, sweatshirts and leggings. In addition, the whole family received many gift cards for restaurants, gas stations, and department stores. We also received a vacuum cleaner, and a couple of baskets filled with food items, as well as various household items like detergent, dryer softener sheets, razors, and you name it. Then to top it off they gave us two huge poster-sized checks indicating money to help pay for our house payment and our car payment to get us back on our feet. We were both crying at this point. I felt so overwhelmed by all the love and support. Then they handed Bob and I this little red package. I opened it up and it was a silver star ornament that was engraved with "The Best Christmas Ever." Every year when I place that on our tree, I always cherish and remember all the love and support, we received the year Bob had his stroke. It changed a difficult time in our life into one of love and joy.

A week later we received another knock at the door. It was Deacon Gary and our whole yard was filled with family, friends and neighbors. Everyone was holding a lit candle. Deacon Gary said, "We are all here to support you and your family." Bob was watching from the inside of our house in his wheelchair, all wrapped in his blanket, and he could not stop crying. He saw all the people, and he was totally speechless.

Mark yelled, "Bobby" in his deep loud voice, everyone was cheering and yelling Bobby's name. At this point, Deacon Gary asked everyone to sing *Silent Night*. It was sung so beautifully. Deacon Gary led everyone in praying the *Hail Mary*. Afterwards, my cousin Bonnie talked and said, "We were all here to support you." She reminded us that we have a huge army around us and will never be alone. At this point, Deacon Gary prayed over Bob and our family. Everyone yelled, "Go Bobby!" That night, our family felt much love from our family and friends. When I rewatched the video from that evening, I saw orbs bouncing back and forth in the video. I think Blake was right there watching his dad and singing with the crowd.

We were also recipients for the "Twelve Days Before Christmas Program" from Saint Ambrose Church. We received a beautiful poinsettia that was dropped off at our front door with a note attached. The note indicated that this gift was from Saint Ambrose, and they were thinking of our family during this holiday season. Each day for twelve days we received a special gift such as a coffee mug with hot chocolate, an ornament, chocolate candy, donuts, a candle, a popcorn packet decorated as a snowman, a book, a Christmas CD (Saint Ambrose Music Ministry), cookies, and a wonderful Christmas picture made by the students at Saint Ambrose School. On the twelfth day it was Christmas Eve, and we received a handmade tied blanket. It was made by layering two pieces of fleece, cutting fringes around the edges and knotting the fringes together. When they put these blankets together, they prayed as they tied each knot. When Bob wrapped himself in the blanket, he felt the warm love and support from Saint Ambrose Parish. Most of the gifts were made by our Saint Ambrose family, and we never felt alone. Each year Bob wraps himself in the blanket and is reminded that even though he faced tough times, he was never alone.

Griswold Home Care helped us out from December all the way through March. That is when Covid hit the whole country, and everything was shut down. This was a blessing in disguise for our family. Our offices were shut, and I worked from home. That was when we didn't need Griswold Home Care any longer. I was able to take care of Bob. As time went by, Bob was improving. When our offices opened back up, Bob was able to be at home by himself.

CHAPTER 11:
HEALING

Healing: The process of making or becoming sound or healthy again. (*Oxford Languages*) "The gift of Healing"

Uncle Jimmy

Bible Verse - 2 Chronicles 7:14 NABRE - "if then my people, upon whom my name has been pronounced, humble themselves and pray, and seek my face and turn from their evil ways, I will hear them from heaven and pardon their sins and heal their land."

After Uncle Jimmy died, I turned away from God. I was mad and very angry that my favorite uncle in the world was not with me. He was my everything. I had a choice, and I turned away from God instead of turning to God.

Later in life, in October of 2011, I finally surrendered to God. I started to heal that day in the woods, when I surrendered everything to God. I heard His voice, and He said He was with me. It was as clear as day: an inner voice that spoke deep into my heart. The healing began; I realized that God was closer than I thought. He was not just this untouchable God that didn't hear my prayers and my cries, he was part of me, within me, and part of my soul. He is Love. I felt His love pouring over me and the whole experience was indescribable, love like no other.

Blake

Bible Verse - Psalm 6:2 NABRE - "Do not reprove me in your anger, LORD, /nor punish me in your wrath."

Our family made it through the first year with Blake in heaven. We had to go through so many "firsts" including his senior year without him in our life.

I learned that we all grieve differently. We have to be there for each other and respect how each one of us grieved. I had to be surrounded by others that lost loved ones and go through the *GriefShare Program* [31] (http:/www.griefshare.org). Bob had to be alone and spend time with Blake at the cemetery. Brent surrounded himself with Blake's friends, had bonfires in the back yard, and would hang out with friends. Brittany surrounded herself with her dance friends, and did a tribute dance in memory of Blake.

I remember the first time Brittany performed the tribute at a dance competition, she walked across the stage wearing Blake's #36 jersey. I had no idea she was doing this. She wanted to surprise me. I couldn't hold back the tears. What courage she had to get up there and dance in memory of her brother. Brittany was only in 8th grade. For her to go through the loss of her brother, and then dance a song in memory of him, was very brave. You have no idea all the emotions that were running through my head: how proud I was of her to be able to do that. She took the words out of the song *Good Riddance – (Time of Your Life)* and replaced them with her voice and her memories of Blake and her times together.

One of Blake's best friends on the football team happened to be at the competition watching his girlfriend perform. When Brittany stepped off stage, he lifted her up, hugged her and they cried in each other's arms. I know Blake was smiling when he watched his little sister perform that number, and when he saw one of his best friends there for Brittany, when she needed a big hug, and to be told it was going to be okay.

Things I did to help me through the year.

I still feel very blessed that God came to me the night that Blake passed away. You only have one wake to say goodbye. Blake never said goodbye; it was always, "See you later." So, Blake, I will see you later. When God revealed Himself to me, I felt peace the night that he died.

God knew that Blake had a very BIG personality as well as lived life to the fullest. His smile and his laughter lit up the room. I was one of those scrapbook moms and I am so glad that I am. At the funeral I placed those big scrapbook pages all around the church for family, friends and classmates to write a memory of Blake. If anyone asked me if I needed anything; I answered, "Could you write me a letter or send me your favorite memory of Blake."

I made a promise to Blake in his freshman year that I would catch up on his scrapbooks. My goal was to have it all completed by his graduation, so I could have all his scrapbooks out at his graduation party.

I kept my promise to him. I was only up to 3rd grade with his scrapbook, when the accident happened. I scrapbooked all the remaining years; articles from the accident, all the letters and memories of his family, friends, and classmates prior to what would have been his high school graduation. Lucky for me, *Facebook* came out before he passed away. If I had a memory or letter from someone, I looked them up on *Facebook.* I copied their picture and placed it on their page. My daughter was calling me a creeper, but I didn't care. I wanted a picture of the person who took the time to write a memory of Blake. I wanted to see their faces as well as the memory they had of Blake. All those letters and memories truly helped me through the grieving process. I laughed and I cried so many times reading those pages! Every anniversary and on his birthday, I went back and reread them, as I went down memory lane.

I feel very blessed that I have all those letters to bring Blake back to me for a day. Someday when I have grandchildren, if God blesses me with grandchildren, I can share all these memories of their uncle with them. I also saved all the articles about what the community did for our families, all the articles on the accident, and how they fixed the road by the railroad crossing the following year. I'm in the thirteenth year of Blake in heaven. I still have not had the courage to read the articles. I read a few here and there and then I have to put it aside, even though it is thirteen years later.

God kept placing on my heart the idea to write a book. Each moment when I feel that calling, I would type a little more. Sometimes in the middle of the night, I got a nudge or an idea. What is crazy, I never thought about writing a book until it was laid on my heart.

Last night, God placed on my heart the idea about the "Longest Blue Line." The collaborative effort to support the families that lost a loved one to the fatal accident or to suicide. I vaguely remember the community getting together for that event. I had to go back to my binders and look it all up. I remember Brittany coming home from school and telling me, "You won't believe this mom, but Kyrie Irving is going to help Brunswick High School raise money." She was so excited. It was nice to see a smile on her face after Blake passed away. She told me Blake would have loved seeing Kyrie come to his school. Kyrie Irving helped raise money and awareness for the Longest Blue Line.

Blake loved the Cleveland Cavaliers (Cavs). We both talked about the Cavs shortly before the accident. Blake, Lexi, Jeff (who were all in the accident), and their friend, Devin went to a Cavs game. My husband, Bob was a realtor for RE/MAX Beyond 2000 at the time and worked with Quicken Loans Arena. He had tickets for the loge and couldn't make it. He asked Blake if he would like to go and bring three friends. Blake was all up for that. Blake had so much fun with all his friends. Then Dan Gilbert walked in. Blake called his dad quickly and said, "Dad, did you know that Dan Gilbert was going to be here?" His Dad said, "It is his loge." So, Blake went up to Dan Gilbert, shook his hand, and said, "Dan Gilbert, hi, I'm Blake Bartchak."

Blake came home and told his dad what he did. Bob said, "I'm sure he will remember you, Blake. Most people probably address him with hello, Mr. Gilbert." Blake laughed and said, "He was a great guy, and they had so much fun." Little did we know, that a few months later, that God would call him home. I'm so glad that he had that wonderful experience with his friends.

The Bible

I also started reading the Bible, God's Word, because I didn't know the Bible that well. I only knew the popular Bible stories and verses. I wanted to know everything about God and His character, because my son was with Him. I wanted to learn everything about heaven. I have a very hard time retaining information and learning, so I decided to write Bible verses on index cards. Every night I would read verse after verse, and I placed them in a box. My box of index cards grew and grew. I decided to categorize them so I could find verses easier. I labeled them on what touched my heart. Categories such as: Prayers, Feeling Abandoned, Afraid, Anger, Betrayal, Blessings, Brave, Brokenness, Gods in Control, Darkness, Decision, Depression, Disciples, Dying, Hardship, Faith, Fear, Forgiveness, Grief, Heaven, God is Near, Suffering, Surrendering, Holy Spirit, Hope, Joy, Lead Us, Praise, Thanking God, St. Therese, Illness, Healing, Judging, Regret, Sin, Temptation, Feeling Unworthy, Love Patience and Joy, Signs, Listening, Reflecting, Revealing, Purpose, Passion and Positive Sayings, and Inspirational Quotes and Life Lessons. I have to admit, I have the most index cards in the following categories: Strength, Courage and Perseverance, Trust, God's Will, Wisdom, and Worry.

I have gone back to these index cards time and time again, and it has helped me through my grief. Then again after my husband's stroke, I relied on them. In the past few years when I look for a Bible verse or something, I use Google: what a difference. It is wonderful. I plug in what I am feeling and just like that, a Bible verse will come up that will guide me for what I am facing. Technology at your fingertips. You got to love it. I truly believe that God wanted me to take in His word, let it soak into my soul, and spend that time writing out those verses. I was able to learn His words in the silence of my prayer room. I have spent an abundance of hours in my prayer room, scrapbooking and writing Bible verses on index cards.

My Prayer Room

I have so many different pictures of Jesus in my prayer room. Right in front of me as I am typing this book, I have a beautiful, approachable picture of Jesus. Jesus my brother - this is the picture I look at to inspire me. Jesus' eyes are so warm, and He looks at me with those deep brown eyes. I can share with Him all my feelings and the loneliness I feel without my son by my side. As I look into His eyes, I know that Blake is by His side, and I find comfort knowing he is with Jesus.

Also, right in front of me, I have a lovely statue of the Blessed Mother holding a beautiful rose. She is all in white, her veil is pale blue, the flower she is holding in her hands has mint green leaves and the rose is pale pink. I have the statue right next to the picture of Jesus that I had described.

I have Blake's candle that they gave us on all Souls Day and a message bottle for tears - with a small card that says, "You keep track of all my sorrows. You have collected all my tears in your bottle. You have recorded each one in your Book"- Psalm 56:8 NLT. The card is tied on the bottle with a burgundy ribbon. In front of the candle is a picture of Blake smiling and holding Bailey, our dog. Blake loved Bailey, and this picture is the last picture that was taken before he died. Next to that I have a 4" x 6" football picture of Blake smiling, and a very silly picture of Blake when he was about 3 years old on his birthday. You can tell he is smiling really BIG with birthday hats all over him. One on top of his head, one on each side of his ears and one for his mouth that looks like a beak. His smiling eyes always bring joy to my heart.

Also, in my prayer room, above my head to the right, I have the *Prince of Peace* picture and Jesus is in white. Above that picture I have stakes in the form of a cross that reminds me of the stakes that were used to hang Jesus to the cross. In this picture, it looks like this is the resurrected Jesus. He has a calmness and a gentle warm feeling on His face. Jesus has a shadow over His face on the left-hand side, but it brings me restfulness and a piece of heaven into my inner soul. I can picture Blake being still and in the presence of God. This is the picture I tried to look at the night Blake passed away, when my light in the dining room would not turn on. I wanted to look in

Jesus's eyes. I felt if I could only see His face, I would be okay. The warmth in this picture of Jesus is very soothing.

To the right of me, I have a picture of Jesus hanging on the cross. This picture brings so much sorrow on how God would sacrifice His one and only son and that He would die for me. He had a purpose, and His purpose was to die for the sins of the world. He loved us so much, He died for us! A very good friend of mine, Mario, drew this picture in his younger years, and I love it. I look at this picture each day and it reminds me of how much God loves me. When I go through deep grief, I look at this drawing and I know how much I am always loved.

Resurrection Cemetery

Another way I healed is spending time at the cemetery. I called this my time for walking in the park with Blake. I would spend hours just walking around and around. My Aunt Jean gave me a little purple iPod that I could hold in my hand. She downloaded a whole bunch of religious songs. I would just listen to them over and over. I loved spending time just being in the presence of the Lord. I would get lost for hours just being outside in the fresh air, thinking about Blake and all the memories through the years. I would always wonder what heaven was like and how happy he has to be.

I remember one day walking around the cemetery, and I came around the corner near the Blessed Mother statue. I remember just crying and wanting to scream at the top of my lungs. "WHY? Why God did Blake have to die?" I couldn't stop crying and the tears kept coming. As I looked up to the heavens, the sun was shining brighter than usual. It was burning my eyes. Then I saw this big bird flying freely in the heavens. The bird had no care of this world. It was just flying freely. I wish I could be a bird, just fly and soar through the open sky. I looked back at the sun. Its radiant light touched upon everything. I thought, wow, in all God's glory His light touches upon all of us. God you are the light and all goodness; in you I will find my joy.

As I mentioned, a bunch of birds came down and they were circling over my head, much like a swarm of bees above me. One bird kept poking down on me, annoying the heck out of me and then suddenly it made me laugh. God, you are truly amazing. The nature that surrounds me, you have created and all these birds are from you. Even the annoying one which reminded me of Blake, and how he used to annoy the heck out of me. He would wrestle all the time, put me in head locks and I would yell, "I surrender," so he would let go. He was my jokester who always made me laugh. So, thank you God for sending all these birds to uplift me, and remind me that Blake is always with me, even among all these crazy birds that are flying over my head.

Another time I was walking around the cemetery and then I sat down next to his tombstone, just looking at his picture. I was remembering Blake playing baseball at Mooney field with all his friends. I remember him going up to bat with his huge grin from ear to ear. I could hear his laughter and his joy as he was getting ready to bat. Suddenly, right in front of me the lights on my car went on and they shined so brightly. How did my lights turn on? I smiled up to heaven. Thank you, God, for shining your light on me and giving me a glimpse of Blake today.

The Memorials

I also spent some time at Brunswick Lake walking around and around the lake. It was so nice that the community dedicated this area to the kids. I felt complete love from the community when I would spend time sitting at the picnic table reading my Bible. They always had music playing and it felt so serene listening to the music.

I would sometimes walk from my house to Saint Ambrose and back behind the church where they dedicated the grotto to the four teens that died. It was nice to see the football field right across from it because that was Blake's passion. Saint Ambrose also held outside masses at the grotto. They have an altar and a wall where they have crosses for Blake, Jeff, Kevin and Lexi and some additional crosses of children that had passed. I love sitting on the steps of the grotto and looking up at Jesus behind the alter with his arms opened wide. The grotto has the Stations of the Cross, the Ten Commandments and a statue of the Beatitudes. There is so much peace back there.

Grief Programs and Study Groups

Another way that was healing for me was attending grief programs and talking with others that went through losing a loved one. I felt connected to them and could share my heart. I felt this was the place where I could be myself and cry. I looked forward to Monday. It helped me make it through the week knowing that *GriefShare* would be in a few more days and I could share how much I was missing Blake.

After attending *GriefShare* at another church, I had a desire to start *GriefShare* at our church, however, Father Bob thought it was too early in my grief process and suggested going through my own grief first. Father Bob suggested that I take a strength finding class first, before starting a ministry, to see if I was a good fit for a grief ministry. It was the best thing that I had ever done for myself. The class had helped me in my everyday life; giving me confidence and a new approach to life.

I loved that class so much, I felt a new energy about myself and confidence that I never knew existed. I then decided to take an *Alpha* [32] course that they offered at Saint Ambrose. I loved getting together with the others and growing in my faith. This was an evangelistic course which seeks to introduce the basics of the Christian faith through a series of videos and small group discussions. They would always start with a meal then watch a movie about Jesus and discuss the movie with the people at your table. I enjoyed all the discussions that we had and became very close with others at my table. Further, it led all of us to learn and grow more in our faith. We decided to take a Bible study class together and learn about the Book of Matthew. I was excited, perfect timing for this class. Blake's middle name is Matthew, and I was led to that chapter in Matthew the night Blake passed.

In the summer, the leader of my Bible Study class was Mark Oldfield, he also led the *Alpha* Course. Mark asked me if I would like to go to *The Fest*.[33] I asked, "Sure, what is The Fest?" He explained, "It was a one-day annual Christian Family Festival held every August. Father Bob is the one that makes this all happen. He brings many people together from all walks of faith. They have live Christian music, food and games." I replied to him, "I would love to go." When I was working at the Alpha table, I met a guy named Bruce Farley who is the Regional Director for Alpha in the Northeast Ohio area. He was full of energy, and I loved his passion for Christ. Mark told him that I lost my son recently and I shared my story with him. He asked me if I would be willing to share my story and do a video that would help others find Christ during a difficult time. At the time, I did not think I could do that. I didn't like to talk in front of people. He informed me that they will tape me and they can edit it. I stated, "I don't like being on camera or even getting my picture taken." He replied, "If you could bring one person to Christ or to know Christ, would you share your story?" I said I would think about it. Well, I prayed on it. I decided that if I can bring one person to know Christ, I would share my story.

Bob

Bible Verse - James 5:14-15 NABRE – "Is anyone among you sick? He should summon the presbyters of the church, and they should pray over him and anoint [him] with oil in the name of the LORD, and the prayer of faith will save the sick person, and the LORD will raise him up. If he has committed any sins, he will be forgiven."

The gift of prayer. So many families, friends and parishioners at our church have been praying for Bob. I could feel the outpouring of prayers when Bob first had his stroke and even to this day.

Bob and I have attended many healing services of *Peter's Shadow Ministry*,[34] and we were both prayed over. I will never forget this one evening when Bob was being prayed over. He had a whole team praying over him and one of them was one of his doctors, Dr. John Carpenter. He prayed over Bob's head where Bob had his stroke. He asked God to heal him from his stroke. Then another younger gentleman was praying, and he saw a vision of a tall, stronger man standing right behind Bob. He kept saying "I believe the person praying over Bob is Thomas Aquinas." He kept saying, "I feel he is right behind you." I felt at peace as they were praying. I looked over and, on his shirt it said, "Light of Christ." It made me smile because I thought of Blake smiling and singing *This Little Light of Mine*, as he was dancing in my image. As he was praying, he also said, "This angel is very strong and he is right next to Bob."

Mary, Dr. Carpenter's wife, started coming over to our group mesmerized. She stood right in front of Bob. She commented, "I see Blake clear as day over Bob." Mary was Blake's 9th grade English Teacher. The young gentleman added, "He is a big, strong young man." Mary responded, "Yes, he is." He said, "That is what I see also. He is standing right over Bob." Dr. Carpenter asked Bob, "How do you feel? Do you have feelings in your leg, can you move it?" Bob's right leg had been causing him many problems, and he could barely walk. Bob also had trouble articulating his words and getting them out with the diagnosis of aphasia. Bob said, "No, but I feel his presence." He said it as clear as day. I leaned down near him, and I asked him how are you feeling? Do you feel anything in your leg, or in your arm, or maybe in your brain. He said, "I feel very holy."

You never know what God can do in your life. Bob and I prayed for a miracle; for God to lift him from this stroke and help him walk again. But it's all in God's own timing. At this time, God healed Bob's faith, drew Bob close to His heart to feel His presence, and to feel God's love pour over him.

What a good and gracious Father we have. Bob experienced God in all His glory, pouring the Holy Spirit upon him.

CHAPTER 12:
BLESSINGS IN DISGUISE

Disguise: Give (someone or oneself) a different appearance in order to conceal one's identity. (*Oxford Languages*)

Make something unrecognizable by altering its appearance, sound, taste, or smell.

God is blessing us during our good times and our bad times. But we can't always see them because too often we will get distracted by the things around us and the suffering that we endure. When things go great and smoothly, we are living the life we want to live, and we are in control. Then something happens, and life turns upside down, and we start to question God. Why is this happening to me? Why is this happening to my family?

Uncle Jimmy

Bible Verse - 1 Peter 4:13 NABRE - "But rejoice to the extent that you share in the sufferings of Christ, so that when his glory is revealed you may also rejoice exultantly."

I didn't see very clearly in my past. I shut out the world and was focused inward. I often wondered why my uncle would take his life and choose to die. I was very angry at that time in my life. It felt like God had abandoned me. I tried many times to look past this, and I tried to figure out why he took his life. In time, I came to realize only God truly knows the answer.

Later in life, I understood that God never abandoned me. I was the one who turned away from God. With the choices I made, I did not see God's glory revealed in this world. I was looking in the wrong place. I searched for answers of why Uncle Jimmy would leave me, instead of asking why and what caused him so much pain. He felt there was no way out but to leave this world and to be with God.

If I turned to God and asked Him to walk with me instead of trying to figure it out on my own, God would have been at my side through the suffering. God would have revealed a part of Himself and would have guided me to find joy through suffering. His glory would have been revealed to me.

As I look back, it definitely was a blessing in disguise. I did spend so many hours pouring out my suffering to God. As He listened, as I cried, God felt my pain. He understood. I spent many years sharing my heart. I realized that

God was the one I ran to; He understood my pain and what I was going through.

Through my suffering, God dwells in my soul. My Lord, my Father, I cry out to you.

He is my Father; He is the one who held my sorrow.

Yes, God, I did lose what was most dear to me when I was in seventh grade. Uncle Jimmy was my world. I felt lost without him in my life. Did I feel blessed for losing him? Absolutely not.

You are blessed when you have your inside world, your mind, and heart put right; then you can see God in the outside world As I look back, I could see God in the outside world. I'm not sure if it is seeing Him in the outside world; I think it's more I feel God in my soul, in my conscious. He has blessed me with the gift of the Holy Spirit. He is with me each day. If I let Him in, I can hear His voice. It's the devil in this outside world that keeps trying to bring me down.

Blake

Bible Verse - Matthew 10:34-39 NABRE – *A Cause of Division* (God led me to this Bible verse the night Blake passed away) – God loves me so much that he gave me one of the hardest Bible verses to swallow that night. I have learned over the last ten years that you should read the whole verse to have a better understanding of the verse. So here is the whole verse:

Matthew 10:16-42 NABRE

Coming Persecutions

"Behold, I am sending you like sheep in the midst of wolves; so be shrewd as serpents and simple as doves. But beware of people, for they will hand you over to courts and scourge you in their synagogues, and you will be led before governors and kings for my sake as a witness before them and the pagans. When they hand you over, do not worry about how you are to speak or what you are to say. You will be given at that moment what you are to say. For it will not be you who speak but the Spirit of your Father speaking through you. Brother will hand over brother to death, and the father his child; children will rise up against parents and have them put to death. You will be hated by all because of my name, but whoever endures to the end will be saved. When they persecute you in one town, flee to another. Amen, I say to you, you will not finish the towns of Israel before the Son of Man comes.

No disciple is above his teacher, no slave above his master. It is enough for the disciple that he become like his teacher, for the slave that he become like his master. If they have called the master of the house Beelzebul, how much more those of his household!" (Matthew 10:16-25)

In these verses Jesus prepares the disciples for the challenges they will face while proclaiming the message of Jesus. Be on guard. In this life, you will have challenges.

Courage Under Persecution

"Therefore, do not be afraid of them. Nothing is concealed that will not be revealed, nor secret that will not be known. What I say to you in the darkness, speak in the light; what you hear whispered, proclaim from the housetops. And do not be afraid of those who kill the body but cannot kill the soul; rather, be afraid of the one who can destroy both soul and body in Gehenna. Are not two sparrows sold for a small coin? Yet not one of them falls to the ground without your Father's knowledge. Even all the hairs of your head are counted. So, do not be afraid; you are worth more than many sparrows. Everyone who acknowledges me before others I will acknowledge before my heavenly Father. But whoever denies me before others, I will deny before my heavenly Father." (Matthew 10:26-33)

In these verses Jesus encourages His disciples to remain bold in their faith and not fear persecution or the judgement of men. He emphasizes the importance of acknowledging the consequences of denying Him. He reminds them that their enemies can only harm their bodies but not their souls. So don't be afraid, you are worth more than many sparrows. If you acknowledge me, I will also acknowledge you before my Father in Heaven.

"Do not think that I have come to bring peace upon the earth. I have come to bring not peace but the sword. I have come to set a man 'against his father, a daughter against her mother, and a daughter-in-law against her mother-in-law; and one's enemies will be those of his household.' Whoever loves father or mother more than me is not worthy of me, and whoever loves son or daughter more than me is not worthy of me; and whoever does not take up his cross and follow after me is not worthy of me. Whoever finds his life will lose it, and whoever loses his life for my sake will find it." (Matthew 10: 34-39)

I read this verse many times, since it was the verse I was led to the night Blake died. Following Jesus will bring division and conflict, even within families. Those who prioritize earthly connections over Christ, will not be worthy of Christ. This verse was very hard to take – Anyone who loves their son or daughter more than me is not worthy of me – God, I cried out, "I know everything about Blake, and I don't know you like I should. I have to love you over my son that just died. This is going to be the hardest thing that I have ever had to do. Oh God, I need you; I want to know everything about you. God, I will take up my cross and follow you."

Rewards

"Whoever receives you receives me, and whoever receives me receives the one who sent me. Whoever receives a prophet because he is a prophet will receive a prophet's reward, and whoever receives a righteous man because he is righteous will receive a righteous man's reward. And whoever gives only a cup of cold water to one of these little ones to drink because he is a disciple — amen, I say to you, he will surely not lose his reward." (Matthew 10:40-42)

Those who choose to follow God, may face personal loss and hardship, but will ultimately find a life that is truly fulfilling. God walks with you, and He helps carry your cross. You are never alone. God desires a heart of obedience, and a desire to do what is right and just. He wants us to love one another as He loves us. When He carries us through troubled times, in return, we are to help our neighbors, and to lead them to the kingdom of God.

"And do not be afraid of those who kill the body but cannot kill the soul; rather, be afraid of the one who can destroy both soul and body in Gehenna. Are not two sparrows sold for a small coin? Yet not one of them falls to the ground without your Father's knowledge. Even all the hairs of your head are counted. So do not be afraid; you are worth more than many sparrows." (Matthew 10:28-31)

Not two sparrows sold for a small coin. Yet not one of them will fall to the ground outside your Father's knowledge. God's love for us is so immense. And even the very hairs of your head are all counted. God is telling us, "Do not be afraid, YOU are worth more than many sparrows."

Blake was called to go home and to be with His Father.

He is also God's child. God knew that this was his day to be called home. Our heavenly Father knows every hair on your head. He knows the time of our death, and He has even appointed it.

Job 14:5 NABRE - "Since his days are determined — / you know the number of his months; / you have fixed the limit which he cannot pass."

I find comfort knowing that this was the day Blake was called home. This is God's child, and I feel Blake lived out his purpose here on earth. God called him home when his journey on earth ended. I also find comfort in Psalm 31:15 NABRE – "But I trust in you, LORD; / I say, 'You are my God.'"

Bob

Bible Verse - 2 Corinthians 12:7-10 NIV

"…or because of these surpassingly great revelations. Therefore, in order to keep me from becoming conceited, I was given a thorn in my flesh, a messenger of Satan, to torment me. Three times I pleaded with the Lord to take it away from me. But he said to me, 'My grace is sufficient for you, for my power is made perfect in weakness.' Therefore, I will boast all the more gladly about my weaknesses, so that Christ's power may rest on me. That is why, for Christ's sake, I delight in weaknesses, in insults, in hardships, in persecutions, in difficulties. For when I am weak, then I am strong."

Many times, through Bob's stroke, he has gone through so many obstacles and trials. The first trial was when he had the stroke. The doctor told us many times that his stroke was very severe, and they gave up hope. Our family fought for life, and we kept praying that if we have faith as small as a mustard seed, watch what our God can do. We were very blessed that they performed surgery, and now he is alive and with us today.

On August 12, 2021, my mom's birthday, and right after our family came back from a wonderful vacation in the Outer Banks with my parents and my sister's family, Bob took a very bad fall. He was brushing his teeth in the master bathroom. We believe he fainted. We had to call for an ambulance to get him up because Brittany and I weren't strong enough. They took his vitals, and his blood pressure was very low. Bob didn't want to go to the emergency room. I wanted him to be looked over to see if he had broken anything. Before this time, Bob managed to get around the house pretty good. He could get up, get himself dressed, and put on his AFO brace. He was walking with his cane, and life was going well for us.

We spent some time at the emergency room. He had X-rays and then they let us go. "Are you sure we can go? He could not even get up or stand on his leg," but they released us. That whole week I had so much trouble getting him out of bed. He was wheelchair bound. I took him to a few doctors' appointments. Each time they kept telling us that he was okay, but I knew something was not right. He was in so much pain and could not even stand. Life as we knew it became very challenging.

One morning I attended mass, and I ran into a very good friend of mine. She is the owner and physical therapist at Millennium Rehabilitation. Trish was wonderful; she came over to my house and she stooped right down to him. She placed her hand on his shoulder and talked directly to him. She asked him where it hurt, and he pointed to his lower leg from his ankle to his knee. He said it's throbbing over and over. She showed him so much love and compassion. She asked him to move his ankle side to side and he did, but he was in tremendous pain. She advised she was about 99 percent sure Bob broke his hip. He needs an X-ray on the hip area. I told her that we had done that already, however, he has an MRI this coming Friday. She said, "Trust me, ask for an X-ray on his hip."

She was right! A month later and many doctor appointments later Bob had to have emergency surgery.

After receiving therapy at Millennium Rehab, Bob was walking again with his cane. Life was starting to become more normal again. But in August a year later, Bob started having spasms in his lower leg. They were so severe that he would cry. At times the pain would last two to three hours. I took Bob back to the doctors. For four months and seeing many doctors, we had a very tough time figuring it out. I went to his Neurologist Doctor, and he witnessed a bunch of spasms happening. The doctor gave him a few shots in the lower leg. That helped for a week or so, but his leg went back to severe spasms. I took him back to see more doctors.

One of my best friends, Kim, who is a nurse, has been my rock through all of this. Almost every day she would call me and check up on Bob. She advised this was crazy, it has to be something. Finally, she referred me to a pain management doctor, and he ordered an MRI. Through that MRI we found out that Bob had three kidney stones. Bob ended up needing two surgeries.

When I found all this out, I couldn't believe it was kidney stones. By this time, just before it was Christmas, and they told me the first surgery that was available was not until February. Kim told me to keep calling and try and get in as soon as possible.

Well, God is so good. A huge snowstorm came to Cleveland on December 23rd, the day before Christmas Eve. I received a call from the doctor's office that an appointment was available. I agreed, "I'll take it." I had to get a pre-surgery appointment done for Bob to make sure he was strong enough to have surgery. He had to get a urine test done along with some other tests. When we woke up that morning it was a blizzard outside, and Bob was fighting with me not to go. I told him we were blessed by God to even have

124

this appointment and informed him we were going. He was not happy about this, and he put up a fight, but I won. We made the appointment and Brittany drove us.

After his first surgery, the doctor told me that it was a good thing you kept calling my assistant to get him in when we did. If we had waited, I'm not sure what would have happened.

What a blessing in disguise. If Bob didn't have spasms in his leg, which also caused him not to be able to walk, (he could barely stand) we would never have known that he had kidney stones. God had to get our attention. He sent pain so we would search for answers. Finally, we had the answer of why he was in so much pain.

In life we are hit with trials. It was through those trials Bob and I have leaned on each other. We cried together, we prayed together, and we reached out to others to guide us through this challenging part of our life. I can't thank Kim enough for her perseverance and her patience with both Bob and me. She loved us when it was tough to love us. I felt like such a complainer, but she realized that Bob was in pain and that it was something serious. She guided me to the right doctor who spent so much time listening to Bob's history, when the pain started way back in August. He decided Bob needed to get to a baseline, to determine where this pain was coming from. This was a time of reflection and pleading with God. Please God be with us to take away the pain.

I would lay next to Bob in bed, and we would listen to very soothing Bible bedtime stories to try and ease the pain. We cried out to Jesus so many times throughout the day and night to take away the pain. I can't even imagine the pain that Jesus endured on the cross for us. Watching Bob go through this, I wanted to change places and take the pain from him. I believe God loves us like that and He died for us to take away our sins and our pain.

So many times, through Bob's stroke, I have cried out to God, why do we have to suffer? Why did this happen? Why are we going through another trial in our life? Maybe we go through trials because that is the time when we are closest to God and we become more like Christ through our suffering. Bob and I have thanked God so many times during these past few years after his stroke. When we give thanks to God, we give God all the Glory and praise.

CHAPTER 13:
GIFTS

Gifts: A thing given willingly to someone without payment; a present. (*Oxford Languages*)

Uncle Jimmy

Bible Verse - Romans 3:23-24 NABRE – "all have sinned and are deprived of the glory of God. They are justified freely by his grace through the redemption in Christ Jesus."

We all fall short of God's grace when we sin. Each sin is something that we have done wrong or wronged someone. Who are we to say what sins are bigger than others? Only God knows and we will all come before Him on judgment day. God with all His glory paid the price. God rescued us from our sins and brought us into His glory. What an incredible gift that He gave to all of us. He sacrificed His one and only son to rescue you. Let that really sink deep into your soul, that God would die for you, and that He would sacrifice His one and only son because of His love for you. That love is something I can't even comprehend. His love is a love that is beyond comprehension.

I believe we are the ones that can't forgive our own selves; that is when we turn away from God and feel we are not worthy of His love. But God loves us **unconditionally** and wants to grow closer to us. He is our Heavenly Father that longs to have a relationship with us. God doesn't force us to love Him. His arms are always open. We are the ones turning our backs on Him. We live our lives recklessly when we choose to sin. God, through the resurrection of His son, Jesus, has set us free.

Life is about choices. Are you going to run to God, or run away from God?

When my uncle passed away by suicide, I was angry that he would leave me. Look at those words, leave me. I agree, I was selfish. I missed him and I wanted all of him. I had no idea he was struggling and he was going through depression. My uncle felt lost in this world, and the pain that he was going through, I can't even imagine.

I know when he felt lost and alone, God never left his side. God knew his pain and his suffering. I believe when he took his last breath, he was in the arms of his Father. I didn't believe this for a very long time. When I spent that time in the woods, I cried out to God, and I heard him say, "Your uncle is with me." All the pain and suffering I have had for so many years had left, I felt at peace. I felt the Holy Spirit dwell inside me. That day in the woods was a remarkable gift from God.

So many times in my life, I ran the other way because I didn't feel worthy of His love. When you take a good look at your own self, and the sins that you have done, the cross has more meaning. When I look at the cross, I have a deeper love for Christ who sacrificed His life to save mine. He rescued me and brought me back into His loving arms.

Blake

Bible Verse - Luke 11:11-13 NABRE – "What father among you would hand his son a snake when he asks for a fish? Or hand him a scorpion when he asks for an egg? If you then, who are wicked, know how to give good gifts to your children, how much more will the Father in heaven give the holy Spirit to those who ask him?"

This is one of my favorite Bible verses. I believe that God loves us so much, especially when we are in pain after the loss of our loved ones. God knows our hearts and feels our pain. He reveals Himself and showers us with His love by sending beautiful gifts from above to let us know that our loved ones are always with us. Our loved ones are part of us, and in our soul. Love is eternal.

I feel very blessed when I have received a beautiful gift from God. If we ourselves can give beautiful gifts, look at what God can do. If God can move mountains, God can also give us a glimpse of heaven and shower us with gifts. Sometimes I wonder if it's just a veil between heaven and earth, and our loved ones are always closer than we think.

The faith I have in Christ allows me to see all these beautiful treasures and gifts that God has given to me.

I have seen so many beautiful rainbows. God sent a beautiful rainbow over Brunswick High School the day of the funeral. I have seen many rainbows on the anniversaries of the accident and on Blake's birthday. I always smile when I see a beautiful rainbow in the sky. I feel Blake is with us always.

I will never forget my sister-in-law's last birthday before she died; it was Blake's Golden Birthday. It was August 27, 2021, and Blake's 27th Birthday. Brittany made a birthday cake for Debby and for Blake, and we sang *Happy Birthday*. Every year we go to the cemetery and sing *Happy Birthday* to Blake. We also release white and blue balloons in the air and have blue and white cupcakes with the number 36 on them. That year it was pouring rain, so we decided to have the party at our house. We ordered a couple of sheet pizzas and Brittany made a cake. We all sang to Debby and Blake.

After we sang *Happy Birthday*, my brother-in-law Todd said someone sent him a text message saying they saw a rainbow. We all went outside to see if we could see it also. We opened the door, and right in front of us was the perfect, brightest rainbow. It was right in front of our driveway, and we could see the beginning and the end of it. We all gathered on the front porch, feeling very blessed that God sent us this fabulous, perfect rainbow on Blake's 27th Birthday. Thank you, God, for always keeping your promise, and loving us so much to send us this special gift from above.

Bob

Bible Verse: 1 Corinthians 13:2 NABRE – "And if I have the gift of prophecy and comprehend all mysteries and all knowledge; if I have all faith so as to move mountains but do not have love, I am nothing."

The day Bob had his stroke, all the doctors and physicians lost hope. I went downstairs in the chapel to pray, and I asked God what I should do. I just kept praying. I kept going back to the Bible verse Matthew 17:20-21 NABRE – "He said to them, 'Because of your little faith. Amen, I say to you, if you have faith the size of a mustard seed, you will say to this mountain, 'Move from here to there,' and it will move. Nothing will be impossible for you.'" I continued hearing that Bible verse over and over in my head.

I am so glad I listened to God and followed my heart! Bob is alive today and he is with us. We are enjoying each other, by growing closer to God.

CHAPTER 14:
SIGNS

Signs: "An object, quality, or event whose presence or occurrence indicates the probable presence or occurrence of something else."

"Flowers are often given a sign of affection."

A gesture, or action used to convey information or instructions. "She gave him the thumbs-up sign." (*Oxford Languages*) Over and over again God blesses me with beautiful signs from above.

Uncle Jimmy

Bible Verse – 1 Samuel 10:7 NABRE -"When these signs have come to pass, do whatever lies to hand, because God is with you."

I remember working at the Holiday Inn in Strongsville when I was in high school. I had to clean the pool area and the restrooms before I left. At the time, I was dating a guy named Dean, and he would help me close up and clean the restrooms so I could get home at a decent hour. He would follow me home to make sure I made it home okay. I remember driving down Howe Road, it was pitch-black. The road was very narrow, and I had a very hard time staying awake, so I rolled down the windows to keep from falling asleep at the wheel. Sure enough, I was so tired I fell asleep at the wheel. Suddenly, I felt someone sitting right next to me, who took hold of the steering wheel. I was going head on with the car on the other side of the road. I swerved quickly and avoided hitting them. As I looked over, I didn't see anyone in my car, but I knew I felt someone right next to me.

At that moment I felt the presence of my Uncle Jimmy with me. I kept saying, "Thank you for saving me." I was touched by an angel that evening. Maybe it was my uncle, and I would like to think that it was, but I know God was watching over me. When I arrived home, Dean asked me what happened. "I saw your head bobbing and you looked like you were falling asleep, then all of a sudden, your head was still down but you swerved, and you missed hitting that car." "I agree, I don't know what happened, but I felt someone was sitting right next to me."

Blake

Bible Verse - 2 Corinthians 12:12 NABRE – "The signs of an apostle were performed among you with all endurance, signs and wonders, and mighty deeds."

Dianna

On June 11, 2013, my friend, Dianna, had her camera film developed from the football banquet. She noticed an orb right by her son, Danny's head. She made an extra copy and gave it to Brent while working at CVS. When I saw the picture, I couldn't believe it. I finally had a picture of Blake. He was the orb in the picture. I know Blake was with his friends that night. That evening, Brad, Danny, Keith, and Eric received $750 each in memory of Blake and Jeff. They received the scholarship award because they were the four captains on the football team; also, they were close friends of Blake. What a great gift from above that Blake showed up in a picture with his football team.

God Calling by A.J. Russell – March 11[35]

March 11 – Seek Beauty

> "Draw Beauty from every flower and Joy from the song of the birds, and the color of the flowers.
>
> Drink in the beauty of air and color. I am with you. When I wanted to express a beautiful thought, I made a lovely flower. I have told you. Reflect.
>
> When I want to express to man what I am – what my Father is – I strive to make a very beautiful character.
>
> Think of yourselves as My expression of attributes, as a lovely flower is My expression of thought, and you will strive in all, in Spiritual beauty, in Thought–power, in Health, in clothing, to be as fit an expression for Me as you can.
>
> Absorb Beauty. As soon as the beauty of a flower or a tree is impressed upon your soul, it leaves an image there which reflects through your actions. Remember that no thought of sin and suffering, of the approaching scorn and Crucifixion, ever prevented My seeing the beauty of the flowers.

131

Look for beauty and joy in the world around you. Look at a flower until its beauty becomes part of your very soul. It will be given back to the world again by you in the form of a smile or a loving word or a kind thought, or a prayer.

Listen to a bird. Take the song as a message from My Father. Let it sink into your soul. That, too, will be given back to the world in ways I have said. Laugh more, laugh more often, and love more. I am with you. I am your Lord."

"The heavens declare the glory of God; the firmament proclaims the work of His hands." – Psalm 19:2

God is so good. Listen to a bird. Take the song as a message from my Father. Thank you, God, for confirming that you love me so very much.

June 29, 2014, Brittany, my mom and dad, Traci, Tara, and I were coming home from our vacation in Florida. On the plane, I prayed to God for a safe trip. Brittany and I sat together on the plane, and my mom and dad were a couple of rows behind us. Traci and Tara were towards the back. While I was on the plane, I was praying and thanking God for a wonderful vacation, and I was thinking of Blake. I thought about heaven and where Blake is, and I thought Blake is in God's world. Blake is surrounded by a place I can't even imagine. It has to be like paradise. A place that nobody can even imagine. I found out after the plane landed in Cleveland that our flight took off at 8:36. When our plane landed, the pilot announced on the speaker that we have landed and we are in Cleveland, and the time is 11:36. When I got off the plane my niece Tara ran over to us and showed Brittany and I a picture she took on the plane. It was a beautiful rainbow right above our heads. She said it was only over us. She looked at the time on her phone, and it was 8:36, just as our plane was taking off. God, thank you for shining your light over us and sending us a rainbow. I know Blake was with us on this trip.

December 25, 2014, another Christmas without Blake. This Christmas was very different from any other. Aunt Debby and Uncle Joe were both sick, Bob had a very bad cold and so did Brittany. We decided to cancel our Christmas. It was Christmas like no other. Bob decided to lay down in bed. Brent went to visit Blake at the cemetery with friends. Brittany went over to her boyfriend's house. I was all alone on Christmas. At first, I started feeling sorry for myself and started to cry. I shook it right off because I knew Blake would not want that for me, so I started praying and talking to Blake and God. Maybe this is what God intended for me, to slow down and spend Christmas with Jesus on His Birthday and to be with Blake. It felt so peaceful, and I felt very connected to heaven. I had tears running down my cheeks, but it was tears of joy, thanking God that He gave me this time to spend with Blake. Then I played my Christian music and just let the music fill my heart. It was the most beautiful Christmas with God and with Blake. I felt God's warm embrace and I felt like I was being hugged.

Brent came home with Kyle, and he had the most colorful bouquet of daisies. Bright purples, pinks, blues, oranges, yellow and white daisies. They were so gorgeous! I was inspired that one of Blake's best friends had time to visit me on Christmas Day. They visited a while and when Kyle left, I thanked God for bringing Kyle my way. I was thinking maybe Blake had something to do with this, and he wanted me to have Christmas flowers. I was not expecting anything, but it truly put life into perspective. That Christmas brought God and Blake to me when I needed them both. This is one Christmas I will remember forever. The flowers truly brightened up my

133

Christmas! The purple and pink ones reminded me of Lexi; the red and yellow ones reminded me of Kevin, and the bright blue and white ones reminded me of Blake and Jeff. A vase full of Christmas flowers from above. This is one Christmas I will treasure forever.

January 3, 2015, the third day of every month hits me and reminds me of June 3rd. I think of Blake always. On the third of every month, I always think of the four angels: Blake, Jeff, Kevin and Lexi. Today Brittany wanted to get her temporary driver's license. I know Blake would have been that big brother and would have loved to teach her how to drive. We went up to the BMV in Medina for her to take her test. When she was called to take her test, I sat in the waiting room area and prayed. "God be with her as she takes her test. Blake, I know how much you loved driving, and this is a very big day for your sister. Please be with her as she is taking her test." When she was finished, she told me she passed. I was excited and nervous all at the same time, because Blake passed away in a car accident. When we were in line getting her temporary license, she told me she had 36 out of 40 correct. I was so excited for her. Brittany said "Mom, look I got 36 right. I know Blake was with me." It felt so good that she felt her brother was with her on this special day. Thank you, God, for shining your light over us always.

Traci Grabowski – (Blake's Aunt)

My sister, Traci was in Iceland with her family on the 6th anniversary of Blake in heaven. It was June 3, 2018. The rest of our family was sitting in church. I heard a text message come to my phone; as they gave the blessings of the four teens, I looked down on my phone. It was a rainbow sent from my sister in Iceland. Even though we were miles apart, God brought us all together in his perfect timing and blessed us with a wonderful rainbow in Iceland. Of course, Blake was with Traci's family and with his cousins on this special day. Blake always wanted to travel.

June 3, 2021, Blake always sends us a rainbow on this day!! Right over my sister's house.

Rick Bartchak – (Blake's Uncle)

My brother-in-law has a way of making Blake's birthday very special. He decorates at Resurrection Cemetery with lots of balloons and he always has candles showing how old Blake would be. I know Blake is smiling from heaven. Rick always sees the #36, and when he hears *Don't Stop Believin'*, or *Good Riddance* by Green Day, he feels Blake is with him.

Dawn Allar (My Cousin)

January 8, 2022, my cousin's son, Drew made All American and was playing in the big game in San Antonio, Texas. I know Blake would have loved to watch him play that game! My basement flooded the week before. I was cleaning up from all the water damage and I came across a bag full of Christmas cards. Brittany was downstairs with me helping me sort out everything. She said, "Why do you keep all these old Christmas cards?" I answered her "I love looking through the years of how my family and friends have grown." She pointed out, "Well it looks like this bag is waterlogged and will probably need to be thrown away."

I opened the bag and on the very top was a picture of Blake's funeral card with his football picture on it - In Memory of Blake M. Bartchak. Right behind it was Drew's football card dated 2012, the year Blake passed away. Blake is in his blue jersey #36 and Drew is in his white jersey from Medina #26 at the age of 8. I know God wanted me to find these cards. It was His way to let me know that Blake has the best seat in the house and is watching Drew from above.

God always has a way of bringing a bad situation into His beautiful glory. I am so blessed that God led me to finding these two cards, right next to each other; all in God's perfect timing the morning of Drew's big game. What a beautiful blessing from above.

January 2, 2023, Penn State played in the Rose Bowl against Utah, winning 35-21. As a freshman, Drew had this wonderful opportunity, and I know Blake definitely had the best seat in the house.

Drew's Boarding Pass. Blake is sitting with Drew #36 B.

Rose Bowl Tickets - 15 Drew's Number - Section/Aisle - 36 - Blake's Number Row/Box

Our family gets very excited when we see the #36. We feel Blake is always with us.

Blake adored football, so we know he was with Drew at this game.

February 26, 2023 - Kelli Corell (My Cousin) – Text Message Between Kelli and I

Hi Cousin Terri, :) I'm seeing the number 36 a lot lately… I always feel like that's Blake's way of asking me to check in with you and let you know you've been on my mind.

I get so excited when I see the number 36.
Half time score!

I'm seeing it everywhere!!! It brings me such comfort!!!

Jean Boylan - (My Aunt)

My Aunt Jean was in Cooperstown watching her grandson, Drew play baseball; he really wanted to get a homerun. It was getting close to the end of the week and still no homers. He was successful at getting on base, but he really wanted that home run. A man sat down next to us with a baseball hat on. On his hat was the number "36". Drew came up to bat. We knew something special was going to happen. The pitcher threw the ball and Drew connected. The ball sailed over the fence. He had his homer! Blake and his "36" are always with us.

My Niece Sarah – Baby Greyson Blake

This little miracle happened two days after Blake died. My niece Sarah had a baby boy, and she named him Greyson Blake. She named his middle name Blake in memory of my son. As Blake was called home, Greyson was entering into this world. What a precious gift from God. Greyson weighed 7 pounds 8 ounces, and he was 21.5 inches long. This equals 36.5 – another miracle from God.

Brad Darlington – Blake's Best Friend

April 1, 2023 - Brad was Blake's best friend since sixth grade and we were invited to his and his wife's baby shower. They asked each person instead of buying a card to get a baby book instead. When Brittany and I went to wrap the gift, we read the book. I know God was shining over us and picked out this book because when you use the letter "B" in a book you usually see the word "B" for Ball or "B" for Baby or something like that. When we opened the book, the word was *Believing*. That was always Blake's word. He had the whole bus singing *Don't Stop Believin'* when they went on their Washington trip. "Bb" is for Believing things will be okay in the end! Even when it is something you usually never see in a baby book - things will be okay in the end!! (With a rainbow in the corner.) Even though Blake is not here to watch Brad and McKenzie's baby grow up; he will be watching from above. I am sure he will be sending little gifts from above to let us know that he is always with us.

Brad and McKenzie's little baby girl was born on June 13th. Brad called me from the hospital and was rolling his little girl back and forth in her little bassinet. He said, "I have some news to share. Our little girl was born today, and we named her Miss Elizabeth "Ellie" Blake Darlington." I started to cry with joy. "You named your beautiful daughter's middle name after Blake." He laughed, "We sure did." I replied, "You are going to have a very special angel watching over her, always and forever." He responded "I know he will always be watching her from above. I always loved Blake's name." I am so excited that his best friend chose his daughter to have the name Blake for her middle name. Blake's name will live on. Little Ellie Blake will discover all that she can be from A to Z. When Brad and McKenzie read the Letter "Bb" is for Believing - they can share that her middle name was picked after a wonderful angel up in heaven, and that things will be okay in the end!

Number 36 Jerseys

I love to see the #36 worn by young kids that want to remember Blake. I have a picture in my house with all my cousin's kids, and they are sitting Indian style with their last names on the back of their jerseys with the #36.

Every year, cousins Michael, Sean, and Ryann pick the #36 jerseys to wear. Although, this past year Michael didn't get #36 because Hunter was a senior, and he picked that number. I told Michael that when Blake was a sophomore, he had a different number. It wasn't until his junior year that he had the #36. I know Blake will be watching from above.

A couple of times Delaney would be handed a running number, and in that number, would be 36. She would always send me a picture and say look who's running with me today. Those pictures always made me smile, knowing that the #36 means so much to our family. They all feel that God and Blake are watching. It always gives us hope and brings us joy.

In our neighborhood, we have a family that reaches out to us and tells us that they are thinking of us. Hunter was very young when Blake passed away. Blake used to run around the neighborhood with our dog Bailey to train for football. I remember Blake coming home from running. He would tell me he was talking to Hunter and Cooper about football and baseball. When Blake passed away, Hunter always picked number 36 in memory of Blake. On Facebook, I would see lots of baseball pictures and football pictures, and it would make me smile when I saw the #36.

The summer that Blake died, I went to Minnesota to visit my Aunt Pat and Uncle Tom, and to spend time with my cousins, Renee and her family, and Rick and his family. One day, we went water skiing. I wasn't sure I'd be able to get up on my skis, so I said a little prayer. I whispered, "Blake, I know you're always with me."

The moment I said that, I rose on my skis, and a dragonfly began flying right beside me. I knew then that Blake was with me.

I know many of our family and friends receive signs of rainbows, dragonflies, the number 36, and songs that remind them of Blake. Each time we receive these signs, we are forever grateful and feel the presence of God.

CHAPTER 15:
PRAYER

Prayer: A solemn request for help or expression of thanks addressed to God or an object of worship. (*Oxford Languages*)

"I'll say a prayer for him."

The word prayer is more than just a word; it is a beautiful connection to our Heavenly Father.

My prayer life changed the day Blake died because I wanted to know all about God and heaven because Blake was no longer with me. I wanted to make sure that Blake was being taken care of because I could no longer be the one to take care of all his needs. It had changed the day that he died.

As I look back on my prayer life, it was quite simple. I realized that throughout my childhood I made the choice to keep God at a distance. I said my prayers, did a check in with God, and I prayed the *Our Father*; the *Hail Mary* and the *Glory Be*; I prayed for my family.

Memories and Heartache

Looking back, I was angry and upset that my uncle was no longer in my life. He was the older brother that I always wanted. He was my protector from all the bullies. He was the person that I shared all my pains, worries, and all my feelings with. He "got me" and I "got him." When he died, a piece of me died with him. I was always looking for that person to be with, but that person never came along. If I knew then what I know now, I would have reached out to God for understanding, and for love. God would have been the one to fill that void, but I did not know that at the time. I was so angry that I could not see past my anger of losing him.

When Blake died, God "showed up" and He was with me. I felt God's presence and I felt loved.

The next day, our family came together to make the wake and funeral arrangements for that entire week; I attended wakes and funerals for Blake, Jeff, Lexi, and Kevin. I was feeling mentally and emotionally drained. Our family, and the other families, experienced so much grief in such a short time of losing our children. Then, for about two months, the community had fundraisers and various events and we felt very supported and loved by our community.

When all the noise died down, and Bob was at the cemetery visiting Blake, I was home all alone. I sat on Blake's bed looking at everything around me. I saw his jersey next to me, I picked it up, and I held it close to my face as I cried tears into his jersey. Then I looked up at the big fathead on the wall, and I looked straight into Blake's eyes. I had a huge lump in my throat as tears rolled down my face knowing that I was never going to see him again and that he would never be sleeping in this bed again. He will never be making plans to go out with his friends again; he will never be spending time with his brother, sister, dad, and me again. This feeling was final. No more seeing Blake in this lifetime. My heart ached with pain, not being able to see him ever again until I see him again in heaven. I will never again experience new memories of him; all I had were all the old memories to hold onto and to keep close to my heart. All the memories of the past went through my head. When he was a little boy playing with his Thomas the Tank Engine; and then when he was older and hanging out with Brent, going through all his football and baseball trading cards and separating them in big, neat piles on his bedroom floor. So many beautiful memories that I will cherish forever. I felt I was broken in a million pieces, and my heart was so empty. Will I be able to pick up all the pieces and move forward?

The pain in my heart was indescribable. I felt lost and afraid. Who am I? I was Blake's mom, Momma B. to some of his friends. I felt so empty and lonely inside; I was longing for something that was missing that I wanted to grab and hold onto, but I knew that I could not hold onto it any longer.

The pain in my heart felt like half my heart was gone. I just wanted to hug Blake one more time and never let him go. The pain was so intense that I could not even breathe. Blake had so many friends; they were such a big part of his life and our world, that would all change now.

I looked all around the room; I loved the spirit in our house and the jokes and his laughter. I loved how Brent and Blake were always together; people would get them mixed up because their names both started with the letter B and when you saw one, you saw the other. A neighbor would **always** say **Brent** is the older **brother** and he would pay the **rent** first and we shared that with others so they would know who the older brother was. I felt so blessed that I had two boys and a daughter.

Blake protected his sister, Brittany, and loved her; they had that brother and sister sibling love that many families have. I will always treasure both of them trying to get attention from both Bob and me. Blake was always trying to make money, and I remember the contracts he would come up with to sell his old Gameboy and PSP – PlayStation handheld games. He would convince Brittany that they were the best games ever. He would sell them to her and make a contract for her to sign, so she couldn't get her money back. She always ended up playing with them and ended up loving them, but it was basically Blake's way of making money and seal it with a contract.

One thing I treasured the most were Blake's bear hugs. He would hug me tightly and never let me go until I would yell, "I surrender." I would give anything to get one of those hugs again. As I looked all around the room, I felt so empty inside and all alone. It felt like a knife went straight through my heart. Will I ever be the same?

As I look back, that pain was so intense, I could barely breathe; I felt lost and alone and half of my identity was missing. Over time, the pain wasn't as bad as that first year, but I still missed him like crazy. When I pass orange cantaloupe I think of Blake and always remember his first-grade teacher calling me up and asking, "What is Blake's favorite food that is orange? He keeps telling me, 'envelope' and I have no idea what he was trying to say." That word was "cantaloupe" and every time I see it at the store or at a party, I just smile, sometimes I cry because I miss him so much in our life and in our world.

As a griever, we have so many triggers, one of my biggest triggers is when I hear the garage door opening. Blake would always come barging in the house, "Mom I'm hungry, I'm feeling Romeo's (pizza restaurant)." Each year on his birthday and on the anniversary of his death, we get Romeo's in his memory.

Blake also loved chocolate chip cheesecake and every time I make it, I think of him. When I hear the song *Don't Stop Believin'* and *Sweet Caroline* on the radio, I always think of Blake. When my family hears those songs, they always call me and that makes me so happy that those songs remind them of Blake. When I found out that Penn State always plays *Sweet Caroline*, I just laughed thinking that Blake had the best seat in the house and was probably down on the field sitting right next to his cousin Drew, who plays on the football team. I'm so glad I have so many wonderful memories that I will cherish forever.

Call to Prayer

Those triggers are always going to come, sometimes they make me smile, and sometimes they make me cry. When they come, sometimes it comes like a tidal wave, and it knocks me down. When it does, I have to call out for God to bring me back into His loving arms or I will get stuck. Sometimes I have gotten in a very bad funk, and it has taken me time to get out. I have learned how to recognize when I am down, and I can get myself back up by reading God's word in the Bible and walking in nature to hear His voice.

When Bob had his stroke, God was truly everything to me. I believe Bob is alive because I spent that quiet time with Him. I thank God all the time for giving us that time together to sit quietly and to hear His voice, "Watch what I can do."

It's not always easy. I have so many days that I feel defeated and uncapable of taking care of Bob. Those are the days I let my own self get defeated by this world. Life is about choices, and I can't let myself feel sorry for myself and get defeated. I have to remember what I have, instead of what I don't have.

God gave me a beautiful blessing; Bob is alive and that is a treasure. I have to remember, on the days when Bob is in pain and can barely move, those are the days we have to call out to God to give Bob the strength to keep on moving forward and to give me the strength. I have to encourage Bob and ask God to be with us through Bob's pain. God feels our pain because Jesus, His son, took all that pain on the cross. Both of us pray, "Jesus be with us during this pain. You know what it feels like, please be with us." Both of our prayer lives have grown from the suffering and pain that Bob has endured. Sometimes when we both look inward and feel sorry for ourselves, we both spin in a downward spiral, but when we call out to Jesus, He brings us back into the light and into His arms.

I have learned that prayer is everything. When we pray, we have a connection straight to our Heavenly Father. It is our choice to reach out to Him or to walk away. So many days after Blake died, I would just talk to God all day long, telling Him all about how I was feeling. The more I talked to God, the more I felt He was close to me. I remember a few years after Blake died, just being still and walking around the cemetery. I was just in the silence, listening to the birds' chirping and the wind blowing. Part of nature becomes part of you, and you can feel God go through you. It's in the silence when you can hear and feel God's presence the most.

Prayer is more than just saying prayers to God. It's having a relationship with God. When you have a relationship, it's sharing your thoughts and ideas. That is when you are in His holy presence. God loves it when you spend time with Him and it's just the two of you. It's a special bond that only you can experience when you open up your heart and you let Him in.

Bible Verse - *The Lord's Prayer* - **Luke** 11:1-4 NABRE – "He was praying in a certain place, and when he had finished, one of his disciples said to him, 'Lord, teach us to pray just as John taught his disciples.' He said to them, 'When you pray, say: Father, hallowed be your name, your kingdom come. Give us each day our daily bread and forgive us our sins for we ourselves forgive everyone in debt to us, and do not subject us to the final test."

In Luke, Jesus teaches the Lord's prayer during his journey to Jerusalem. As their Rabbi, the disciples saw Jesus as an example of a man of prayer. One of his followers asked him for instruction in prayer, and Jesus gave them the Lord's Prayer.

Why did the disciples ask Jesus to teach them to pray? The disciples asked Jesus to teach them to pray because they noticed the importance and priority of prayer in His life. They took note that Christ's prayer life was, in many ways, the source of His holiness and power.

How did God answer prayer in the Bible?

Matthew 21:22 NABRE – "Whatever you ask for in prayer with faith, you will receive."

Mark 11:24 NABRE – "Therefore I tell you, all that you ask for in prayer, believe that you will receive it and it shall be yours."

John 14:14 NABRE - "If you ask anything of me in my name, I will do it."

Why do we pray? Prayer is important because it helps us to stay close to God. When we pray, we are opening our hearts to Him. He can work in us and through us. Prayer also helps us to grow in our relationship with God. The more we talk and spend time with someone, the more we come to know them.

The Lord's Prayer has a strong focus – It prays for the coming of the Kingdom of God and maintaining the will of God until such coming. Jesus' disciples must live within God's shadow and depend on God's will and strength.

What is the meaning of Luke 11:1-4? The idea is that unless we forgive others, God will not forgive us; unless we come to Him "really" forgiving all others, we cannot expect pardon.

This is how I prayed when my uncle passed away. Every night before I went to bed, I prayed *The Our Father* (The Lord's Prayer), *The Hail Mary,* and *The Glory Be.*

As I look back on my childhood, I was reciting the same prayers over and over each night and then going to sleep. I remember thinking our world has so many people that God doesn't have time for my simple needs in this big world. Does He even know I am here? I thought that my prayers were vague compared to everyone else around the world. Why would God want to connect with me when He has bigger problems to face each day?

Blake

Bible Verse - Proverbs 4:20 NABRE – "My son, to my words be attentive, / to my sayings incline your ear;"

When Blake died, I wanted to know everything about God and everything about heaven. It was so hard to let him go, to let God have His child back. At that time in my life, I was just starting to get close to God and building a relationship with Him. Then suddenly, the carpet was pulled right underneath my feet.

That first year, when Blake passed, I dug into the Bible and God's word. I wanted to know all about God and everyone in heaven. I looked for anything that I could hold onto because my world was turned upside down. All I knew was that I brought Blake into this world, he was my child, and I couldn't imagine a world without him in it. Our family seemed broken and incomplete. Each morning, I felt lost without him in it. He was the one who brought so much joy and laughter into our home.

I started opening my Bible each morning, then it became a couple of times throughout the day. I was searching for answers. Why did he have to die? What is heaven all about? I wanted to know it all. I have always heard that all your answers can be found in the Bible. I became lost in God's words. So much of it was over my head, and I was trying to understand what God was saying in His scripture verses. The more I read, the more curious I became. I was fascinated by so many of the Bible stories.

When I decided to take a Bible study class, my parents and my sister also joined. We learned about the Books of Matthew, Mark, Luke and John as well as many other studies we did together. Mark Oldfield brought the Bible to life for all of us.

A few years later I was in a Bible study group with Deacon Gary and his lovely wife Shari. We read the book, *Pray 40 Days - The Personal Relationship with God You Have Always Wanted* [36] by Father Michael J. Denk. (http://www.theprodigalfather.org) If you want to grow spiritually and learn the Bible, I highly recommend purchasing this book. It changed my prayer life, and the scripture verses came alive with the teachings from his book. Father Michael Denk also wrote *PRAYADVENT - The Personal Relationship with God You Have Always Wanted.* [37] This book prepares you for the coming of Jesus during Advent. Again, you experience scripture through his teachings of how to pray.

Father Michael Denk did a mission session at St. Ambrose at the perfect time in my life. It was a few years after Blake passed away. I was looking into growing and learning more about the Bible. To be honest the Bible was very intimidating for me. I had a very difficult time understanding what I was reading. I always wanted to read the Bible, but I didn't know where to begin. Do I start at the beginning? Do I skip around?

Father Denk taught us many ways to pray, and my favorite one was using our senses. I can picture myself walking with Jesus and the other disciples, feeling the dust on my feet, the hot breeze on my neck and tasting the salt in the sea spray. If you are interested in experiencing the Bible and growing in your faith, look into *Pray 40 Days.*

One of the things Father Denk teaches in this book; *Pray 40 Days,* is how to prepare yourself before you pray. In the back of the book, there is a prayer exercise. He has different ways to pray including Guided Meditation, Contemplative Prayer, Lectio Divina, Praying Like a Pirate, Praying with Your Senses, and Spiritual Relaxation. I am going to share my favorite ones that have drawn me in a closer relationship with God.

> "Preparation – It is very important when we go to pray that we are already prepared in some way to enter prayer." (p. 26)

I love praying in the morning when I first get up and I thank God for my many blessings. I also love praying on my way to work, as I ask God to be with me, and help me throughout my day. If I run into difficult situations or feel overwhelmed, I take a break from work and go to a quiet place. I ask God for guidance to help me through the day. In the evenings before I go to bed, I love thanking Him for the day and reflecting on what went well. In addition, I recall areas where I am disappointed in myself, and I give it over to God. He already knows me, and what happened, it's good to talk it over with Him. I love talking to God about my day. It's just like talking to Bob in the evenings about what happened throughout my day. I like to share my day with God each evening.

> "Place" – This is very important – Find a place that is the most sacred place where you can pray. You can go to your church and pray before the Eucharist, or in nature. Wherever you feel closest to God.

I have a room right off my bedroom that has pictures of Jesus, and I have spent many hours in this room reading my Bible and writing down scripture verses on index cards.

> "Posture – We pray with our bodies. There are four traditional postures for praying: standing, sitting, kneeling, and prostrating. – When we stand it is symbolic of standing before God in wonder and awe with great attention. When we sit, it is a more relaxed posture which allows us to receive God's Word. When we kneel, we are humbling ourselves before God in a very intense and deliberate way. By kneeling we are inviting God to bless us. In prostrating, which is lying face down, we surrender to God." (p. 29)

The following are just a few types of prayer (he has more in his book.)

> Contemplative Prayer – "This is ultimately the closest to heaven we will ever experience on earth. It is not something that we can "make" happen; however, we can prepare ourselves to have this experience every time we pray with Scripture. We just need to be simply aware and mindful of God in our midst at every moment of our lives and focus on Christ. "(p. 219-220)

> "It is the simple expression of the mystery of prayer. It is a gaze of faith fixed on Jesus, attentiveness to the Word of God, a silent love. It achieves real union with the prayer of Christ to the extent that it makes us share in his mystery (*Catechism of the Catholic Church*: [38] 2724)

> "Contemplative prayer is also the pre-eminently intense time of prayer. In it the Father strengthens our inner being with power through his Spirit that Christ may dwell in (our) hearts through faith and we may be grounded in love" (*Catechism of the Catholic Church*: 2714)

> "Contemplation is a gaze of faith, fixed on Jesus, 'I look at Him and he looks at me.'"

"Contemplative prayer is the simplest of prayers; it is just being in the presence of God. What makes contemplative prayer difficult for us is learning how to spend time in silence and solitude."

Guided Meditation "is a form of prayer that uses quiet reflection on a scene from Scripture or from everyday life. It is led by a person (guide) who describes the scene and the actions of those in the story. The purpose of guided meditation is to relax so that you are free to use your senses and to imagine a personal encounter with Jesus." (p. 221)

Lectio Divina - A Latin phrase meaning "divine reading" dates all the way back to the third century. Lectio Devina consists of four steps - 1. Lectio (reading), 2. Meditatio (meditation) 3. Oratio (pray), 4. Contemplatio (contemplation). (p. 229)

You will learn so much about different ways of praying when you dig into *Pray 40 Days*. Father Denk also has a Podcast that Bob and I listen to during Advent and during Lent.

Praying like a Pirate ARRR!!! – "(This is a type of prayer that Michael J. Denk learned from Msgr. John Esseff.) In this prayer, you **A**cknowledge, **R**elate, **R**eceive, and **R**espond to God. In the first step of this type of prayer, you acknowledge whatever is in your heart. Whatever your desires or feelings are, acknowledge them. After you acknowledge it, you will relate those feelings to God. Tell Him how you are feeling. After you acknowledge and relate, you need to receive God's message. This requires you to be silent to hear what God has to say. Once you receive God's message, you will want to respond to Him in some way. Perhaps it is saying 'Yes, Lord, I will do that,' or 'Yes, God I can.'" (p. 230)

Praying with the Senses – "The idea of this type of meditation or contemplation is to get us out of our thinking mind and into a way of concentrating with our senses." (p. 230-232)

- See – "Use your imagination to try to see everything in the Scripture passage. It has come to life. Ask the Holy Spirit to help you to see."

- Hear – "Try not only to hear the sounds of the people, places, and things but what they might be saying; what God may be saying to you."

151

- Smell – "Smell and taste are so closely linked together, but it can be very beneficial to try them separately. The phrase "stop and smell the roses" works well here. We have to slow down, be gentle and delicate with ourselves and with the Word of God so that we can smell the fragrant aroma of the scene."

- Taste – "The notion here is to savor and relish in the "dolce" or sweetness of God's Word. 'How sweet to my tongue is your promise, sweeter than honey to my mouth'" (Psalm 119:103)

- Touch – "Scripture is filled with our need to touch and be touched by God. This is what the Incarnation is. The Word became flesh so that we might experience God in the flesh."

"When we pray with our senses and our imagination through the Holy Spirit we can enter into God and allow God to enter us."

My favorite type of prayer is just reading the scripture and placing myself as one of the characters in the book and imagining myself in the story. All my senses come alive, and I feel like I am actually walking with Jesus. I can see the homes and places Jesus takes the disciples. I can hear the sounds around me like the storms coming in and rain coming down. I can smell the fish cooking, and I can taste the bread that is divided, broken and shared and the wine that is poured.

Scriptural Relaxation – "Faith and reason go together. We have learned much from psychological discipline. One of the current approaches most translating to prayer is Cognitive Behavioral Therapy (CBT) because it deals with our mind and body. A person can be aware of their thoughts and then change those thoughts through CBT. When the thoughts change, the behavior will follow." (p. 232-233)

"For example - If our thoughts tend to be negative, they will produce anxiety. When we are anxious, we behave like Martha, 'Martha you are anxious. Mary has chosen the better part'" (Luke 10:41-42)

"Jesus tells us repeatedly 'Do not be Afraid' One way to do that is to be aware of our thoughts and then change them."

"As you do Scriptural Relaxation remember you are in God's presence through His Word. Begin by reading the whole passage first, memorizing as much as you can to help you focus as you go through relaxation. The steps are simple but remain focused. Find a place that's comfortable holding the book so that you can move on to each step easily."

If you want to grow closer to God, I recommend reading the book, *Pray 40 Days*. Gather with some friends and discuss it because God tells us in Matthew 18:20 NABRE – "For where two or three are gathered together in my name, there am I in the midst of them."

The scriptures came alive when I learned how to pray.

What also helped me through my grief was reading poems and things that I saw on Facebook. One morning I read this, and it really spoke to me:

The day my child died,
I became somebody new,
A totally different person,
Someone I never knew.

I am not who I used to be,
I am definitely not the same,
The only thing that hasn't changed
Is the spelling of my name.

I cry more than I ever did,
I break down quite a lot,
My heart hurts everyday,
The pain will never stop.

A mother gives a child life,
And a love unlike no other,
When that is taken all away,
She then becomes a grieving mother.

By Lisa McCann
FB October 23, 2024

Prayer for a Grieving Mother

"Father God," I come to You in this time of need.
I know that despite the pain and grief I feel

153

from losing my child, You are with me.

You are my refuge and strength, a present help in times of trouble.
Lord, be near me now more than ever as I navigate
life without my son here on Earth.

Help me to keep their memory alive by sharing the stories
and moments I shared with them. Let me find peace in
knowing that one day when my time here is done,
we will be reunited again in Your presence.

Comfort my heart and soul during this difficult time, Lord God.
In Jesus' name, I pray, Amen

From the Angels

As I mentioned earlier, my Grandma Boots had a love for the Blessed
Mother. She had her little blue book – *Mothers' Manual* by her reading chair.
I was very blessed that my mom gave me her little blue book on Blake's first
Birthday in heaven.

Here are some of the prayers from *Mothers' Manual*:

For a Bereaved Mother

Mary, what can I say now that my child is gone?
Mother of Sorrows, to you I turn for help and comfort.
I have lost my child, just as you lost your son Jesus,
when you stood beneath the cross and saw him die for our sins.
You suffered so much, Mary, and you have to know what I am suffering.
I do not understand why God has allowed this sorrow to come into my life.
Yet I know that He is all good. I have to be patient and trustful.
Heavenly Mother, pray that I may have strength.
What are those words, so gently and consoling,
I seem to hear you say? Yes, my child is happy in
heaven, or will soon be in heaven.
Someday we are going to meet again
where there will be no more sadness, no more parting.
Until then I will look to you holding your divine Son
in your arms and I know you will help me to understand and bear sorrow.

My Mother, My Trust!
At the Death of a Child

Most sorrowful Mother, your only son
was called the fairest of all the sons of men.
And you lost your boy in death on Calvary.
Mary, my child is gone now, too
–and in this earthly life I shall never see my dear one again.
And still, I would not have it otherwise because I know that God
wished to take my son away young and innocent,
before this would have cast its shadow upon that precious soul.
And I am grateful for the assurance that my child is safe with
Jesus and close to you.
Yet, dear Mother, I have to carry on here below.
Remind your divine Son of the emptiness that my
Mother's heart has to now know in this loss, and ask with me that I may
have the strength and comfort that I so greatly need.
May I in faith, like you, be humbly submissive to the end.

I can relate to the Blessed Mother as she had to suffer the loss of her son, and she knows how I am feeling.

I remember right after my Uncle Jimmy passed away, my grandma was very upset with the Blessed Mother, and she wouldn't pray to her for a while. She was missing her son. I know that the Blessed Mother never stopped loving and watching over my grandma. She knew her broken heart and the trials and the suffering that she endured. When my grandma was ready, she returned to the Blessed Mother, and she started reading her little blue book again. She felt the comfort that she needed through God and the prayers that she prayed to the Blessed Mother. I will always treasure all the conversations I had with my grandma as well as her love for the Blessed Mother. She would always tell me that the Blessed Mother understands the pain that I am going through. When nobody else understands, she will always understand.

A mother's love for her child is the greatest gift that God has given us mothers. The Blessed Mother endured the most painful sorrow when she had to watch her own son be sacrificed to save the lives of all us sinners. What a sacrifice both God, Jesus and Mary had to go through to rescue and save all of us.

God gave Mary the most incredible gift, to conceive Jesus and bring Him into this world. But He also gave her the most difficult task of all, and that was to watch the crucifixion of her beloved son. All the disciples didn't even have the courage to watch their friend die, only John. When I am suffering

155

and missing Blake, I turn to God as a father figure, I turn to Jesus as a brother who can comfort me, and I also turn to Mary. She is a mother just like me. She can relate to how I am feeling as one mother to another mother.

I believe God gave us the Holy Family so we can turn towards God for comfort, especially during difficult times and when our heart is suffering.

Grandma Boots

My grandma always told me that every Tuesday she would pray ten *Hail Marys* before noon and something wonderful would happen.

The day my grandma passed away, I will never forget. She was surrounded by her whole family and all her grandchildren. She hung on for almost a week. We had so many wonderful memories. Whenever our family came together, it took forever to say goodbye. We would say bye and talk some more, and then say bye and talk some more, finally, we would go around hugging everyone and talk some more. When my grandma passed away it was the same way. We all gathered around her bedside eating snacks, talking and hugging and saying goodbye many times. We were telling grandma it's time to see your beautiful son in heaven; we will take care of grandpa. She was still hanging on.

I was sitting right next to her holding her hand. I leaned over to my grandpa, and I said, "Grandpa you need to say goodbye to your beautiful wife." He looked at her and then looked at me and he quietly stated, "I can't let her go." "I understand, I know we all love her." Then he brushed her hair back and looked into her eyes and said, "Carmalita, I will always love you, you were always my beautiful pearl. You go up and see Jimmy and I will stay down here and take care of all your daughters." My grandma looked into his eyes, and you could see all the love that they had for each other. My Grandma squeezed my hand three times like she always did when I was younger and gave me candy from her pocket. I smiled down at her because she remembered our little three-squeezes love-shake. She gently passed away.

I was able to hold her hand before God was able to hold her in heaven. I feel so blessed that I had her in my life. She was my role model and the best grandma ever. God also blessed me with letting her slip away slowly out of my life with having Alzheimer's. If she was taken from us by a heart attack or something else, I wouldn't have all the time I had loving her and saying goodbye.

At her funeral we were saying goodbye. It was a Tuesday morning and all ten of her grandchildren prayed ten *Hail Marys* in memory of our special Grandma Boots. You are reunited with your heavenly Father, family and friends.

My Scripture - Prayer Index Cards

When going through the trials and suffering in my life, spending quiet time alone with God, this is where I feel His love and His comfort.

I want to share a sample of my prayer index cards. I am hoping that some of the prayers will help you just like they have helped me. They have drawn me closer to know and to love God with all my heart.

The Bible truly shows us the importance of prayer through His word:

Mark 1:35 NIV – "Very Early in the morning, while it was still dark, Jesus got up, left the house and went off to a solitary place, where he prayed."

On many mornings I would wake up, go to the cemetery and spend the mornings with God and with Blake. I loved just closing my eyes and walking around the cemetery. I loved hearing the birds sing and being in nature. I would walk around and just be. The silence of just being with God felt very comforting. At times I would listen to my Christian music and feel lifted up. Some songs would bring me to tears, but I needed to feel the sorrow and the loss, because it was real. Other songs invigorated me and I felt God's love pouring over me.

Romans 8:26-27 NABRE – A piece of truth from Paul – "In the same way, the Spirit too comes to the aid of our weakness; for we do not know how to pray as we ought, but the Spirit itself intercedes with inexpressible groanings. And the one who searches hearts knows what is the intention of the Spirit, because it intercedes for the holy ones according to God's will."

So many times, I don't know what to pray, especially when my heart is filled with the loss of Blake. However, God knows my heart and what I am feeling. Sometimes I just pray, "You know what I need."

Luke 5:16 NABRE – "…but he would withdraw to deserted places to pray."

It's very easy to get distracted by the worries and noise of life. The enemy of your soul wants to rob you from hearing God's voice. God is always with you. Give yourself time to spend with God, and to receive His comfort, peace and strength.

Isaiah 18:4 NABRE – "For thus says the LORD to me: / I will be quiet, looking on from where I dwell, / Like the shimmering heat in sunshine, / like a cloud of dew at harvest time. "

I love spending time just lying in the grass, feeling the warmth on my face, and looking up in the heavens. That is when I can feel God's love pouring over me. I feel His warmth on my face and His strength run through me.

My dear friend Leslie, who once worked with me, often shared inspirational quotes and heartfelt prayers. Some time ago, she sent me a beautiful prayer that her grandma had written when she was just a young girl. It touched my heart deeply, and I have cherished it ever since. Her words continue to remind me of faith, love, and the timeless beauty of a prayer written from the soul.

> I'm just the place where God shines through,
> For He and I are one, not two.
> He wants me where and as I am,
> I will not need not, fret or plan.
> If I will be relaxed and free,
> He'll carry out His plan through me.

Jane Bartlett Walter
Sunrise Magazine, October/November 1999

> We try to be good so that others will love us. Consciously or unconsciously, we think it is the same with God. While we may say that God's love for us is not determined by our actions, our behavior often says that we believe that God loves us only when we keep his commandments. We try to be virtuous so that God will love us. However, God loves us UNCONDITIONALLY. His love is freely given to us.

Imaging Ourselves as LOVABLE

When we suffer from a poor opinion of ourselves, we are inclined to assume that God and others share this opinion. If we don't see much love in ourselves. We will find it difficult to believe that God sees much love in us.

Such a belief will keep us at a distance with God.

The reason we end up with a poor self-image is because we allow destructive words to enter and shape the core of our being.

Example: Someone might say you are stupid or you will not amount to much. Unfortunately, we tend to believe that person and that lie. Those words become part of how we see ourselves and become a destructive force in our lives because we dwell on them, ponder them, and reflect on them to our core. We need to change that perception and the feelings, and know we are loved by God.

Come to prayer, with a heartfelt sense of God's compassionate love for us. We don't have to prove anything, dress up nicely, or be formal; we are loved just as we are.

Our Father says to us: Come as you are. Be yourself, enjoy your time with me. If you want to pour out your heart to me about something, that's okay. If you want to rest in my presence, snuggle up in my lap and in my arms, that's okay too. I am always here for you.

Prayer is the raising up of the mind and heart to God.

We pray or call out to God because He has moved us to prayer and not because **we** think it is a good idea to contact God. In Him we live, move and have our being. We call out to God only because He has first called out to us. We find God because he has been looking for us. We move toward God because He is inviting us to come and enabling us to move in His direction. Prayer is learning to listen to what God is saying and where He is guiding us.

Make every encounter a spiritual exercise through which we grow in our relationship with God. The more we do this, the more real God will become for us. God will become a companion with whom we shall share all of our life.

I love our Irish heritage, and this is one of my favorite prayers.

Saint Patrick's Prayer

Christ be with me, Christ within me,
Christ behind me, Christ before me,
Christ beside me, Christ to win me,
Christ to comfort and restore me.

I have read many of Matthew Kelly's books. Once I was able to meet him when he came to St. Ambrose for one of our Lent Missions. He changed Blake's life. I remember how excited Blake was when we came home that evening. He said, "Mom I know I can make a difference, and I am going to start by taking care of myself." I answered, "That sounds like a great idea, what are you going to do?" He commented, "Well, first off when Matthew Kelly asked, 'Would you feed a racehorse a hamburger or anything that is not good for the horse to win a race?' That opened my eyes. I'm going to stop drinking pop and start eating better." He listened to every word that Matthew Kelly said and from that day forward he changed. Blake was always positive, but he had a new glow about him and more confidence in himself. Teachers even approached me and said that they have seen a change in Blake, and he is becoming a great leader and role model.

In my index box, I have many quotes from Matthew Kelly. My favorite book that he wrote that has changed my life is the *Rhythm of Life.*[39] The quote in his book that I love the most, that was a game changer in my life, was "Becoming the Best Version of Yourself".

Here are some of the quotes that I have in my prayer box under the heading, Prayer.

"In prayer we learn who we are and what we are here for, what matters most and what matters least."

"Through prayer we discover the best versions of ourselves."

"Through prayer we learn how to love and be loved."

"We have always been loved, are loved, and will continue to be loved by God."

"The unexpected good or bad reveals character. How do we prepare for the unexpected? Prayer helps us develop awareness, virtue, and character that are essential when life gets turned upside down."

"He used to pray and plan out his whole day. 'Listen up, God, your servant is speaking.' Then he had a very difficult situation, and he prayed, 'God, what do you think I should do? Speak, Lord, your servant is listening.' Before, he was only interested in telling God what his WILL was. The second time, he was asking God to reveal His will. God, what do you think I should do?"

This transformed my life - We can find joy, peace, and contentment within ourselves. This peace comes from God regardless of the outcome and regardless of other people's opinions. The only opinion that matters is God's opinion.

> "What is the difference between two trees side by side? One is blown to the ground and the other continues to stand tall."

> "A tree with strong roots can weather almost any storm. A tree with deep roots bears great fruit for it can source the weather and nutrients it needs from the earth."

> "Sink the roots of the daily habit of prayer deep into your life."

> "Is there a storm coming? Are you ready? Life has taught me that when the storm arrives it's too late to start sinking those roots. Prayer life is an essential daily habit."

Matthew Kelly has inspired me to live the best version of myself. I hope if you would like to be inspired, you will take time to read his books or listen to his podcasts. They are very inspiring.

Another encouraging book is *13 Powerful Ways to Pray,*[40] by Eamon Tobin:

> "I don't want to listen too closely to God in prayer because I'm afraid of what the Lord might say to me. He might ask something of us that we are not ready to give, or He may reveal to us something about ourselves that we would prefer not to hear. Growth in self-knowledge is an essential ingredient of human and spiritual growth. We all create a certain idea." (p. 51)

> "I don't want to get too serious about prayer because consciously or unconsciously I'm afraid of losing control over my life. At the heart of authentic prayer is surrender to the will of God. Because we fear this surrender and where it leads to the cross, most of us keep God at arm's length. We pray frequently, say prayers, read scripture, but we may not listen properly because we are afraid of giving God control over our lives." (p. 51)

WOW!! He truly says it like it is. It may be what we are all thinking, but when you see it written, it hits you harder. I think I do try and keep God at arm's length because I am afraid of giving God control over my life. It is a constant struggle for me to give God total control.

161

I have learned, prayer is to my spirit what food is to my body. It is the bread of my spiritual life. To quit or neglect prayer is to quit or neglect to care for the core of my being (my spirit), and its deepest desire (intimacy with my creator). Without prayer I would be a person without the source of life.

This was another amazing book for me; I added so many more quotes to my index cards.

John 15:5 NABRE – "I am the vine, you are the branches. Whoever remains in me and I in him will bear much fruit, because without me you can do nothing."

Luke 22:19-20 NABRE – "Then he took the bread, said the blessing, broke it, and gave it to them, saying, 'This is my body, which will be given for you; do this in memory of me.' And likewise, the cup after they had eaten, saying, 'This cup is the new covenant in my blood, which will be shed for you.'"

Jesus stated, I am dying that you may live. I love you so much that I am ready to pour out my blood (my life) for you. Every time we receive communion (the Eucharist), we are confirming and given the opportunity to affirm our belief in Jesus' love for us. Our "Amen," is "Yes Lord, I do believe you love me."

Mark 14:36 NABRE – "...he said, 'Abba, Father, all things are possible to you. Take this cup away from me, but not what I will but what you will.'"

Jesus is acknowledging two major aspects of His relationship with God.

1. God loves Jesus as a father and wants the best for Him.
2. Jesus owes God his submissive obedience as a son does his father.

Ephesians 1:4 NABRE - "...as he chose us in him, before the foundation of the world, to be holy and without blemish before him. In love..."

God knew that Adam and Eve would sin in the garden. He knew their descendants would be unable to choose to obey Him. When the Holy Trinity made the world, they knew the Son would have to sacrifice His life for their creation. In order to be a substitute for humans, the Son had to become human. He knows that suffering would be horrible, but short lived. He knew suffering will result in God glorified and humanity saved. When Jesus gives the cup to His disciples at the last supper; they are taking on the life His blood provides. Both the persecution that comes to His followers and everlasting life in paradise.

Matthew 26:36 NABRE – "Then Jesus came with them to a place called Gethsemane, and he said to his disciples, 'Sit here while I go over there and pray.'"

Matthew 26:39 NABRE – "He advanced a little and fell prostrate in prayer, saying, 'My Father, if it is possible, let this cup pass from me; yet, not as I will, but as you will.'"

Jesus prayed to his Father in heaven, before He knew He would die on the cross for our sins. Can you imagine praying that hard and asking God to be with you? Jesus, even to the end of His life has taught all of us how to pray.

John 17: 1-2 NABRE – "When Jesus had said this, he raised his eyes to heaven and said, 'Father, the hour has come. Give glory to your son, so that your son may glorify you, just as you gave him authority over all people, so that he may give eternal life to all you gave him.'"

Bob

Bible Verse - Romans 8:5 NABRE – "For those who live according to the flesh are concerned with the things of the flesh, but those who live according to the spirit with the things of the spirit."

Living in the flesh is so difficult each and every day. We live in a fallen world. Each day I wake up and I want to give my life over to God to live in the Spirit, but I fall short. I know that God gives me grace, and I am trying the best that I can.

John 15:5-8 NABRE - "I am the vine, you are the branches. Whoever remains in me and I in him will bear much fruit, because without me you can do nothing. Anyone who does not remain in me will be thrown out like a branch and wither; people will gather them and throw them into a fire and they will be burned. If you remain in me and my words remain in you, ask for whatever you want and it will be done for you. By this is my Father glorified, that you bear much fruit and become my disciples."

Every day I return to this verse. God you are the vine, and I am your branch. I have to always lean into this verse that you remain in me, and I remain in you. Your words overflow in me and even when temptation comes, through God your words pull me closer to you.

I have learned various lessons through the loss of my uncle, the loss of Blake, and through Bob's stroke as well. In addition, I believe God has shown me His character.

These last couple of years, I have learned just how precious life is. I have surrendered over to God to take the pain away from Bob, and to give it to me. I hate watching him in pain. I would rather have it happen to me than to him.

Some days I struggle; I get so tired, and I get very short with him. When that happens, I ask God for grace. Please God, help me place myself in my husband's shoes, and realize that he is doing his best. I have to remember that I am human, and I live in the flesh. In this life we are going to have struggles. So, I pray, "God be with me, I surrender it all over to you."

My friend, Laura, and I have had this discussion, especially after her husband passed away. She told me some days were very difficult. She suggested to pray to St. Therese of Lisieux (also known as the "Little Flower") and her "little ways." So, when I do feel overwhelmed, I remember that I am not alone. I ask God for grace and to think of St. Therese and her little ways. That gives me the strength to keep moving forward and to take care of Bob with love and understanding.

Prayer of Consecration to Merciful Love – **St. Therese of Lisieux**

"I, (name), choose, on this day, with the help of your grace, to strive with all my heart, to follow the Little Way. And so, I firmly intend to fight discouragement, do little things with great love, and be merciful to my neighbor in deed, word, and prayer."

When I feel overwhelmed and discouraged, and when my heart fills up with self-pity, I will turn my heart to follow St. Therese' Little Ways. God will give me the grace to live in the spirit and not in the flesh.

(So many times, I turn over to the surrender prayer, "not my will, but your will be done.")

"O Jesus, I surrender myself to you, take care of everything. (repeat it ten times)

Jesus be with me, comfort me and give me strength.

O Jesus, I surrender myself to you"

As you can see from this prayer, much of what our Lord wants is contrary to normal human inclination and reason. We can only rise into this level of thinking through the grace of God, and the help of the Holy Spirit.

We have to let go of our problems; stop worrying and stop trying to resolve problems ourselves. We have to believe, trust, and allow our Lord to rescue us from ourselves and to supply our wants and needs; for Him to resolve our problems as only He can.

"Jesus, you take care of it," should be the first words that come to mind and then flow from our lips. After all, we have tried to do things our way and look where it has gotten us.

Just do as the prayer says, open your heart and mind in love, close our eyes in trust and ask Jesus to take care of it. He will.

Matthew 11:28-29 NABRE - "Come to me, all you who labor and are burdened, and I will give you rest. Take my yoke upon you and learn from me, for I am meek and humble of heart, and you will find rest for yourselves."

I have this inspiring Surrender Novena Card. It has ten days of prayer, and after each day of prayer, it says:

"O Jesus, I surrender Myself to you, take care of everything." I say it ten times.

I went through a lot of depression when Bob came home from the hospital. I felt unworthy to take care of him. I was overwhelmed with fear. I turned to the book *Miracle Hour: A Method of Prayer That Will Change Your Life* [41] by Linda Schubert.

"**Miracle Hour** - Five minutes for each section" (p. 2)

1. Give Praise to God
2. Sing to the Lord
3. Spiritual Warfare
4. Surrender
5. Release of the Holy Spirit
6. Repentance
7. Forgiveness
8. Scripture Reflections
9. Wait for the Lord to Speak

10. Intercessions
11. Petitions
12. Thanksgiving

I recommend this little prayer book. It has helped me to grow closer to God and to get me out of my self-pity.

CHAPTER 16:
GOD'S LIGHT

Light: The natural agent that stimulates sight and makes things visible.

"The light of the sun."

An expression in someone's eyes indicates a particular emotion or mood.

Verb – "Provide with light or lighting; illuminate." (*Oxford Languages*)

Light is a type of electromagnetic radiation that allows the human eye to see or makes objects visible. It is also defined as visible radiation to the human eye. Photons, which are tiny packets of energy, are found in light. Light always moves in a straight line.

The Bible Definition of Light - Abstract. In the Bible, light has always been a symbol of holiness, goodness, knowledge, wisdom, grace, hope, and God's revelation. By contrast, darkness has been associated with evil, sin, and despair.

As I reflected on the past, I remembered the times when I was in the dark and I couldn't see the light.

I decided after I wrote this story, that this chapter was missing something. What this chapter was missing was the time when I was in the dark, and I couldn't see the light. I needed to be honest with myself and with you to share the moments when all I saw was darkness, and the light was very hard to find.

I remember sitting in my room when I was in middle school after my uncle died. I felt alone and afraid. I just got bullied again, and I would lie in my bed crying, wishing my uncle were with me to take away all the bullies and to make me laugh again. Why did he have to die? Why did I have to live without him in my life? All those years, as I looked back, sitting in my room by myself, in my own pain and sorrow, wishing my uncle was there to share life together and to be with me. I was in the dark, and I chose to be in the dark. I didn't let anyone in; I kept it all to myself. The more I cried and felt sorry for myself, the more I got deeper in my own pain. I didn't know how to release this pain. I just kept it buried deep in my soul. I cried and yelled at God so many times, but I kept Him at a distance because I was mad at Him for not protecting my uncle and for letting him die. "Why God? Why would you take him away from me when I needed him the most?"

I was in the dark for so many years, trying to find out these difficult answers, keeping all that pain and sorrow in my own heart and never reaching out to anyone for help. All I saw was darkness, and God was very far away. I was a very positive person and very blessed to have a wonderful family. I received so much love and support and lived a very good childhood and adult life, but when I was alone, I had to face the darkness of this world, and I chose to isolate myself and suffer alone. I stayed focused inward on myself, and I couldn't look beyond my own pain. I died to self instead of searching for God and finding His inner peace and His love for me.

Then another tragedy hit my world when my son Blake died. I remember so many days walking in the cemetery wanting to be close to Blake and to God. Some of those days at the cemetery, I cried out to God, questioning why Blake had to die. I sat by his grave, looking up at heaven and wondering what heaven was like and what Blake would be doing. I spent many hours just lying on the grass, just so I could be close to him. The real world would sometimes be too much for me to handle. I wanted to spend time being close to Blake and God, so I could escape my world and be in a world that I wanted to learn more about. I felt helpless as a mom, that I couldn't be the one taking care of my son; I had to depend on God to take care of Blake. I had to remember that Blake was God's child; I had to let him go. When I spent time at the cemetery, we could all be together in His embrace.

As time went by, I had many days when I had an extremely hard time getting up and moving. I thanked God that I started *GriefShare* because that allowed me a way out of my pain and to help others, but some days I felt sorry for myself and "got in my own head." Feeling sorry for myself is when I would see the darkness, and it was tough to see the light. I kept telling myself, "Search for God, look for the light, and get yourself out of this," but that's not as easy as you think at times. Your mind plays tricks on you and leads you to dark places. In those dark places, I would scroll on Facebook and see everyone living their life with their whole family; my family felt broken because half of my heart was missing, because my beautiful son Blake was not here. I felt like someone took a melon scoop and scooped out half of my heart, and I felt very empty inside.

I first saw everyone getting ready for the school year, the year that Blake could not wait to be a part of. Senior year was his year to shine under those big lights on the football field. We missed seeing Blake being part of the Blue Devil football team. When that football season ended, I would see all the holiday pictures of Thanksgiving and Christmas, with everyone enjoying spending time with family; with my family, my son was missing from all the holiday cheer. Then I would scroll again, and it was prom time.

Blake talked about prom since he was in middle school. He wanted a big party at the clubhouse in our development to start it off, then to be picked up in a limo and brought to his senior prom. Those months leading up to prom were so hard, when I saw each child being asked to prom. Nowadays, when someone is asked to the prom, it's posted all over Facebook in a very clever way. I wondered how Blake would have asked his prom date to the prom. I know Blake would have thought of a very clever way to ask his prom date; then I wondered who he would have brought to his senior prom.

As time went by, I would scroll through graduation day, the day that marks you completed a big milestone in your life. Then you see pictures on Facebook from when they got on the school bus in kindergarten, and now, the picture of them on their last day of school. Side by side, you see them as a little child, then all grown up. I was never able to take that picture of Blake on his last day of school, because he was no longer part of this life and was in heaven. So many experiences that I did not get to capture and be a part of with my son.

Then college came, and everyone was leaving to follow their dreams. Blake was planning to attend Cleveland State, and he wanted to get into the business world. I know that he would have loved it because Blake was a go-getter, and he loved to work. He was dedicated to everything that he wanted to do. As time went by and I scrolled through the years, I looked at pictures of his friends. I saw them getting married and having children. I wondered if Blake were alive, would he be married? Would he have children? You can't do that to yourself because that leads you into the dark and out of the light. You have to bring yourself back to your own reality; and remember that you know where he is, he is in heaven with his heavenly Father.

Then you start questioning again and your mind goes back to the dark. I was left alone, clutching onto the jersey that lays on his bed and looked up at his fathead picture and saw his eyes shining bright and looking back at me through his helmet. Then I noticed his signed helmet on the shelf with all his friends and classmates' names all over the helmet. I was left with his friends' signatures and memories that filled my head with happy times, full of love and laughter. I wondered what life would had been like if Blake was in it. I can't go there because it brought me further in the dark and far away from God's light.

I have to remember the promise that I made the night that Blake died. How God came to me in this same room and told me to get Blake's Bible with the football cover. I needed to remember how God showed up on my hardest day; that He was with me, and He will always be with me.

God had taken me downstairs and led me to one of the hardest Bible verses. I have to love God over everything, and that if I can see God, He would help me through my toughest days. When I looked outside and I saw that ray of light leading up to heaven, I wanted to walk up that ray of light, and peek in and see that Blake was okay, then I would be okay. I looked at that ray of light and I made a promise to God that I would live for the both of us; I would be God's ray of light because He shined His light on my hardest day.

I made the choice to pick the light over the darkness and to live for the both of us because Blake was my ray of sunlight. His personality lit up the room and lit up my life. Blake's name meant "Father of Light." It was a choice you had to make, to get yourself out of the darkness and into the light. I had to call out to God and say, "Jesus bring me into your light and guide me back to you."

Then I had another tragedy and that is when Bob had his stroke and almost died. When the doctors gave up hope on him, I went to the chapel to be alone with God. After spending quiet time with God and surrendering, "Not my will, but your will be done," I heard the voice of God in my inner soul. He said, "Watch what I can do." God was with me, and now Bob is with me today.

In the beginning, it was not easy. I went through so much darkness, especially when Covid hit, I was isolated and surrounded by the outcome of Bob's stroke 24/7. I started questioning myself if I could do this. My life consisted of taking care of Bob and all his needs. I took him to physical therapy, occupational therapy, speech therapy, took care of everything that Bob needed, took care of the home, cooked, and paid all the bills that were stacked up. Well, Brittany cooked. I was so blessed that she liked to cook.

My life was no longer my life. I was living my life for both of us. I was one person living two lives. Bob needed everything done for him and I was his hands and feet. I felt so much pressure all around me; then with Covid, I felt physically and emotionally isolated from my parents, sister, brother and all my cousins and aunts. I just wanted to scream. I wanted to jump out of my own reality and out of this world. I desperately needed a hug from my mom and to see my sister again. I felt the entire world crashing down on me. I just could not take it anymore.

I remember sitting in my big brown recliner looking outside. It was an extremely hot day with the sun shining bright, but on that day all I saw were black clouds and the room closing in on me. The room kept getting smaller and I was sinking further down in my recliner. I did not see any light at all. My thoughts turned toward my Uncle Jimmy and Blake not being in my life. I started thinking about taking care of Bob and all his needs and the responsibilities that were in front of me. I wanted to close my eyes and wake up and be somewhere else. I just did not care; I wanted to leave all that behind me and escape my reality. I did not care about anything. I was numb as I sunk further into the darkness. I felt like I was being pulled under, like I was standing in quicksand that was taking me down further into a deep dark hole.

I missed Blake, and my heart was broken and empty. I could not see him, I was crying and screaming in my head, "Get me out of here." Then I heard in my inner voice, "Grab your phone, just grab your phone." I grabbed my phone and in my inner voice I heard, "Talk on your phone and say, 'play *Breathe* by Michael W. Smith.' Place the phone on your shoulder, let it rest with your phone close to your ear."

The song started playing. At first, I was very restless and then, little by little, I let the music fill my heart and soul. As I kept listening to the words, "This is the air I breathe," then again, "This is the air I breathe. Your holy presence living in me." At that moment, I felt like I could breathe again. Then I listened to the next verse, "This is my daily bread, This is my daily bread, your very words spoken to me." I thought, "God was with me, and I heard His voice." The next verse got me, and I felt a huge lump in my throat. "I, I'm desperate for you and I, I'm lost without you." Then the song went back to, "This is the air I breathe, this is the air I breathe. Your holy presence living in me." I kept listening to those beautiful words! I needed to breathe and feel Gods presence near me. Then, the next verse again, "I, I'm desperate for you, and I, I'm lost without you." Repeatedly, I said, "God I am lost without you. God I am so desperate for you. I need you to hold me, and I am so desperate for you."

If you feel lost, afraid, and missing your loved one, cry out to God and He will bring you into the light and out of the darkness. I was desperate for God, and I needed Him to get me out of the darkness, into God's light and into His loving arms.

Here are a few Bible verses that helped me when I was in the dark and I needed to see God's words and have Him bring me back in His light and into His arms.

Genesis 1:3 NABRE – "Then God said: Let there be light, and there was light."

The good news: Light is hope, wisdom and goodness - God brings us that and it'll never go away.

Psalm 18:28-30 NIV - "You Lord, keep my lamp burning; my God turns my darkness into light. With your help I can advance against a troop; with my God I can scale a wall. As for God, his way is perfect: The Lord's world is flawless; he shields all who take refuge in him."

Darkness: The partial or total absence of light.

Wickedness of evil. "The forces of darkness."

What did God call the darkness? God called the light "day," and the darkness he called "night." There was evening and there was morning in one day.

John 1:5 NABRE – "the light shines in the darkness, / and the darkness has not overcome it." The good news: regardless of how bad things may seem or how bad things could get, there is always hope.

1 Corinthians 10:13 NABRE – "No trial has come to you but what is human. God is faithful and will not let you be tried beyond your strength; but with the trial he will also provide a way out, so that you may be able to bear it."

The Lord is our Light.

Psalm 18:28 ESV – "For it is you who light my lamp; the Lord my God lightens my darkness."

Psalm 27:1 NABRE – "The LORD is my light and my salvation; / whom should I fear? / The LORD is my life's refuge; / of whom should I be afraid?"

Isaiah 60:1 NABRE – "Arise! Shine, for your light has come, / the glory of the LORD has dawned upon you."

Micah 7:8-10 ESV – "Do not gloat over me, my enemy! Though I have fallen, I will rise. Though I sit in darkness, the Lord will be my light."

Revelation 21:23 NABRE – "The city had no need of sun or moon to shine on it, for the glory of God gave it light, and its lamp was the Lamb."

John 3:19-21 NABRE – "And this is the verdict, that the light came into the world, but people preferred darkness to light, because their works were evil. For everyone who does wicked things hates the light and does not come toward the light, so that his works might not be exposed. But whoever lives the truth comes to the light, so that his works may be clearly seen as done in God."

John 1:7 NABRE – "He came for testimony, to testify to the light, so that all might believe through him."

God always calls us out of the darkness and into the light.

Isaiah 9:2 ASV – "The people who walked in darkness have seen a great light; they that dwelt in a land of the shadow of death, upon them hath the light shined."

John 12:35-36 NABRE – "Jesus said to them, 'The light will be among you only a little while. Walk while you have the light, so that darkness may not overcome you. Whoever walks in the dark does not know where he is going. While you have the light, believe in the light, so that you may become children of light.'"

John 12:44-46 NABRE – "Jesus cried out and said, 'Whoever believes in me believes not only in me but also in the one who sent me, and whoever sees me sees the one who sent me. I came into the world as light, so that everyone who believes in me might not remain in darkness.'"

2 Corinthians 4:6 NABRE – "For God who said, 'Let light shine out of darkness,' has shone in our hearts to bring to light the knowledge of the glory of God on the face of [Jesus] Christ."

Acts 26: 17-18 NABRE – "I shall deliver you from this people and from the Gentiles to whom I send you, to open their eyes that they may turn from darkness to light and from the power of Satan to God, so that they may obtain forgiveness of sins and an inheritance among those who have been consecrated by faith in me."

Turn to God and away from the darkness. Return to God's guiding light. I have sat in the darkness many times and I have had to call out to God, "Please shine your light over me."

The devil tries so many times, to place us in darkness and far away from God. He knows our weakness and will pull on us, over and over, to bring us down. When this happens, ask God to shine his light over you and pull you out of the darkness. God's light is much stronger than the darkness.

Mark 14:36 NABRE – "…he said, 'Abba, Father, all things are possible to you. Take this cup away from me, but not what I will but what you will."

We have a choice, and we can choose to let God into our heart and let Him hold and take care of us, or we can choose to be angry and mad at God and keep Him at a distance like I did when my Uncle died. God has big shoulders, and He understands your pain because He himself watched His one and only son die on the cross.

173

It is your choice, and I feel so blessed that when Blake died, God showed up and He was by my side. God carried me through my toughest days, and He was my light. I knew the difference when I was trying to figure it out on my own; I felt lost, alone, and afraid. I saw the difference and I knew what to do when I start feeling sorry for myself. It's then I knew that I had to listen to music that drew me closer to God, or I knew I needed to open up my Bible to read His love story and to encourage me to keep moving forward. I also knew that I could listen to the *Amen App* or other Apps that drew me close to God, instead of falling into the darkness. I could also choose to go for walks in nature, and I could be with Blake at the cemetery. It is your choice and you decide if you want to stay and be in the dark, or you can call out to God and ask Him to be with you through the pain. In time, He will hold you and bring you into the light and into His loving arms.

CHAPTER 17:
DOES GOD PREPARE YOU FOR THE TOUGH DAYS TO COME?

Prepare: Make (something) ready for use or consideration. (*Oxford Languages*)

Prepare a summary of the article.

Make (someone) ready or able to do or deal with something.

Schools should prepare children for life.

Uncle Jimmy

Bible Verse - Matthew 24:36 NABRE - "But of that day and hour no one knows, neither the angels of heaven, nor the Son, but the Father alone."

Matthew 24:42 NABRE - "Therefore, stay awake! For you do not know on which day your Lord will come."

Matthew 24:44 NABRE - "So too, you also must be prepared, for at an hour you do not expect, the Son of Man will come."

Luke 21:36 NABRE – "Be vigilant at all times and pray that you have the strength to escape the tribulations that are imminent and to stand before the Son of Man."

I was not prepared for my uncle's loss. It took me by surprise. God tells us in these verses to be prepared for you do not know the hour when your loved one will be called home. At that time in my life my prayer life was simple, and I did not have a relationship with God. God calls us to pray and to get to know him so we are not alone.

Blake

Bible Verse - Ephesians 2:10 NABRE – "For we are his handiwork, created in Christ Jesus for the good works that God has prepared in advance, that we should live in them."

After Blake passed away, I knew that I could not do this alone. I attended a grief program and met so many wonderful people who poured out their hearts. I became very close to many people. One of these was Denise Golan, who became a good friend of mine. I met Denise at a grief program after she lost her mother-in-law.

Father Bob agreed to let us bring this program to St. Ambrose, and with the help of Denise, Pat Drum, who had many losses, and Nancy VanGieson, who lost her husband, we started our first *GriefShare Program.*

After the loss of my Uncle Jimmy, both of my grandparents, and then my son Blake, I felt God's calling for me to walk with others who were grieving. I could feel their pain, and we could walk together on this journey.

This program was a blessing in my life. They all helped me through the loss of my son; together as we shared our pain, it led us to God and how much He pours out his love over us.

After seven years of facilitating *GriefShare*, Brittany approached me right after Christmas. She said, "Mom, I love you so much, but I have to ask you something. I hope you don't get mad at me for saying this." I replied, "Sure, what is it?" "Do you think you do *GriefShare* because it is easier to listen and help others with their grief, so you don't have to go through your own grief?" I told her, "I love *GriefShare*, and I believe God led me to help others." Brittany informed, "I see that you are helping so many people, but Dad is still taking it hard, and we need you here." A few months passed, I couldn't stop thinking about what Brittany said to me. She might be right. It was easier to ignore my own pain.

I decided that when the current thirteen-week session ends, I would turn it over to Denise and have her run the program with Kathy and Gloria. They both were participants who suffered a loss of a loved one.

That summer proved to be wonderful. Bob and I, Brent, and Brittany would spend many nights sitting on the front porch with our dog Bailey. We would share funny stories, get Honey Hut ice cream, and enjoy nature.

As I looked back, I realized that God prepared me for Bob's stroke. The doctors gave up hope and said he would not amount to anything. I knew differently. I had looked into my husband's eyes, and I could see life in his eyes. He was talking to me through his eyes, and I had hope for him.

Bob

Bible Verse: Mark 13:32-33 NABRE – "But of that day or hour, no one knows, neither the angels in heaven, nor the Son, but only the Father. Be watchful! Be alert! You do not know when the time will come."

This verse is very similar to Matthew 24:36 – No one knows the day or the hour, only the Father.

I repeated it in my head - However, no one knows the day or hour **when these things will happen - when that time will come, be on GUARD! STAY ALERT!**

God gave me the grace to see that Bob loved sitting on the front porch with his family and his dog at his side before the stroke. That memory helped me make decisions when Bob had the stroke. Now, after the stroke, we still have each other.

I also believe God prepared me for Bob's stroke and gave me the opportunity to work at Oak Tree Holdings LLC. Every year when the kids were little, we used to get a real live Christmas tree at Fred's Tree Farm in Valley City. Blake would often tell me, Mom, you need to work closer to home. Working downtown Cleveland is so far away.

After Blake passed, my friend, Kristin, mentioned that they were hiring new employees at her company. I used to work with Kristin at PwC in the tax department. I told her that our company was going through some transitions, and I felt that this might be a good time to make a change. I worked at PwC for almost 28 years. They were family to me, especially after Blake passed away.

I had an interview with Kristin, and she offered me the job, but she didn't know the benefit package. She mentioned that she would look into it for me. At that moment, I also remembered Blake telling me that he always wanted me to work close to home. I told her that I had to think about it because I loved working at PwC.

Well, that Sunday at church, the homily at mass truly spoke to me. The homily was about two rock climbers, Tommy and Kevin, who wanted to climb El Capitan at Yosemite National Park. Everyone said it could not be done. They planned to use only their skill and strength. The sheer rock wall they wanted to climb was 3,000 feet straight up. Again, they were told it would be impossible; however, Tommy and Kevin did the impossible. They reached the summit only using their hands and feet. When asked if they had

177

a message to tell the world, Kevin said that he hoped everyone would take the time to scale their own mountain, to achieve something big that they dream of, and never give up.

I thought of Blake - He always told me, "Mom, Go Big or Go Home." He always pushed himself to the limit, and this reminded me of Blake.

And I think the same could be said of the men we encountered in today's gospel. People thought the apostles were crazy, or maybe just stupid.

A traveling preacher passed by on the seashore, and these fishermen dropped everything to follow him. They abandoned their income, their security, their families; they set out (so to speak) without any ropes to begin the greatest "free climb" adventure in history. They set out to scale mountains they never imagined.

They would, like Tommy and Kevin, know fear, disappointment, uncertainty and dread; climbing a mountain is like that, however, so is a life of faith. It takes tenacity - and it takes trust. Trust in God. But also trust in one another. Tommy and Kevin knew they couldn't scale El Capitan alone, solo. Jesus knew His disciples couldn't do it alone, either, which I think is why he first called them two by two: Andrew and Simon, James and John…In this gospel, we're reminded again how the commitment of the first apostles was with complete trust. One phrase stands out in this reading, "They abandoned their nets and followed Him."

They walked away from their job, a livelihood. I don't think they asked Jesus about His dental plan, or retirement benefit, or paid vacation. They just went. They left what they knew and what was familiar to them. They went into what they did not know, followed Jesus, and lived differently.

I was thinking - I just had an interview at Oak Tree Holdings LLC. I don't know what the pay is, and I have no idea about the benefits, but I think God is calling me to make this change in my life. Blake always wanted me to work close to home. Should I leave my family at PwC and take this chance?

Can you imagine doing anything like that today? We should, because whether we realize it or not, that is the choice facing each of us. All of us are like those first followers of Christ. Not all of us, of course, are fishermen, but we all have nets.

Sometimes, our nets are strong and hold us together, but sometimes, they are flimsy and hold us back. Those nets are the world we know and what we are comfortable with. I was very comfortable at PwC.

Those things that we are used to and are familiar with us, may be keeping us from becoming true followers of Christ.

That Sunday morning the homily was really speaking to me. "God, are you guiding me to make a change and to work at Oak Tree Holdings LLC?"

I decided to take the job, and I truly believe God prepared me. God led me to a company that places God first. Upon my first visit, they took me into a conference room. I noticed a Bible was on the credenza. At that very moment, I knew for sure that God led me there because they had a love for Christ. After I signed some papers, I went on a tour and was brought into the boardroom. On the wall, they had a very large picture from the Bible with the verse Ecclesiastes 3:1-22 listed.

Ecclesiastes 3:1-8 NABRE - "There is an appointed time for everything, / and a time for every affair under the heavens. / A time to give birth, and a time to die; / a time to plant, and a time to uproot the plant. / A time to kill, and a time to heal; / a time to tear down, and a time to build. / A time to weep, and a time to laugh; / a time to mourn, and a time to dance. / A time to scatter stones, and a time to gather them; / a time to embrace and a time to be far from embraces. / A time to seek, and a time to lose; / a time to keep, and a time to cast away. / A time to rend, and a time to sew; / a time to be silent, and a time to speak. / A time to love, and a time to hate; /a time of war, and a time of peace."

I felt a presence of God all around the room. I knew without a doubt that God led me here.

When Bob had his stroke, I needed to keep working. I hired a caregiver to take care of Bob for four hours a day. This was very expensive. When Covid happened, we started working from home, and I didn't need a caregiver. What a timely and beautiful blessing for me, as I really couldn't afford the caregiver.

Does God prepare us? God, I cannot thank you enough for loving me and for taking care of me. I am so blessed that you led me to Oak Tree Holdings LLC. Now, I can work close to home and take care of Bob. I cannot even image if I still worked downtown, how I could manage to take care of Bob.

God prepared me for another situation that happened in our family. I wasn't going to mention this one, but God keeps placing it on my heart, so even though the outcome was different, God still prepared me.

On October 31st, 2021, I woke up around 3:00 a.m., crying and shaken up. I had many shuddering feelings rushing through me. I had a dream of Jesus praying to his Father in heaven. As he was praying, I could feel this loneliness and emptiness after his friends abandoned him and didn't stay awake in Gethsemane. He asked them to pray, and they fell asleep. I felt Him trembling and shaking. I felt His terror knowing that He would die on the cross for all of us, to take away our sin. I felt His pain and loneliness and how scared He felt. He was crying so hard and praying to His Father, "If it is possible, may this cup be taken from me. Yet not as I will, but as you will." As he was crying and praying, I felt His fear in my heart, which caused me to jolt up, shaking and crying. What does this dream mean? How could I feel all this pain? Jesus prayed so hard and asked His Father to take away this cup.

God, is something going to happen to Bob? Bob has been feeling good lately. Is something going to happen to one of my parents, or to my mother-in-law? Jesus prayed so hard, and He died for us. Not His will, but as the Father willed. I know many people pray, and prayers are not always answered the way we hope, sometimes. I was shaken to the core. I woke up and walked around downstairs, thinking about the dream I just had. I decided to open my Bible and search for God's word. God loves us so much that He would die for me.

I went into my prayer room and looked at a copy of a picture that Mario, one of my *GriefShare* participants, drew. This picture was of Jesus, after He passed away on the cross for us. I just could not keep my eyes off this picture. At that moment, as Jesus was dying on the cross, the Bible tells us that (Matthew 27:46) "At about the ninth hour Jesus cried out with a loud voice, saying, *'Eli, Eli, lema sabachthani?'*" This means, "My God, my God, why have you forsaken me?" I kept looking at the picture and what came to me is that Jesus said to His Father, why have you forsaken me? As a mother, I could never watch my child pass away in front of me. As a mother, who lost her son, I would die for him, and I would take his place.

I believe at that same moment when Jesus cried out to His Father, His father turned away because the pain was overwhelming. At the same time Jesus was taking on all the sins of the world and felt all excruciating sin. When He felt all the sin. He drew away from His Father. Because when you sin you don't feel worthy of God's love. Jesus is God and God is Jesus, but at that moment Jesus felt what we feel, which is the sin of the world. He felt the betrayal you feel when you draw away from yourself, and away from the Father. In this picture after it is finished - Jesus looks totally at peace, He is home with His Father.

I continued looking at the picture of Jesus. Mario had passed away from Covid and I am very close to his wife, Barb, who was helping me edit my story. I feel so blessed that Mario had given me this picture because I turn to it always to give me strength; to understand how much God loves me, that He would sacrifice His one and only son for me, and all of us. What a true gift. I have a God that would die for me. That is what gets me through the toughest days.

I decided to get dressed and go to 7:30 a.m. Sunday mass. When I arrived at mass, I could not take my eyes off the crucifix. God, are you trying to prepare me for something? Is Bob going to have another stroke? Father Andrew was leading us in mass that morning. After mass I was going to talk to him about my dream and what I felt, but I didn't know what to say or what the dream truly meant, so I decided not to say anything.

The next morning, Monday, my brother-in-law, John, called me around 7:00 a.m. He said, "Terri, we need lots of prayers, and you are a prayer warrior." I said, " I can pray." I asked, "What is happening?" John replied, "Debby just had a stroke, and Joe is at the hospital. I can't believe this is happening."

I thought immediately about the dream I had the other night. I thought something might happen to Bob, my parents, or to his mom, and here it was Bob's sister.

My sister-in-law, Jean called, and she couldn't stop crying. I could barely make out what she was saying. She pleaded, "You and Bob need to go to the hospital. Show them that my brother had a stroke and he pulled through. You have to convince them not to give up on her, to move her to Cleveland Clinic Akron General where Bob was at." I told her to try and calm down and we should pray together. After crying and talking so fast she thought that was a good idea. I relayed to her that I lit Blake's candle, and I prayed. I also have been listening to music to be near God. She suggested, "Play me a song that helps you the most." I proposed to play *Breathe* [42] by Michael W. Smith. It always helps me calm down and focus on Christ. So, we listened to this song together. When the song was over, we prayed together.

Again, she stressed, "You and Bob have to get to the hospital. You have to show the doctors how good Bob is doing and tell them that the doctors didn't want to perform bone flap surgery, however, they did do the surgery and look he is alive."

Bob and I went to the hospital. When we were getting off the elevator, Father Andrew from our parish was about to get on the elevator. I said to him, "What are you doing here?" He said, "Father Bob told me about your sister-in-law and I just saw her." I asked how she is doing. He answered, "My prayers are with all of you." I was just thinking, yesterday Father Andrew had the mass, and I wanted to tell him about the dream that I had and what he thought it meant. Here he is, right when we got off the elevator. So, I decided to tell him about my dream. He said, "Terri I would go in and pray with Debby, and God will be with you."

Bob and I went in to see her. My heart was aching for her and for her wonderful husband, Joe, who was sitting by her side. Bob was in his wheelchair, and he just held onto her hand, and said "Debby I am here." I held her hand along with Bob's hand, and I prayed God please be with Debby. As I looked down on Debby I kept thinking about when Bob had his stroke. This didn't seem the same. When I looked into Bob's eyes, I saw light in those eyes, and I could tell that he was with me. Debby's eyes were closed, and I didn't see or feel anything.

I prayed to God, please shine your light and give me a sign that she is with us. I kept looking down on Bob holding onto his sister's hand. Just two years prior, Debby was holding onto Bob's hand and praying over him. God please be with Debby and all of us. As I held onto Debby's hand, I looked up at Joe, looking at Debby. This was me just two years ago. I could feel the pain that was running through him and all the love that he had for his beautiful wife.

182

I looked over at Bob and saw tears rolling down his cheek as he was holding onto Debby's hand. "Why God, why is this happening?" I kept praying over Debby and looking over at Joe. Then I heard the voice of God, stating the dream was not for you, that dream was for Joe. I thought of my dream and how Jesus prayed to His Father in heaven. "If it is possible, may this cup be taken from me. Yet, not as I will, but as you will. Not my will, but your will be done."

As I looked over at Joe looking into Debby's eyes, I didn't have the courage to tell him. I looked back down at Bob holding onto Debby's hand, and his thumb was rubbing back and forth giving her comfort as much as he knew how. I felt helpless and so scared for Joe. My heart burned for Bob who was holding his older sister's hand and holding onto hope. Joe looked over at me and asked, "Terri, is this like Bob's stroke?" I looked into his eyes, and I answered, "no," as tears were rolling down my face. I walked over to him and hugged him. We both walked over to the side of the room, we just hugged each other tightly and cried together. Joe said "I don't know what to do? So, you don't think this is like Bob's stroke. It was so hard for me to tell Joe that I didn't think this was the same. I finally softly mentioned, "I saw light in Bob's eyes and a glimpse of life. Debby's eyes are closed and when I hold her hand I don't feel anything. I am so sorry." He agreed. He didn't want to admit it, but he felt it was different also. He brought up when the doctors gave up hope but I never did. "Why did you want surgery? He is not going to ever be able to walk again or talk again," the physician's assistant kept coming back asking.

Debby, Jean, and Rick, Bob's siblings, were fighting for Bob's life in hope and prayer. John, Jean's husband and Joe were on the fence. Joe had said to me at that time when Bob had his stroke, that if he placed himself in Bob's shoes, he would not want to live like that. I remember telling Joe that Bob was different from you. You and John are very active and work out. Bob works out, but not like both of you. Bob loves to sit and watch TV. I can picture us sitting on the front porch with our dog Bailey, living a very simple life. I remember telling Joe that this was the hardest decision that I had to make. I didn't know if Bob would be mad at me later for keeping him alive.

Joe asked me, "What made you decide to have surgery?" "I cannot imagine giving up on him when I saw him with his eyes open. I didn't get a chance to fight for Blake because he passed away in a car accident, but I can fight for Bob, and I have a chance. I then went down to the chapel to pray. I prayed, 'God not my will, but your will be done.' I kept looking up at the cross and thinking of Jesus and how he died for us. I kept returning to the Bible verse about having faith as small as a mustard seed and God can move

183

mountains. I took the coin out of my pocket, and I pressed it in the palm of my hand and at that moment I felt God's love pour through me. I knew that God could move mountains, and in my heart, I already accepted that if he dies when he is having his surgery, that God is calling him home. If he survives that God has a different plan for him and for our family."

Joe looked at me, and stated, "I don't want to give up on Debby. What should I do?" I reminded Joe that this was not the same. We both cried in each other's arms. I looked in Joe's eyes and explained that I had a dream the night before. When I was praying over Debby, I heard the voice of God telling me that the dream was for you and that I had to share what I felt. He said, "Please tell me." I related to Joe that this was very painful, but I thought the dream was for God to prepare me for something that would happen to Bob. Joe asked again to please share it with me.

I stated, "The night before I had a dream of Jesus praying in the garden of Gethsemane. Jesus was afraid to die on the cross. He asked his Father in heaven to take this cup away." I told him everything that I felt about the dream. I looked in Joe's eyes, and I mentioned, "Joe, I am so sorry this is happening, but Jesus prayed. I believe some of our prayers don't get answered the way we want them to, but God truly knows what is best for us." Joe hugged me so tightly with tears in his eyes. He said, "Thank you so much for sharing this with me because I was afraid that I was giving up on her. You are giving me a message from God that He is calling her home."

When prayers go unanswered it can rip a big hole in our heart. We wonder if God really hears our prayers.

Matthew 27:46 NABRE – "And about three o'clock Jesus cried out in a loud voice, *'Eli, Eli, lema sabachthani?'* which means, 'My God, my God, why have you forsaken me?'"

No response came from Heaven for Jesus, and often no response comes for us.

God spoke, assuring He was attentive and listening, but during the darkest moments of Christ's earthly life, God answered only with silence and darkness.

Jesus' response to unanswered prayer was commitment.

Luke 23:46 NABRE – "Jesus cried out in a loud voice, 'Father, into your hands I commend my spirit'; and when he had said this he breathed his last."

184

Jesus was giving us an understanding that we can trust God even with unanswered prayer.

CHAPTER 18:
SURRENDERING OVER TO GOD

Surrender: Cease resistance to an enemy or opponent and submit to their authority. (*Oxford Languages*)

When you surrender everything over to God, you live for Him and not your own selfish ways. When you make decisions, you look through the eyes of Christ, you live in the spirit and not in the flesh, being human and living in this world, life is very hard with the demands and the lifestyle of today's world. You are living in the flesh. I believe you have forces against you, and the devil is also living in this world. I feel that the devil is going to try harder to bring you down, the closer you become to God.

We have to remember we are human, and we live in a fallen world.

Uncle Jimmy

Bible Verse - James 4:7 NABRE – "So submit yourselves to God. Resist the devil, and he will flee from you."

Repeatedly the devil was telling me lies in my head. Your uncle didn't love you. Look, he is not here with you. I kept listening to his lies, but in this verse, God is telling us to resist the devil, and he will flee from you.

Blake

Bible Verse - Matthew 16:24 NABRE – "Then Jesus said to his disciples, 'Whoever wishes to come after me must deny himself, take up his cross, and follow me.'"

Luke 9:23-24 NABRE - "Then he said to all, 'If anyone wishes to come after me, he must deny himself and take up his cross daily and follow me. For whoever wishes to save his life will lose it, but whoever loses his life for my sake will save it.'"

This cross (the death of my son, Blake) is the hardest cross I had to bear. I had to surrender many times to God to give me the strength to get up and keep moving. Only God truly knows all the pain that I am enduring. It is at the cross where I see God's glory. God at this moment knows my pain; He sacrificed his one and only son for us - for me. If I lean on His understanding and follow Him, He will lead me on the straight path. I think we all have crosses to bear. Each of us knows with what we are suffering, and God knows our heart. We can be honest with ourselves, deny ourselves, and take up our cross daily to follow Him to the cross. God lays out His word and He gives us the Ten Commandments. He gives us the free will to live our life, but we are human and live in the flesh. We do what we want, when we want, when it fits into our lifestyle. It's up to us to deny ourselves earthly pleasures and come to follow Him.

What does Luke 9:23-24 mean? - It means that a death takes place in your life. The old goes away; the eyes are fixed on Jesus, and you follow him. It's very radical, and it's very, very decisive .... carrying the cross, denying yourself, fixing your eyes on Jesus, and living for His glory.

Philippians 3:7-11 NABRE – "[But] whatever gains I had, these I have come to consider a loss because of Christ. More than that, I even consider everything as a loss because of the supreme good of knowing Christ Jesus my Lord. For His sake I have accepted the loss of all things and I consider them so much rubbish, that I may gain Christ and be found in Him, not having any righteousness of my own based on the law but that which comes through faith in Christ, the righteousness from God, depending on faith to know him and the power of his resurrection and [the] sharing of his sufferings by being conformed to his death, if somehow I may attain the resurrection from the dead."

I believe there is power in the resurrection and Jesus' suffering on the cross for our sins. When we grieve the loss of a loved one, we become more like Jesus in His suffering, because our heart is suffering. We are brokenhearted, and we feel a pain that is so deep in our souls.

Bob

Bible Verse - Matthew 26:39 NABRE – "He advanced a little and fell prostrate in prayer, saying, 'My Father, if it is possible, let this cup pass from me; yet, not as I will, but as you will.'"

When Bob had his stroke, I gave it ALL over to God. I said, "Not my will, but your will be done." God only you know what is best for Bob. He was your child before he was my husband. If he is meant to be with you, I will accept and let him go. If you decide for him to live, I will take good care of him. We will live out your purpose and find the true meaning of this life we are in.

CHAPTER 19:
CHOICES

Choice: An act of selecting or deciding when faced with two or more possibilities.

The choice between good and evil. (*Oxford Languages*)

This definition reminds me of the cartoon characters of Tom and Jerry. I always remember Jerry the little mouse choosing to annoy Tom and having Tom chase him all over the house. Tom's job was to protect the house, but both characters always seemed to have episodes regarding choosing between good and evil.

Uncle Jimmy

Bible Verse - Deuteronomy 30:19-20 NABRE - "I call heaven and earth today to witness against you: I have set before you life and death, the blessing and the curse. Choose life, then, that you and your descendants may live, by loving the LORD, your God, obeying his voice, and holding fast to him. For that will mean life for you, a long life for you to live on the land which the LORD swore to your ancestors, to Abraham, Isaac, and Jacob, to give to them."

Colossians 3:8-10 NIV – "But now you have to also rid yourselves of all such things as these: anger, rage, malice, slander, and filthy language from your lips. Do not lie to each other, since you have taken off your old self with its practices and have put on the new self, which is being renewed in knowledge in the image of its Creator."

What this Bible verse meant to me/When I was Angry at God

I chose to close out the world. I chose not to let anyone see the pain that was building up inside. It was easier to escape than to accept what happened. I was very angry at God for not protecting my uncle and saving him so he could be with us. I remember going to church when I was in middle school just looking at the crucifix and staring at it. One day I remember sitting in my room crying and saying, "Why did this happen? Tomorrow will be another day." I blocked Jesus from my life in the years I was in pain. I chose to be angry at God because He didn't save my uncle. As I look back this was not God's doing. This was my uncle's choice. I didn't want to be mad at my uncle, because he was everything to me. I wanted to blame God and not my uncle for him not being in my life. As I grew older, I understood more how complicated his life really was.

As I reread this last paragraph about eight years later, two years after Bob's stroke, I realized that all those years in middle school, and through high school I was with God the whole time. I was shutting out the world because I was in pain, but who I turned to was God. I would go into the woods, walk for hours and share my pain with God. I would ask, "Why Uncle Jimmy, why did he have to die?"

At times I remember the wind roaring like a lion and taking me by surprise and almost knocking me over. That pain was echoing into the bottom of my soul. If I could just let myself go, and start yelling at the top of my lungs, I would have, but the pain strangled me. Those windy days felt amazing as they blew me all around and the sound would be piercing in my ears. The sound of the wind would take me away. I felt much like the wind. I felt God's nature all around me. The strong wind beneath my feet. Maybe it was God's way of telling me that it's okay to be mad. Here is the wind to show you how you can feel. It's okay to be angry. The wind can be angry. What I felt was God's strength in those winds. But those winds let me feel the pain. Eventually when I was in my late 40's I finally was able to yell at the top of my lungs, "WHY? – Why did you have to DIE?" I realized it's okay to be mad. Let it all out. It's okay not to be okay. Don't let it absorb into your soul. As I looked back, I felt comfort in those winds. God let me feel His strength and His power. I could be with my uncle and be with God. The pain was so overwhelming I felt God's comfort alone in the woods.

After I cried, there were times I didn't feel afraid. I would have loved it to just be swept up and taken home. I remember being down on my knees in the thick of the woods clutching the dirt in my hands and just crying. I felt a sense of peace in those woods and in those years, I let the pain sink into my soul. I let every hurt become me, but I realize now that I was not alone. God was with me. The pain that I felt, God felt it also. I didn't want to be mad at my uncle, but I wanted to blame someone, so God seemed like a good one to blame.

Blake

Bible Verse - Philippians 4:13 NLT – "For I can do everything through Christ, who gives me strength."

This Bible verse reminds me of Kevin Fox. Right before he passed away this was the Bible verse, he turned to for insight. Also, this is the Bible verse many athletes and businessmen turn to when they are looking for strength.

We all turn to God to give us strength to play that important football game, or to write that good speech that we have to present at work. I have read this verse many times because I have a plaque with these words on it. It has a football player down on one knee with his head down. It is right next to Blake's football picture and among all his scrapbooks in my reflection room. As I contemplate on this Bible verse, what it means to me especially after the loss of Blake is that only you, God, can give me the strength which allows me to do everything through you. God you truly are my strength.

Life is all about choices. Blake lived each day, full of laughter and joy. I made a promise to myself, the night that he died, that I would shine my light for the both of us. I asked God to shine His light through me to give me strength, so I can do everything through Christ.

Bob

Bible Verse - Matthew 19:26 NABRE -"Jesus looked at them and said, 'For human beings this is impossible, but for God all things are possible.'"

So many times, during Bob's stroke, we could have thrown the towel in, but Bob kept fighting the good fight with me fighting alongside him. Life is all about choices. We continued to stay positive and focused on God. Some days were harder than others, however, each morning when I woke him up, I went into his room with lots of energy, laughter and smiles in my voice. I believed a joyful heart would cheer him up and bring him happiness.

Father Bob from Saint Ambrose Church was amazing, and this couldn't have come at a better time in our life with all Bob's struggles this past year. Father Bob's theme song for this year was *Day by Day* [43] originally written by Lina Sandell-Berg. Each morning when I get Bob up, we sang the song *Day by Day*. This gave us both the strength we needed to keep on going and moving day by day, and one step at a time.

DAY BY DAY

Day by day,
Day by day,
Oh, Dear Lord,
Three things I pray.
To see thee more clearly,
Love thee more dearly,
Follow thee more nearly,
Day by day.

Life sometimes seems impossible, but with God, He gives us the strength to make life possible day by day.

CHOICES - We Live in a Fallen and Broken World

We live in a fallen and broken world. We are all struggling with something. I never realized this until I started seeing so many people around me dealing with various struggles in their life. It seems like we keep facing the same challenges repeatedly. Maybe, just maybe, God is trying to teach us lessons. I believe that in this life, there is a force between God and the devil. I feel so torn every second with thoughts in my head. It's like that Tom and Jerry cartoon that I used to watch. Tom the cat would see an angel on his one shoulder and the devil on his other shoulder, or was that, Jerry? I can't remember, but I always thought sometimes I feel torn between both, when I am making decisions. I feel the devil is very good at knowing our weaknesses and he will try to get us down every chance he can.

What do you struggle with in this lifetime? Life is about making decisions every second of the day. When the alarm goes off, do you get up and start your day, or do you go back to sleep? Do you have breakfast and grab something healthy that will be a good source of energy for your body, or do you grab a cookie? Do you contemplate all the many tasks you have to do, or do you just conquer and get them done one project at a time? Do you meditate? Do you pray? What do you do? Lately, I wake up about an hour before my alarm goes off. I lie in bed thinking about God and I thank Him for my many blessings. I ask God to be with me and to walk with me. I ask Him to guide me throughout the day, so I can make clear, wise choices throughout the day.

I take a good look at my day, and I ask Him to be a part of it. I know if I try and do it myself, it will be all about me and my selfish ways. I believe God wants to be part of our life each and every step of the way. I never knew that until Blake passed away. I thought I had everything under control, at least everything seemed to be going my way.

I started realizing that every second, we are truly making decisions. Does my mind wander? It sure does. I'm not sure if your mind wanders. I will be at work and my mind sometimes drifts. Stay focused, please stay focused. My daughter calls me a little squirrel and wonders how I get everything done. I have to agree with her. It sure does wander. Does anyone else feel that way? Our mind is very powerful and what do you do, to feed your mind? I know that when I focus on God and I want to live for Him, my decisions seem very clear. With each thought that pops into my head, I ask myself would God be pleased with this decision. If the answer is yes, then I won't have any regrets. I won't worry about the decision that I made. If the decision does not seem pleasing to God, then I realize that I'm not being true to the person I want to become. God created us in His own image. When we try to control our own destiny, and do what we want, we are pleasing our own selves. God made you and me to love one another. When we don't follow and turn away from the way we were designed by God, we fall away from ourselves and away from our creator. We are living for us and not for how God intended us to live our life. When we fall short of who we are meant to be, and don't fulfill our purpose in life, we feel like we don't measure up.

When I was a child, I was looking for validation from my parents. I wanted to feel that they could be proud of me, and I always wanted them to love me. We are all searching to be loved and love one another. We are also searching for our purpose in life. When you don't feel loved, you feel empty inside. When you have God in your heart, He fills you with all those securities and your heart is overflowing with acceptance and love.

Think of your teenage years, when you thought you had all the answers. You wouldn't dare go ask your parents for advice because you felt you were always right.

Did you ever do something that you were so afraid to tell your parents because you thought if they ever found out they would be so disappointed in you? Just think what would happen if we shared our worries with our parents. Our parents love us for who we are, and they would help us through it. God already knows every thought before you think it. God already knows what you are going through in your life. The question is, why do we shut Him out? Why do we turn away when we feel we let Him down? When we have disappointed ourselves, we don't feel worthy of God's love. The truth is that we are harder on ourselves. We let it get us down and we are the ones that never get over it. Jesus died on the cross for our sins and He paid the price for us. God has forgiven you for what you have done. So why do we beat ourselves up when it happens to us? It's hard to forgive, especially when it comes to forgiving yourself. We are our own worst enemies.

Good decisions, bad decisions, they are always lurking around us. That is when the devil gets into your deepest thoughts. It is a definite struggle between good and evil and for me this is real. I don't know about you, but I want to do what is best for me. But why are we so tempted all the time with decisions that might not have the best outcome for us? I feel we have to stay true to ourselves and listen to the heart of God guiding us in the right direction. We do this for ourselves and for God. When you choose to listen and hear His voice, you are drawn closer to His heart. If you choose to do your own will, it draws you further away from God.

CHAPTER 20:
FEAR

Definition of Fear

Noun: an unpleasant emotion caused by the belief that someone or something is dangerous, likely to cause pain, or a threat.

Verb: Be afraid of (someone or something) as likely to be dangerous, painful, or threatening. (*Oxford Language*)

Uncle Jimmy

Bible Verse - Psalm 23:4 NABRE – "Even though I walk through the valley of the shadow of death, / I will fear no evil, for you are with me; / your rod and your staff comfort me."

I went through the deepest of valleys when my uncle passed away and let fear win over me during this time. Life is about choices, and you can choose to let God near you and comfort you, or you can choose to run away and be lonely and afraid. I had so much anger inside that I let that anger get the best of me. I did cry out to God in my sorrow, and he listened, but I know I had a guard up and I didn't let him comfort me all the time, I only let him know how painful and angry I felt.

When I facilitated *GriefShare* this was one of my favorite poems that I passed out. We all go through valleys in our life and God is always with us. I believe God himself endured this when His one and only son died on the cross.

It's in The Valleys I Grow

Sometimes life seems hard to bear,
Full of sorrow, trouble and woe
It's then I have to remember
That it's in the valleys I grow.
If I always stayed on the mountaintop
And never experienced pain,
I would never appreciate God's love
And would be living in vain.
I have so much to learn
And my growth is very slow,

Sometimes I need the mountain tops,
But it's in the valleys I grow.
I do not always understand
Why things happen as they do,
But I am very sure of one thing.
My Lord will see me through.
My little valleys are nothing
When I picture Christ on the cross
He went through the valley of death;
His victory was Satan's loss.
Forgive me Lord, for complaining
When I'm feeling so very low.
Just give me a gentle reminder
That it's in the valleys I grow.
Continue to strengthen me, Lord
And use my life each day
To share your love with others
And help them find their way.
Thank you for valleys, Lord
For this one thing I know
The mountain tops are glorious
But it's in the valleys I grow!

(This poem was written by Jane Eggleston who currently lives in Virginia. Her son Jeff states, "She is a wonderful person, loves Jesus and has been the best mother anyone could ever ask for." What a fitting tribute to any mother.)

Blake

Lord, even when your path takes us through the valley of deepest darkness, on the night our son passed away, Bob and I were frantically looking for him; fear conquered all of us. Bob was out looking for him in the car, Brent was making lots of calls, and I was pacing back and forth in the house. God, I know that you were watching over our family and you kept us close to your heart. I kept praying, "My God, my God, where is Blake? Please take care of our son and bring him back home to us." When the police officers came to our house and told us that Blake passed away, my knees dropped to the floor, and I cried. Then I stood up and fell into Bob's arms and we cried together. We couldn't believe this was happening. "God, you remained close to our family, and you remained close to me through it all. That evening when everyone went to bed, you led me to the Bible verse that I needed to hear; you led me in your arms, so you could comfort me during the most difficult day of my life."

Bible Verse - Psalm 27:1 NABRE – "The LORD is my light and my salvation; / whom should I fear? / The LORD is my life's refuge; / of whom shall I be afraid?"

When God came to me the night that Blake passed, I did not fear. I had a calmness that came over me. It's very hard to wrap my head around it, but I felt an inner peace that God was carrying me. I kept hearing that song in my head. "Be Not Afraid - I go before you always come, follow me and I will bring you rest." On the toughest day of my life, God held me and conquered the devil. He put him to rest. God held me close and didn't let him near me. I feel very blessed that God loved me so much that He took care of me the night that Blake passed away. That is why I want to bring others to know that we have a God that loves us.

Bible Verse - Isaiah 43:1 NABRE– "But now, thus says the LORD, / who created you, Jacob, and formed you, Israel: / Do not fear, for I have redeemed you; / I have called you by name: you are mine."

God called Blake by name, and he is God's child. He was created by God, and for God. He calls each one of us by name, and we are His. How beautiful that verse is that He calls each one of us by name, and we are His.

Bob

Bible Verse: Psalm 46 1-2 NIV – "God is our refuge and strength, an ever-present help in trouble. Therefore, we will not fear, though the earth gives way and the mountains fall into the heart of the sea."

I have to remember to choose faith over fear. When Bob had his stroke, so many times fear would overcome me, and I believed the devil's lies.

Bob always took care of the kids and me. He was the cook in our household while I worked downtown. He always had dinner ready when I got home from work. Bob handled all our finances and did so much around the house, and I am forever grateful. When the stroke happened, I felt very overwhelmed and not competent to take care of Bob with his illness, on top of being the one to cook and oversee all the finances. I'm so blessed that Brittany loves to cook and she took that stress away from me.

I repeatedly believed the devil's lies. Those silent voices in my head that repeatedly told me that I can't do this; that I'm not good enough. I could not take care of Bob. "Who are you kidding? You can't cook, you can't figure out all your financing and how are you going to work and take care of Bob?

You think you can have a caregiver take care of Bob, but how are you going to afford her? Just place him in the nursing home. You know you can't do this by yourself." Over and over the devil would torture me and make me feel worthless. "How are you going to work full-time and take care of him?" All lies, and I believed those lies, it was very hard to get him out of my head. The more I heard those thoughts, the more I believed them.

Then Covid hit and we were isolated. I was surrounded by Bob's stroke 24/7. We were working from home and because we were working from home, I didn't need the caregiver, so that was a blessing in disguise, as I really couldn't afford her. That was one very good thing that came out of Covid.

But what came with Covid was isolation, and anyone that knows me knows that I love to be surrounded by people. Covid left me stuck in my house and isolated from society, and this was torture for me. Guess who came at me with full force. You guessed it - the devil. He whizzled right into my inner thoughts and tortured me. I went through major depression and didn't realize I was going through depression. My friend Jayne called me one afternoon and she told me, "Terri, I think you are depressed." I said, "No, I never get depressed, Jayne. I am always uplifted and happy." She said it again, "Terri, I think you are going through depression." She said, "Do you feel tired all the time and not wanting to do things?" I said, "Yes, sometimes." She mentioned a few other things and the light bulb went off in my head. "I think you are right" So many times, I would just sit in my chair looking outside and I didn't care about anything some days. I remember one day not caring if I even lived. It wasn't like I wanted to take my life. I just didn't care about living in it. She informed, "Yes, that is depression." "Thank you, Jayne, for caring. I have to find my joy again."

When I got off the phone with her, I realized that she was right. I have to find my joy again. Then I remembered one of our training sessions with Dobie Moser up at St. Ambrose. He said if you can name it, you can go through it. I couldn't name it because I didn't see that I was depressed. When Jayne said it out loud and named it, I realized that she was right. I needed to hear those words.

What a game changer that was for me. When I could name what I was feeling, I was able to conquer my fear which was depression and the devil's lies. I needed to get my life back. "Get away Satan. God take care of me."

A few days later I came across this poem on Facebook and I felt God led me to this poem.

Letting Go

Happiness is letting go of what you assume your life
is supposed to be like right now
and sincerely appreciating it for
everything that it is.
At the end of this day,
before you close your eyes, smile and be at peace
with where you've been and grateful for what you have
Life is good.

By Angel Chernofff

This is what I truly feared. I let fear overcome me. It was not just taking care of Bob and having all these new responsibilities, it was everything in this poem that was holding me back. I am going to name it and be honest with myself. I have gone through some tough times. I lost my favorite uncle from suicide which has so many layers of grief and is very hard to understand. My son Blake died, and he missed his senior year, the year he couldn't wait to experience, especially football season and going to prom. My husband had a stroke and almost died. I realized that I have to let go of what I assumed my life was supposed to be like and live for today.

To find happiness means letting go of what you assume your life is supposed to be like. I couldn't name it, and after reading this poem, it hit me hard. Sometimes you need to see it in writing, so you can go through your pain and feel what you need to feel.

As a young girl, I dreamed of my wedding day and who I would marry. I talked all night with my sister about names that we wanted to name our children. We would live next door to each other and have a pool extended between both of our yards, so we could swim all day and be together raising our family. We lived in a bubble, and thought every family was like ours.

When I got in high school, friends would tell me your family was like *Leave it to Beaver*[44] and the *Brady Bunch*.[45] I thought all families were like ours. I came to find out, I wished they all were like ours because that life is easier than the life we are really in. I was blessed with amazing grandparents who loved each other, and they showed that love to their children. My parents showed that love to my sister, brother, and me. My parents are truly the best. They never miss date nights. Every Saturday from the day they got married, they would go on date nights even to this day. We always had babysitters, and we loved spending time with them, while our parents had their date night. My dad adores my mom and will do anything for her.

197

My dad was our baseball coach, and he always made our team laugh. He picked up half the neighborhood, and we were all on the green team. He would pretend he was Charlie, and we were his angels from *Charlie's Angels*.[46] We won the Championship baseball game a few years in a row, and I think it was because my dad loved the game, and we always had fun. We played tennis together on the weekends; one of his favorite sports of all time and he still plays today. When I decided to go out for track, he ran with me in the mornings. I have to agree with my friends, my family was like *Leave it to Beaver* and the *Brady Bunch*. I wish I could live that fantasy life again.

I know my daughter always tells me that she wishes she was born when my grandma lived. She said I would love to be a stay-at-home mom and take care of the kids while my husband worked. I would clean the house and cook and have everything ready when he got home from work. It was a time when life was simple, and you didn't need two cars, and you would spend time together as a family.

We all have dreams of how we think our life is supposed to be; and then life happens. We have to accept what comes our way. We can still dream, and I still do. That is what hope is. When you have faith, love, and hope, it brings you joy.

After I finished typing this chapter I looked up at the cross I have right over my head:

> Faith to give you Strength
> Hope to get you Through
> Love to Lift you up
> All these
> I pray for you

This is a reminder that God is with me through it all. He is my Strength for the journey.

When you let God into your heart, faith conquers fear.

I mentioned that you have to name your feelings and when you can name "it" you can conquer "it." Dobie Moser taught me this concept, and when I see this written, I can conquer my fear and the lies the devil keeps placing over me. I have to call out to God to rescue me.

Dealing with feelings:

1. First, name the feeling. By simply naming an intense feeling that is controlling us, we immediately rob it of some of its power.
2. Express the feelings - The very act of forcefully expressing our true feelings defuses their intensity - Give expression to our feelings before we pray.
3. Own the feelings and accept them as part of who we are. We feel better when we choose to talk to an enemy in our external lives. Also learning to relate to our inner voices, feelings and figures; learning to befriend the enemy within.
4. Talk to Jesus about these feelings and seek His healing. Remember, Jesus was fully human; he experienced at times all the feelings with which we feel uncomfortable. Example, If you feel angry, remember the scripture of Jesus being angry with the buyers and sellers. Pray to the Lord and ask him to help us. Learn to be at home with Jesus bringing our whole selves before God; our messy selves, confused selves; and learn to talk to God.

CHAPTER 21:
FAITH & HOPE

Faith:

Definition of faith.
1. Complete trust or confidence in someone or something.
2. Strong belief in God or in the doctrines of a religion, based on spiritual apprehension rather than proof.

Uncle Jimmy

Bible Verse - 1 Peter 1:6-7 NABRE – "In this you rejoice, although now for a little while you may have to suffer through various trials, so that the genuineness of your faith, more precious than gold that is perishable even though tested by fire, may prove to be for praise, glory, and honor at the revelation of Jesus Christ."

I have heard it said many times, "It's all in God's perfect timing." I grieved many years after the loss of my uncle; I lost my faith in God, and He still opened His arms to me and listened. I believe faith is knowing that God is for you and not against you. I mentioned before, many times that God revealed himself that day in the woods on October 15th, 2011, about 7 months before Blake passed away. God came to me, and I heard His voice, "Your uncle is with me." I heard it as clear as day. I asked again and He said, "He is here." I knelt on the ground and cried. Then my inner voice said you have to let go of the pain, forgive and you will find me. Each day I grew closer and closer to God. I started helping with the children's program and fed the hungry on the streets of downtown. I was able to break out of my own pain, out of my head and started helping others. After God revealed himself to me, I felt I needed to let this pain go; grieve the loss of my uncle and forgive. If I didn't go through this pain I would never have made it through the loss of Blake. My relationship with God was growing and I felt His love.

Blake

Bible Verse -1 Peter 1:8-9 NABRE - "Although you have not seen him you love him; even though you do not see him now yet believe in him, you rejoice with an indescribable and glorious joy, as you attain the goal of [your] faith, the salvation of your souls."

What does faith mean to me? Faith means knowing that I have a Heavenly Father that never leaves my side. He gave us the most precious gift when He gave us the gift of the Holy Spirit. That inner voice is the voice that leads us straight to Him. He gives us free will, and if we lean on Him, and call out His name, He is with us.

Faith is believing who God is and what he would do for us. I can't even imagine all the love He has for me and the fact that His hands crafted me with each little detail, from the color of my eyes, and the color of my hair, to my height, and the structure of my body. God took and instrumented each little detail and designed me in His own image. I am His daughter. Let that sink in, that I am His daughter, and He created me. He designed every delicate detail. I am amazed at how much He loves me; a love I can't even imagine or comprehend. That He would send his one and only son, sacrifice Him to rescue and to save me. I cannot even grasp in my head that He loves me that much. Faith is believing that God sent us to live in this world. Even though we cannot see Him, He sees us. If we grow closer to Him, we see Him, we can hear His voice, and He is ours. We are also His. Be still and know that He is God. He created you in His own image and you are His child. The more desperate I am for Him, He reveals himself to me. I can feel His warm embrace and that is what faith is; it's having a relationship and capturing the love God has for us.

When Blake passed away, I wanted to know everything about heaven and all about God. Each night I spent time writing out Bible verses to find more about God and His character. The more I read the Bible, the more I realized how much He loves us. He is always comforting us and rescuing us from evil. Bible story after Bible story, you see faith come into play.

Hebrews 11:7 NABRE - "By faith Noah, warned about what was not yet seen, with reverence built an ark for the salvation of his household. Through this he condemned the world and inherited the righteousness that comes through faith."

God spoke to Noah and he listened and acted with faith.

Hebrews 11:8 NABRE – "By faith Abraham obeyed when he was called to go out to a place that he was to receive as an inheritance; he went out, not knowing where he was to go."

Hebrews 11:11 NABRE – "By faith he received power to generate, even though he was past the normal age – and Sarah herself was sterile – for he thought that the one who had made the promise was trustworthy."

Story after story, God spoke, and His people listened and acted by faith.

Bob

Bible verse - 2 Timothy 4:7 NABRE – "I have competed well; I have finished the race; I have kept the faith."

Over and over, I see Bob fighting the good fight; he never gives up. Every night we lay together in bed before he goes to sleep. Bob's aphasia is pretty bad, and he can't make out words sometimes. He may say, "Can you get me a pillow?" When he means, "Can you get me a blanket?" I always understand what he means. Every night we pray *The Our Father* and The *Hail Mary* and *Glory Be.* By repetition through the years and his faith, he knows every single word. I just discovered this new amazing App called *Amen* [47] and every night before we go to bed, we cuddle up next to each other, and we listen to the *Sleep Story App.* It is so peaceful; sometimes a man narrates, and sometimes a woman narrates. They talk very softly, and they start with a meditation, and they share a Bible verse. When they speak, they lay it all out for you to imagine, including the scenery of what is happening in the Bible verse, even the smells that you would smell. I can picture myself walking in that time and space. I feel like one of the characters in the Bible and they bring it to life in my mind. It is very serene and when I look over at Bob, he is at peace. No pain, no suffering, pure peace.

This poem is mentioned in the *GriefShare* videos, and I have passed it out during that session to participants. We all go through good times and tough times. It's called "The Weaver." The poem is very appropriate. God is our creator and weaves each one of us into a beautiful masterpiece through the ups and downs and the challenges we face.

The Weaver
by Grant Colfax Tullar (1869-1950)

My life is but a weaving
Between my God and me.
I cannot choose the colors
He weaveth steadily.
Oft' times He weaveth sorrow;
And I in foolish pride
Forget He sees the upper,
And the underside.
Not 'til the loom is silent
And the shuttles cease to fly,

Will God unroll the canvas
And reveal the reason why.
The dark threads are as needful
In the weaver's skillful hand,
As the threads of gold and silver
In the pattern He has planned.
He knows, He loves, He cares;
Nothing this truth can dim.
He gives the very best to those
Who leaves the choice to Him.

"Weaving is the ancient art of recognizing health and wholeness as the primary state and overcoming the blockages of seemingly broken connections. Weavers are healers of the unbroken whole — connecting people and place in elegant tapestries of shared meaning and visions of a world that works for all." (Feb. 13, 2018)

God weaves various threads into our life. The colorful ones are the times when life brought us joy and fun times. The darker colors are the times we lean on God. He comforts us and guides us through life.

Hope:

Definition of Hope - A feeling of expectation and desire for a certain thing to happen.

He looked through her belongings in the hope of coming across some information.

Verb - Want something to or be the case. (*Oxford Languages*)

He's hoping for an offer of compensation.

Hope is an optimistic state of mind that is based on an expectation of positive outcomes with respect to events and circumstances in one's life of the world at large. As a verb, its definitions include: "expect with confidence" and to cherish a desire with anticipation.

The Bible defines hope - Hope is commonly used to mean a wish: its strength is the strength of the person's desire. But in the Bible hope is the confident expectation of what God has promised, and its strength is in His faithfulness.

Uncle Jimmy

Bible Verse - Isaiah 40:31 NABRE - "They that hope in the LORD will renew their strength, / they will soar on eagles' wings; / They will run and not grow weary, / walk and not grow faint."

No matter what you are facing, if you hope in the Lord, He will give you strength for your journey. Jesus is the one that will bring you hope.

My uncle attended St. Edward High School. Every time in the Bible when I see "soar on eagles' wings" or hear the song – *On Eagles Wings* [48] I always think of my uncle. St. Edward High School is known as "The Mighty Eagles."

When God showed up in the woods the day I was crying out to God, in my inner soul I heard His voice, and He said, "Your uncle is with me." I was given the **HOPE** that we will see our loved ones again.

Blake

Bible Verse – 1 Peter 5:10 NABRE – "The God of all grace who called you to his eternal glory through Christ [Jesus] will himself restore, confirm, strengthen, and establish you after you have suffered a little."

Romans 15:13 NABRE – "May the God of hope fill you with all joy and peace in believing, so that you may abound in hope by the power of the holy Spirit."

Peter 1:3 NABRE – "Blessed be the God and Father of our Lord Jesus Christ, who in his great mercy gave us new birth to a living hope through the resurrection of Jesus Christ from the dead."

God, through the Holy Spirit, brings us joy and peace. He fills our hearts and soul with His love. What helps with our suffering is knowing that we have a God that loves us. He gives us hope in the promise that God called us to His eternal glory in Christ. When Jesus died and rose again, it gave us hope that we will see our loved ones again in heaven. God restores us and makes us strong.

Bob

Bible Verse - Habakkuk 3:17-19 NABRE – "For though the fig tree does not blossom, /and no fruit appears on the vine, / Though the yield of the olive fails / and the terraces produce no nourishment, / Though the flocks disappear from the fold / and there is no herd in the stalls, / Yet I will rejoice in the LORD / and exult in my saving God. / GOD, my Lord, is my strength; / he makes my feet swift as those of deer / and enables me to tread upon the heights."

Explanation - No matter what happened nor what God chose to do, Habakkuk could still rejoice, for his hope and faith and joy were in God alone. In His time, God would deliver the righteous and fulfill His covenant promises. Until then, God was the source of his strength; strength which would sustain him in the dark days ahead.

One of the hardest days of Bob's stroke was the day he was coming home. My heart was pounding. I could not sleep the night before because I was worried about taking care of Bob, with all that responsibility. I remember that morning, when everything was being dropped off. A younger man brought in a wheelchair, a cane, the commode, and a hospital bed. He had to set up the bed in a room that was changed from our office to his new bedroom. He gave me a remote for his bed to go up or down. He asked if I had any questions. Then he turned around and said, "Good luck."

Here I was behind the door after all this equipment was dropped off and I just sobbed. I fell to the floor and just cried. Then I heard a knock on the door right behind me. I thought he forgot to give me something else. So, I opened the door and it was Mark, from a few doors down. He saw me crying and he hugged me. He stated that he was so sorry that our family had to go through all this. I shared what I was feeling, that having all this dropped off today is a reminder that I am going to have to take care of Bob and I was very scared. He hugged me again. I told Mark most people in their 50's are going through midlife crisis and they want a sporty red Corvette, or a motorcycle, or that speed boat and a house in Florida. Here I am with Bob's new wheels. I just couldn't stop crying. I thanked Mark for being with me on that very tough morning.

Something Was Wrong – Another Trial

After a few years of taking care of Bob, I remember another trial we faced. Bob and I will never know why we had to go through months of pain. Maybe God wanted us to grow closer to Him. I took Bob to so many doctor appointments. We had many discouraging days of them telling us it's the stroke and his leg is having spasms. Or it's probably because he is sitting all day. I would tell them If I could get him to stand I would, but he is in excruciating pain that he can barely stand. We lost so many months because when you are a stroke patient, each day matters.

I had a feeling deep down in my soul that it was something more, and my intuition was correct. I know that the hospitals are very busy, and they can only do so much. As caregivers we have to keep on looking for answers. In the end, we found out that he had three kidney stones and that he needed surgery. So many days I felt helpless and very discouraged. I cried out to my sister, Traci and my friend Kim. I'm sure they became sick of me crying to them, but I didn't know what else to do. It's so hard watching your loved one experience so much pain. I would do anything to switch places with him. Every day when Bob wanted to scream and swear, I told him to cry out to Jesus and surrender to God. Bob would clutch his teeth and cry out to God, "God, you are our strength and our hope."

What a difference it was, especially after his second surgery, when the kidney stones were removed. The joy came back on his face, and he could breathe again. Sometimes God allows suffering, and through that suffering, you become more like Jesus Christ, as He is the one that gets you through the pain.

CHAPTER 22:
SUFFERING

Suffering: The state of undergoing pain, distress, or hardship (*Oxford Languages*)

At some time in your life, we will go through suffering, but God can give us grace to overcome those trials and to fulfill our purpose. When we suffer that is when we are most like Christ.

Uncle Jimmy

Bible Verse - Genesis 50:20 NABRE – "Even though you meant harm to me, God meant it for good, to achieve this present end, the survival of many people."

God sometimes allows us to go through suffering to reach a greater purpose. God calls on each one of us to bring heaven to earth and for us to get to know Christ. When we go through suffering, allow God to hold you, and He will bring healing to your heart.

John 16:13 NABRE – "But when he comes, the Spirit of truth, he will guide you to all truth. He will not speak on his own, but he will speak what he hears, and will declare to you the things that are coming."

I look back and I know that I held so much pain in. It was all in God's perfect timing. I cried out to God and became very close to God, right when I needed Him the most in my life. I had to go through the loss of my uncle, forgive, and let that go. I know I struggled with so many insecurities. I was very blessed that I had wonderful parents that poured out their love, because if I didn't have that wonderful foundation, who knows where I would be today. Being angry and keeping it all deep inside my soul meant only God saw all the pain. He was the one that was comforting me all along. It was through my suffering that He gave me the strength and the courage when Blake died; God had prepared me. I was able to lean on Him and He would be there for me when Blake passed away.

Blake

Bible Verse - Romans 5:3-5 NABRE - "Not only that, but we even boast of our afflictions, knowing that affliction produces endurance, and endurance, proven character, and proven character, hope, and hope does not disappoint, because the love of God has been poured out into our hearts through the holy Spirit that has been given to us."

Every time I see this Bible verse; I remember the first time I read it. It was a few months after Blake passed, and I was thinking, maybe in a few years I will be able to rejoice in my sufferings. I have come across this Bible verse many times since, and I can see how suffering can produce character, and character produces hope. After a loss, you can choose to shut down, or you can choose to reach out. I decided to trust God and reach out. When I would cry out in desperation, the closer God became more real to me. He poured out His love over me and comforted me. God dwells in my soul. So many times, your faith is tested. That is when you have to give it all over to God, then you can feel the Holy Spirit within you, holding you up. That gives you hope in heaven, that you will see your loved one again.

Bob

Bible Verse - 2 Corinthians 12:9 NABRE - "…but he said to me, 'My grace is sufficient for you, for power is made perfect in weakness.' I will rather boast most gladly of my weaknesses, in order that the power of Christ may dwell with me."

These past couple of years Bob has gone through so much pain and suffering. Through his pain we choose to surrender to God. He clutches his teeth, even though he really wants to scream, he bears down, and he calls out to God. "Jesus be with me; Jesus be with me always." Sometimes the pain lasts an hour to two hours, but he knows that Jesus is with him.

I learned so much from my neighbor, Mary Abel when she had cancer. She told me one afternoon, "Why shouldn't I have cancer." I was surprised that she said that to me, and I listened. She said, "Jesus has done so much for me, and the Roman officials tortured Him and crucified Him. When my suffering gets unbearable, I look to Jesus at the Garden of Gethsemane. I know that I am not alone, that Jesus suffered for me, and I can suffer for Him." She has taught me so many life lessons, as well as this important lesson, that I will treasure always. Even though she passed away, she gave me the wisdom of surrendering over to God. She gave Bob and I both the strength to look at the crucifix.

God gave Paul something better than removing the thorn. Paul received grace to deal with his weakness. His grace can grow there, and His strength can sustain us. So, we can learn to lean on Him and try to understand that through suffering you depend on and need your Heavenly Father to get you through.

2 Corinthians 12:7 NABRE - "...because of the abundance of the revelations. Therefore, that I might not become too elated, a thorn in the flesh was given to me, an angel of Satan, to beat me, to keep me from being too elated,"

A thorn like Paul had is anything that makes us feel we are not in control of our lives. They are a part of our fallen world. Our thorns produce pain and suffering. We need to lift them up to God in prayer, so we can be content with God's answer.

Fear will not control me, and the devil will not win. You have to surrender and give it all to God.

Matthew 27:46 ESV - "And about the ninth hour Jesus went to his father in heaven and he cried with a loud voice, saying, '*Eli, Eli, lama sabachthani?*' that is, 'My God, my God, why have you forsaken me?'"

Jesus was in horrible pain, and he was suffering terribly. He begged his Father to save Him and to take a different path. God turned the other way and did not respond. Jesus overcame His fear with His faith and trust. Three days later Jesus had risen, and He defeated death.

CHAPTER 23:
TRUST

Trust: Firm belief in the reliability, truth, ability, or strength of someone or something: Relations have to be built on trust.

They have been able to win the trust of others.

Acceptance of the truth of a statement without evidence or investigation. (*Oxford Languages*)

What keeps us from trusting? Fear.

Why did Jesus risk everything at the cross? For the joy set before Him. What was His reward? To sit down at the right hand of the Throne of God. The bigger the risk, the bigger the blessing!

Fear is a Feeling - Trust is a choice.

Psalm 56:3 ESV – "When I am afraid, I put my trust in you."

Uncle Jimmy

Bible Verse - "Psalm 37:7 ESV - Be still before the LORD and wait patiently for him, fret not yourself over the one who prospers in his way, over the man who carries out evil devices!"

The meaning behind Psalm 37 verse 7 - Patience, like silence, requires discipline, but when we are patient, we begin to see that God is at work in our life. Even when I'm not sure how I should go, may I commit my life to you, living for you each day, trusting you in every part of my life. May I know in mind and heart that you are honored as I wait for you, seeking your glory above all else. Amen.

Because I lost faith and I lost hope, I was afraid. I missed my uncle, and I will never understand why he took his life; I realized that it's not for me to understand until I get to heaven. I have to trust Gods plan.

Blake

Bible Verse - 2 Corinthians 5:7 ESV – "For we walk by faith, not by sight."

Message from God

Walk by faith not by sight. As you take steps of faith depending totally on me, I will show you how much I can do for you. When I gave you my spirit, I empowered you to live beyond your natural ability and strength. The issue is not your strength, but mine, which is limitless. By walking close to me, you can accomplish my purpose in my strength.

I realized after the loss of Blake, I would have to walk by faith and not by sight. This was a very tough journey without having Blake by my side. God had to show me, with His beautiful gift of the Holy Spirit, that I was never alone. That God was walking close to me every step of the way. With God's guidance, I was led to *GriefShare* to help others with the loss of a loved one, and to *Stephen Ministry* [49] and so many other beautiful ministries at our parish. God gave me the strength to help others and bring others to know and to love Christ. I learned to trust that God will get you through your toughest days.

Psalm 63: 7-8 NIV – "Because you are my help. I sing in the shadow of your wings I cling to you. Your right hand upholds me."

These are gifts from God, reminding us to rely on Him alone.

Bob

Bible Verse - Matthew 14:28 NIV – "LORD, if it's you, Peter replied, tell me to come to you on the water."

Matthew 14:29-31 NIV - "'Come,' he said. Then Peter got down out of the boat, walked on water and came toward Jesus. But when he saw the wind, he was afraid and, beginning to sink, cried out, 'Lord, Save me!' Immediately Jesus reached out his hand and caught him. 'You of little faith,' he said ,'why did you doubt?'"

When Bob had his stroke, God pulled him through. I thanked God. When Bob came home, I started to doubt that I could not take care of him. God was telling me about having little faith. I had to keep on praying to find God, to confirm that I can do this. I had to block out the lies the devil was telling me. I had to trust God. When I started trusting God, I saw that I could do this. I thanked God for walking with me, giving me faith and strength, to keep my eyes fixed on Him.

Bible Verse – Proverbs 3:5-6 NABRE – "Trust in the LORD with all your heart, / on your own intelligence do not rely; / In all your ways be mindful of him, / and he will make straight your paths."

Accept the race that God has marked out for you. Do not allow your heart to become bitter but keep yourself in God's love. Ask God to help you to know the comforting love and gentle whisper of the Holy Spirit. Learn to run freely in God's love and call on Him in your life.

This life is not for us to understand. Only God understands and until we get to heaven, we will have to wait for the answers to those very difficult questions, such as why my uncle died from suicide? Why did our son die at a very young age? Why did Bob have a stroke? Why did we have to suffer?

Only God knows why.

Romans 8:31 NIV – "What then shall we say to this? If God is for us, who can be against us? He who did not spare his own son but handed him over for us all, how will he not also give us everything else along with him."

God so loved the world that He gave His one and only son. I trust God with all my heart because I have Jesus that would die for me.

CHAPTER 24:
JOY

Joy: A feeling of great pleasure and happiness.

Tears of joy.

True joy is a limitless, life-defining, transformative reservoir waiting to be tapped into. It requires the utmost surrender and, like love, is a choice to be made. (*Oxford Languages*)

The Biblical Meaning of Joy - Having joy includes feeling good cheer and a vibrant happiness. But joy is fuller, a spiritual meaning of expressing God's goodness, involves more. It is a deep-rooted, inspired happiness. The Holy Bible says, "The joy of the Lord is your strength." (NEH 8:10)

Jesus brings joy to those who follow Him. He encourages us to follow Him, and we will find true Joy.

What is the difference between joy and happiness?

Happiness is an emotion in which one experiences feelings ranging from contentment and satisfaction to bliss and intense pleasure.

Joy is a stronger, a less common feeling than happiness. Witnessing or achieving selflessness to the point of personal sacrifice frequently triggers this emotion.

Uncle Jimmy

Bible Verse - John 16:24 NIV – "Until now you have asked nothing in my name. Ask, and you will receive that your joy may be complete."

Hiding from God leaves you lonely and afraid. When you ask God to be with you, He fills your soul with joy.

Blake

Bible Verse – James 1:2-3 NABRE– "Consider it all joy, my brothers, when you encounter various trials, for you know that the testing of your faith produces perseverance."

Romans 12:12 NABRE – "Rejoice in hope, endure in affliction, persevere in prayer."

Peter 1:8-9 NIV - "Though you have not seen him, you love him, and even though you do not see him now, you believe in him and are filled with an inexpressible and glorious joy, for you are receiving the end result of your faith, the salvation of your souls."

The night Blake passed away I experienced the greatest pain of losing my son. But when God showed up, God let me feel the greatest joy. When God fills your heart and soul with His love, joy conquers the darkness. His love for us conquers death. Even though I did not see Him, He loved me. Even though I couldn't touch Him, He reached out to me. Even though I couldn't hear Him, I heard Him in my inner thoughts and He was near. God is with us, even though we cannot see Him, or touch Him, or hear Him. God our Father has given us a very special gift. The gift of himself. He is part of us, and we are a part of Him, if you only let Him into your soul and into your heart. You are one.

John 16:22 NIV – "So, with you: Now is your time of grief, but I will see you again and you will rejoice, and no one will take away your joy."

Ecclesiastes 3 NIV – "There is a time for everything, and a season for every activity under the heavens: A time to be born and a time to die, a time to plant and a time to uproot, a time to kill and a time to heal, a time to tear down and a time to build, a time to weep and a time to laugh, a time to mourn and a time to dance, a time to scatter stones and a time to gather them, a time to embrace and a time to refrain from embracing, a time to search and a time to give up, a time to keep and a time to throw away, a time to tear and a time to mend, a time to be silent and a time to speak, a time to love and a time to hate, a time for war and time for peace."

The Bible is God's love story.

There is a time for everything. There is a time to weep and a time to laugh, a time to mourn and a time to dance. So many times, as a Christian, I felt I had to be strong. If I cried, others might think that I don't have faith and that I don't believe. God in this verse says there is a time to weep and a time to laugh. We can always grieve over the loss of our loved one, and you can still find your joy and laughter. Our loved ones know that we miss them, and they want us to find our joy and be happy. They want to see us dance again. We are the ones that hold ourselves back, and we think if we have fun without them that we are moving on without them. They are already in paradise, with their heavenly Father. We have to keep on living, to find our joy in Christ, and the promise that God has given to us that we will see them again.

Bob

Bible Verse – Philippians 4:4 NABRE – "Rejoice in the Lord always. I shall say it again: rejoice!"

Many times, I thanked God when Bob pulled through his stroke and recovered from so many situations that had caused him pain. Over and over, we both rejoiced and gave God all the Glory.

Hebrews 12:2 NABRE – "...while keeping our eyes fixed on Jesus, the leader and perfector of faith. For the sake of the joy that lay before him he endured the cross, despising its shame, and has taken his seat at the right of the throne of God."

There are many days and evenings, but it seems mostly in the evenings when Bob has many bathroom issues. One evening I will never forget. I was so exhausted and just wanted to go to bed. He had to go to the bathroom, and I had to help him. I had to keep reminding myself and placing myself in his shoes. I had to ask God over and over, "Please God, don't let me lose my patience, please give me grace." I had to also ask St. Therese, with her Little Ways, to be with me, and to remind me that he is the one that has to let me do this for him. As much as I wanted to be angry and just scream, I placed myself in his shoes. God himself did that when he came down to walk with all of us. He walked in Jesus' shoes and became human. He did not take the easy road and walk like kings walk. He walked with us, and He sacrificed himself for us. When we place ourselves in other people's shoes, it gives us the humility and strength to be more Christ-like, and to be patient and kind like Jesus.

When I placed Bob in bed that evening, I laid down next to him. We listened to the *Amen App* to the soothing Bible verse of the prodigal son. It relaxed both of us and then we prayed the *Our Father* and the *Hail Mary*. When I was about to get up and go into my room he grabbed my arm, and he looked into my eyes, and he said, "Thank you." I said, "You are welcome." He said, "No, I truly thank you." When I went into my room I just cried. I think this is what God meant when He said, "You will suffer, but you will find joy." I believe that pain and joy can coexist. My heart was filled with joy, pain, and being uncomfortable, but God's love conquered the darkness. Peace and joy were found when we looked to the crucifix and asked God to be with us.

The Bible teaches us that joy is a gift from God; He shines His light through us.

Followers of Christ understand that joy and happiness are not the same. Happiness is the feeling you have when things are going well; it's based on your circumstances. Joy is a deep sense of pleasure, delight, gladness, and well-being, it is independent of circumstance. (I heard this from the James River Church)

Romans 8:28 NIV "And we know that in all things God works for the good of those who love him, who have been called according to his purpose."

The word "joy" is used 93 times in the Old Testament. It's a Hebrew word that means "glee" or "exceeding joy." God wants you to be joyful! Perhaps, you feel as if you have lost your joy; how do you get your joy back?

Psalm 40:4 NLT – "Oh, the joy of those who trust the Lord."

Placing our trust in God brings joy. We have a God who loves us more than we can imagine. a God who is more powerful than we can comprehend, and who has promised to help us if we put our trust in Him.

Chris Stefanick [50] once said, "Joy is not what happens when life is going perfectly. It is knowing that you are loved perfectly even when life is a mess."

Joy is a choice. We have to choose to find joy in our hearts. When you turn to God, His love shines over the darkness.

CHAPTER 25:
PURPOSE

Purpose: The reason for which something is done, or created, or for which something exists. (*Oxford Languages*)

One of the greatest fears is knowing that we are going to die. What we fear at the end of our lives is the great impact that we have on the world. That we did what we were born to do. Death is a part of life, but to embrace death, we have to know we have lived.

What is your purpose? Are you living to your full potential? What is holding you back? Do you keep saying I will start tomorrow and tomorrow never comes?

The biggest fear at the end of life is that you did not do everything you could have done, that you have never really lived. If we want to prepare to die, we have to choose to live fully so that we leave no regrets.

I know one thing: we don't live forever. Someday it will be our turn to die. Maybe we are all here to learn from each other and grow closer to God. We are on a journey traveling through this life. We are born into this world, and we have our parents to take care of us, or maybe it's grandparents, or an aunt and uncle, or maybe you were adopted. This is where it all starts out for us. We are who we are from those that take care of us.

On this journey we travel, we come across many individuals that shape our life. You never know who is going to inspire you and make you the person that you are today. When I look back on my life, the individuals that I gravitate to are the ones that inspired me to be the best person I can be. They lifted me up instead of pulled me down. I hope that you surround yourself with people that lift you up. For those individuals that suck the life out of you and discourage you, I hope you pray for them. If it's time to move on, I hope you move on. So many individuals have touched my life and made me the person that I am today. I pray in return; I can impact others and make a difference like they did for me.

When Blake passed away, I thought that he would be known for playing football, and for his athletic ability. I realized through his death that he was much more than that. His life might have been only seventeen years, but he has touched so many lives in a short period of time. More than I will in a lifetime. Even today I have seen my family, friends and neighbors that have been touched by Blake; they have grown closer to know who God is. I see them following their passion and doing what God has created them to be. I have grown even closer to God. I have found a passion to help others during the loss of losing my son. I started a *GriefShare* program at my church where we all come together and share our losses. They helped heal my broken heart by opening and sharing their stories. We are all on this journey together. We all need each other to get through the hard times in life. I also helped get the *Stephen Ministry Program* up and going at our Church. All the training and lessons that I learned to become a Stephen Minister helped develop who I am today.

Through this time of sorrow, my heart has grown to know God. He hears my cries, and He reaches out and holds me close. I have a personal relationship with Him, instead of Him being a figure high up in the sky and impossible to know. At one time, I thought God was the person you would say prayers to, and hope that He answers them when you send them over to Him. I realized that God is much more than that, He feels our pain. He is for me and not against me. I don't think Blake had to die for me to grow closer to God. However, through his death, I realized Blake's legacy, and I realized how much God truly loves me.

I have a relationship with God now; He knows me and is there for me. I bring Him all my pain, all my suffering, all my joys, and happiness. He knows me inside and out, because I share everything and anything with Him. I am true to myself, and I let Him in. God has revealed himself to me, as I have revealed myself to Him. That is what love is. Love is sharing your whole self, the good, the bad and everything about you. I learned that God has always been there, and I was the one closing Him out. I did not include Him like I should. I thought He was so far away and untouchable, and through the loss of Blake I realized there He was, right inside of us. He lives in us; He is a part of us. He is the Holy Spirit guiding us every step of the way. We just have to keep our ears open to hear His voice. I thought He would never really care about me because He had this whole world to care about. God loves us so very much and wants to have a relationship with us. It's up to us to let Him into our hearts, to have a loving and close relationship with Him. I never felt this close to God until the day my son was called home to be with God. God has never left my side since.

The night that Blake passed away I was given an amazing gift, a gift that I thank God for every day.

When I die, I know God knows everything about me. He created me. When I look into God's eyes for the first time, I want to say, "Thank you God, for walking on this journey, and lifting me up every day! God, I do know you. I know you love me, and I can't thank you enough for loving me so much that you would sacrifice your one and only Son to rescue me."

We all have a purpose, and it's so difficult to know what that purpose is. Maybe my purpose is to write this book. I decided to write this book because God came to me about three years after Blake passed away. I heard His voice telling me to write a book. I told Him, "I can't write a book." I had a tough time in school, and I never even wrote a report. My mom always helped me with my homework. I kept hearing His voice inside me, and I continued ignoring Him.

I have been journaling since Blake passed away. I just kept writing in my journal, until I continued hearing God's voice telling me to write a book. I decided maybe I should try it. It truly helped me go through my grief and to let it all out. I stepped away from journaling for a few years.

After Bob's stroke, I again heard God's voice telling me to write a book.

Well, nudge after nudge, with God giving me ideas on what to write, I decided to listen to His calling.

Maybe this is my purpose, to share how much I love God and how much He is part of my life; that at one time I closed Him out of my life, and through the tragedies in my life He has become everything to me.

CHAPTER 26:
WHAT IS LOVE?

God is all love. The day He came down from heaven He gave himself. He came down as a little baby and had to depend on Mary and Joseph to take care of him.

He showed us the way to live a beautiful life. God walked the walk to guide us on our journey. Jesus taught us the way to pure joy, to find peace, and how to find Him.

If you follow Jesus and apply these five very important lessons that he taught us, you will find the true meaning of life.

1.   Love God and your neighbor – When asked which commandment was the most important, Jesus said,

Matthew 22:37-39 NIV - "Jesus replied: 'Love the Lord your God with all your heart and with all your soul and with all your mind'. This is the first and the greatest commandment. And the second is: 'Love your neighbor as yourself.'"

When you love God with all your heart and love your neighbor as you love yourself, you will find peace. Your heart will be filled with joy.

2.   Treat others the way you want to be treated.

Matthew 7:12 NIV - "So in everything, do to others what you would have them do to you, for this sums up the Law and the Prophets."

When you love others as you would love yourself, your relationship(s) will grow stronger. You will find true love over anger and bitterness, and you will find joy.

3.   Have faith in Jesus Christ.

John 3:16 NIV - "For God so loved the world that he gave his one and only Son, that whoever believes in him shall not perish but have eternal life."

When you see how much God loves you and that He would die for you, God gives you a heart like His own. Having faith in Jesus Christ is believing in Him and His teachings. When you let God into your heart, you find true joy.

4.   Jesus taught us to Pray.

Jesus taught by example that we should pray to our Heavenly Father.

Luke 11:1 NIV - "One day Jesus was praying in a certain place. When he finished, one of his disciples said to him, 'Lord, teach us to pray, just as John taught his disciples."

In scripture we read that Jesus left the crowd and would go off and pray and spend quiet time with God. This is what God wants. He wants to be with you and spend one on one time with just you. This is His special time to shower you with His love and for your relationship to grow stronger every day.

Psalm 91:14 NABRE – "Because he clings to me I will deliver him; / because he knows my name I will set him on high."

5.   Jesus taught us to Forgive.

Matthew 18:21-22 NABRE – "Then Peter approaching asked him, 'Lord, if my brother sins against me, how often must I forgive him? As many as seven times?' Jesus answered, 'I say to you, not seven times but seventy-seven times.'"

Jesus loves us. When we freely offer forgiveness to others, love and forgiveness is returned in our own lives.

Luke 23:34 NABRE - "[Then Jesus said, 'Father, forgive them, they know not what they do.'] They divided his garments by casting lots."

Last night I attended a video series at our church called *The Search* [51] with Chris Stefanick. At one point in the video, they mentioned that Peter was in his fishing boat while Jesus was speaking to the crowd. Peter never looked over at Jesus. Suddenly, Jesus showed up and was standing in his boat. As scripture tells us, Jesus told Peter to cast his nets. Peter told him, "Jesus, we have been doing this all day, and we have not caught any fish." Peter did what Jesus asked of him. His net was overflowing with fish. Peter looked at Jesus and said, "I'm a sinner."

Peter did not feel worthy of Jesus. However, Jesus does not look at us as sinners. He sees our potential. We ourselves, see that we have fallen short, that we are sinners. Jesus only sees us as His child, and He loves us unconditionally.

After the video we broke into our groups and discussed the video. The instructor brought us all back together and asked us a simple question. Has

God ever entered your boat? The room was silent. He asked if anyone wanted to share.

I couldn't believe it, but I started sharing my story when God came to me when I was questioning my faith, and I asked God where was my Uncle Jimmy?

I had so many questions of who God was at that time in my life. As I shared earlier about the day in the woods, I screamed out to God, "Where is my uncle?" He said, "He is here with me."

As I look back from that day in the woods, trying to grasp why my uncle died, then going through the loss of Blake and then Bob's stroke, I see God has been with me through it all.

I cried out to God, and He showed up in my boat. For me, He showed up in the woods at North Park in the small City of Brunswick, Ohio. If I didn't cry out, where would I be today?

As I reflect on the first time God became real to me, I realized that I changed my dining room to a reflection room. I have all my scrapbooks in that room, with Blake's portrait. Every day I jump into my boat, (that is my nice, big, brown recliner), and I look up at the cross that is diagonal from me. It is hanging in my kitchen. (This past Christmas I replaced my cross with a new cross that was made for me by my niece, Sarah's husband, Travis. He made me a homemade cross that I look at all the time and it reminds me that Jesus was a carpenter. Now I have this beautiful cross that was made for me.) The bottom portion of my walls in my reflection room are painted blue. When I am sitting in my nice brown "boat," surrounded by the "water," I can reflect on scripture, place myself in that time period, and walk with Jesus. My favorite part of the day is when I get to spend it with Jesus in my "boat," surrounded by the waves of this journey that I am on. Even when I am going through troubled waters, God knows how to calm the sea and bring me peace.

God opened my eyes and became very real to me, that day in the woods when I was questioning my faith and was missing my Uncle Jimmy.

On Easter morning, almost eleven years later, I read the Beatitudes in Blake's Bible, and it was an eye opener for me.

I read it a couple of times and realized that Jesus is radical and it's the opposite way of how I think.

He promised us mercy, He promised us comfort, "I will be with you. I will help you. I will give you the strength to persevere."

Most people don't feel blessed when they have lost someone dear to them.

Matthew 5:1-12 NIV

Introduction to the Sermon on the Mount
God loved to spend alone time with his disciples, and this is what he said.

The Beatitudes
He said:

"Blessed are the poor in spirit,
for theirs is the kingdom of heaven.
Blessed are those who mourn,
for they will be comforted.
Blessed are the meek,
for they will inherit the earth.
Blessed are those who hunger and thirst for righteousness,
for they will be filled.
Blessed are the merciful
for they will be shown mercy.
Blessed are the pure in heart,
for they will see God.
Blessed are the peacemakers,
for they will be called children of God.
Blessed are those who are persecuted because of righteousness,
for theirs is the kingdom of heaven."

"Blessed are you when people insult you, persecute you, and falsely say all kinds of evil against you because of me. Rejoice and be glad, because great is your reward in heaven, for in the same way they persecuted the prophets who were before you."

This last one is so hard to understand. For in the same way, they persecuted the prophets who were before you.

God became real to me when I was searching for answers and trying to figure out who God is. I screamed at God and said, "Are you even real?" I heard His voice in my inner soul, and He said, "Your Uncle Jimmy is with me." God said open your Bible and He led me to Matthew 5:4. (*The Message*). After reading this verse, I wrote the following in my journal.

You are Blessed

"You are blessed when you feel you have lost what is most dear to you. Only then can you be embraced by the One most dear to you."

When I read that, I told God, "I do not understand. I do not feel very blessed that I lost my uncle."

When Blake died, I turned to God to comfort me. I spent so many nights crying as He held onto me. I would get up in the middle of the night and journaled. It turned into getting up and listening to God as I typed what He was sharing with me, which I believe became our love story. Through my pain and sorrow, I felt the love of God that He had for His son Jesus, as well as the suffering and pain that He endured watching His own son die on the cross. God let me feel His pain, and He felt my pain after the loss of my son. God gave me a heart like His heart. A heart to feel the pain of losing someone you love.

I read a few more verses, and I wrote down Matthew 5:8 (*The Message*)

"You are blessed when you get your inside world - your mind and heart put right. Then you can see God in the outside world."

For the first time, God became real to me. I always thought of God as this powerful figure up in Heaven who would not have time for a person like me. I realized through my pain that He was this warm, gentle Father who talked to me and held me. After the day in the woods, I started to see God in the outside world. Everything around me started looking brighter, and I started understanding who God is.

One day in *GriefShare,* someone asked, "What do you call someone that lost a child? When you are a woman whose spouse has died, you are called a widow, and a man whose spouse has died is called a widower. When you lose both parents, you are called an orphan. What is the word when you lose a child?" The word is **Blessed**. You are blessed that you brought this beautiful child into the world to love and to take care of. When you look at Mary, the mother who delivered God into this world, she was given the name of the "Blessed Mother." She was a mother who raised Jesus, and she is the mother who watched her son die on the cross. I was blessed because I had a son that I raised and that I got to love and take care of. We are all blessed with the people in our lives who mean the world to us. God showed us what love is when He sacrificed His one and only Son for us.

I feel blessed that God came to me in the woods and revealed Himself. God became real through the tragedies in my life. God himself suffered, and through His suffering and His loss, we are saved. I realized that I am blessed; that when I lost what was most dear to me, I found my heavenly Father. I am His child.

The Disciple Peter

Look at Peter. Peter was one of Jesus's disciples. Take a look at these scriptures:

John 13:31-38 NIV- Jesus **Predicts Peter's Denial**

"When he was gone, Jesus said, 'Now the Son of Man is glorified, and God is glorified in him. If God is glorified in him, God will glorify the Son in himself and will glorify him at once.'

'My children, I will be with you only a little longer. You will look for me, and just as I told the Jews, so I tell you now: Where I am going, you cannot come.'

'A new command I give you: Love one another. As I have loved you, you have to love one another. By this everyone will know that you are my disciples, if you love one another.'

Simon Peter asked him, 'Lord, where are you going?'

Jesus replied, 'Where I am going, you cannot follow now, but you will follow later.'

Peter asked, 'Lord, why can't I follow you now? I will lay down my life for you.'

Then Jesus answered, 'Will you really lay down your life for me? Very truly I tell you, before the rooster crows, you will disown me three times!'"

Jesus tells us that He is going to die, and that Peter cannot go with Him. He also tells Peter that he will deny Him three times.

Luke 22:60-62 NIV – "Peter replied, 'Man, I don't know what you're talking about!' Just as he was speaking, the rooster crowed. The Lord turned and looked straight at Peter. Then Peter remembered the word the Lord had spoken to him. 'Before the rooster crows today, you will disown me three times.' And he went outside and wept bitterly."

Jesus taught his disciples this very important lesson:

"A new command I give you: Love one another. As I have loved you, you have to love one another. By this everyone will know that you are my disciples, if you love one another."

Jesus loved us so much that He gave up His life for us. He guided all his disciples and taught them how to love one another.

I reread this passage:

Jesus replied, 'Where I am going, you cannot follow now, but you will follow later.'

Peter asked, 'Lord, why can't I follow you now? I will lay down my life for you.'

Jesus indicated that Peter would follow later, which Peter did. Peter died for Christ. His love for Jesus was passionate. He shared his love and who Jesus was to everyone that came along his path.

Peter, later on in his life laid down his life for his faith in Jesus, along with all the other disciples, except for John. Even Paul was persecuted for his faith in Jesus.

Since Blake passed away, I have grown closer to God through scripture. I learned all that I could about God, the disciples, and all the characters God wanted us to learn from. Each person that God mentions in the Bible guides us on this journey. They all have fallen short of God's grace, but God loves them unconditionally. Even David committed adultery and murdered his lover's husband. Many other times when David had fallen short of God's grace, God saw his heart and loved him.

Thomas doubted Jesus and wanted to see the holes in His hand and place his finger in His side. At times we are like Thomas, and we doubt Jesus as well as ourselves. Jesus even gave us Judas. Judas' betrayal was a necessary part of God's salvation plan.

Matthew 26: 14-15 NIV – "Then one of the twelve – the one called Judas Iscariot – went to the chief priests and asked, 'what are you willing to give me if I deliver him over to you?' So, they counted out thirty pieces of silver. From then on, Judas watched for an opportunity to hand him over."

Matthew 26: 20-25 NIV – "When evening came, Jesus was reclining at the table with the twelve. And while they were eating, he said, 'Truly I tell you, one of you will betray me.'

They were very sad and began to say to him one after the other, 'Surely you don't mean me, Lord?

Jesus replied, 'The one who has dipped his hand into the bowl with me will betray me. The Son of Man will go just as it is written about him. But woe to the man who betrays the Son of Man! It would be better for him if he had not been born.'

Then Judas, the one who would betray him, said, 'Surely you don't mean me, Rabbi?'

Jesus answered, 'You have said so.'"

Matthew 26: 47-50 NIV – "While he was still speaking, Judas, one of the twelve, arrived. With him was a large crowd armed with swords and clubs, sent from the chief priests and the elders of the people. Now the betrayer had arranged a signal with them: The one I kiss is the man: arrest him. Going at once to Jesus, Judas said, 'Greetings, Rabbi!' and kissed him.'

Jesus replied, 'Do what you came for, friend.'"

Matthew 27:3-4-11 NIV – "When Judas, who had betrayed him, saw that Jesus was condemned, he was seized with remorse and returned the thirty pieces of silver to the chief priests and the elders. 'I have sinned,' he said, 'for I have betrayed innocent blood.' 'What is that to us?' they replied. 'That's your responsibility.' So, Judas threw the money into the temple and left. Then he went away and hanged himself. The chief priests picked up the coins and said, 'It is against the law to put this into the treasury, since it is blood money.' So, they decided to use the money to buy the potter's field as a burial place for foreigners. This is why it has been called the Field of Blood to this day."

Judas tried to make it right, and the high priests turned their heads.

As I reflect on this. Jesus' last word to Judas – "Do what you came for, **Friend.**"

Jesus was all love. Jesus died for our sins. He died for you and for me.

God loved us so much that he came down from heaven to teach us how to love and to be loved. He created us in His own image. You hear in scripture that God is our shepherd, and we are His sheep. He is looking to comfort each one of His sheep and bring them to Him.

Jesus walked with his disciples for three years. He taught them many lessons on how to live life, to walk with those who are suffering and those who are lost and alone.

The big question that I have asked over and over again in my head. Did Jesus forgive Judas, who betrayed Him, and that would send Him on the cross to die for all of us?

Jesus called Judas a friend. He never gave up on Judas, but Judas gave up on Jesus. He turned his back on Jesus, and that is probably the biggest lesson Jesus has taught all of us. When we turn away from God, or when we turn away from family and friends, our hearts harden. God has taught us a better way to live. Love yourself as I have loved you. Forgive yourself as I have forgiven you.

When Jesus was dying on the cross and in Luke 23:34, Jesus' words were "Father, forgive them, for they do not know what they are doing." Jesus walked with Judas and taught him so many lessons of life. They were friends. Jesus taught him a better way, but God gave us free will, and Judas turned away from Jesus. God is always trying to draw us to Him. Even in his final kiss, He loved Judas and called him a FRIEND. Jesus taught us to love ourselves as I have loved you. Judas fell away from himself, his friends, and was alone and afraid. In turn, he took his own life because he did not feel worthy of Jesus' love and friendship.

God did not take the easy road when He came down to walk with us.

God became human so He could feel our pain. Jesus felt all of our pain and even felt Judas' pain when he betrayed Him.

Jesus asked his disciples to pray in the Garden of Gethsemane to be with Him because He himself was afraid of dying on the cross.

Mark 14:32-42 NIV – "They went to a place called Gethsemane, and Jesus said to his disciples, 'Sit here while I pray.' He took Peter, James, and John along with him, and he began to be deeply distressed and troubled. 'My soul is overwhelmed with sorrow to the point of death,' he said to them. 'Stay here and keep watch.'

Going a little further, he fell to the ground and prayed that, if possible, the hour might pass from him. 'Abba, Father,' he said, 'everything is possible for you. Take this cup from me. Yet not what I will, but what you will.'

Then he returned to his disciples and found them sleeping. 'Simon,' He said to Peter, 'Are you asleep? Couldn't you keep watch for one hour? Watch and pray so that you will not fall into temptation. The spirit is willing, but the flesh is weak.'

Once more he went away and prayed for the same thing. When he came back, he again found them sleeping, because their eyes were heavy. They did not know what to say to him.

Returning the third time, he said to them, 'Are you still sleeping and resting? Enough! The hour has come. Look, the Son of Man is delivered into the hands of sinners. Rise! Let's go! Here comes the Betrayer!'"

Jesus was overwhelmed with sorrow to the point of death. He knew that He was going to suffer and die on the cross for our sins. He prayed to his Heavenly Father, "Everything is possible for you. Take this cup from me. Yet not what I will, but what you will." He walked with these disciples to prepare them, grew close to them, and they all fell asleep.

I can't even imagine how Jesus felt that when He needed them the most, they all let Him down.

He tells them that the time has come. Look, the Son of Man is delivered into the hands of sinners. (We are all sinners and fall short of God's grace.) RISE! Let us go!

God can feel our pain. He felt alone, abandoned, afraid, and He had no one by his side. They all fell asleep.

Luke 23:34-46 NIV - "Jesus said, 'Father, forgive them, for they do not know what they are doing.' And they divided up his clothes by casting lots.

The people stood watching, and the rulers even sneered at him. They said, 'He saved others; let him save himself if He is God's Messiah, the chosen one.'

The soldiers also came up and mocked him. They offered him wine and vinegar and said, 'If you are the King of Jews, save yourself.'

There was a written notice above him, which read: This is the King of The Jews.

One of the criminals who hung next to Him hurled insults at Him: 'Aren't you the Messiah? Save yourself and us!'

But the other criminal rebuked him. 'Don't you fear God,' he said, 'Since you are under the same sentence? We are punished justly, for we are getting what our deeds deserve. But this man has done nothing wrong.'

Then he said, 'Jesus, remember me when you come into your kingdom.'

Jesus answered him, 'Truly I tell you, today you will be with me in paradise.'

It was now about noon, and darkness came over the whole land until three in the afternoon, for the sun stopped shining. And the curtain of the temple was torn in two. Jesus called out with a loud voice, 'Father, into your hands I commit my spirit.'

When he had said this, he breathed his last breath.

It took Jesus dying on the cross for those who didn't believe, and those who crucified Him, to witness that Jesus was so much more than a man.

Luke 23: 47-49 NIV - "The centurion, seeing what had happened, praised God and said, 'Surely this was a righteous man.' When all the people who had gathered to witness this sight saw what took place, they beat their breasts and went away. But all those who knew him, including the women who had followed him from Galilee, stood at a distance, watching these things."

It takes strength and courage to watch someone go through pain and suffering. God is always with you through your pain and suffering, but who was with Jesus to watch Him go through His pain and suffering. Jesus asked His disciples to pray and be with Him and they all fell asleep.

John 19:25-27 NIV - "Near the cross of Jesus stood his mother, his mother's sister, Mary the wife of Clopas, and Mary Magdalene. When Jesus saw his mother there, and the disciple whom he loved standing nearby, he said to her, 'Woman, here is your son,' and to the disciple, 'Here is your mother.' From that time on, this disciple took her into his home."

Jesus walked with twelve disciples and now there was only one. John had the courage to walk with Mary and to walk with Jesus to His death. That is what love is. John walked the walk with Jesus and held onto His pain and suffering. He endured the impossible to watch his friend, his teacher, his savior die on the cross for all of us. Jesus, when He was dying on the cross, looked at John and said, "Here is your mother." He asked John to take care of His mother. To His mother, "Here is your son." John had courage to be with Jesus through it all. Jesus asked His friend to please take care of His beautiful mother. He trusted John and loved John. He knew that John loved Him in return.

This was a fulfillment of what Jesus had prophesied at the Last Supper. "You will **ALL** fall away because of me this night." Though the twelve disciples initially scoffed at the notion that they would abandon their Shepherd and Lord.

Matthew 26:56 NIV - "But this has all taken place that the writings of the prophets might be fulfilled. Then all the disciples deserted him and fled."

However, John remained and watched Him die on the cross.

God walked the walk. God felt what it was like to be human. He was alone and betrayed, and He suffered horribly. He poured out His love to each one of His disciples and they let Him down, but He forgave.

Little by little God keeps revealing more of himself. He led me to this understanding with Judas, Peter and John. He revealed this in my heart a few months after Blake passed away, but I didn't understand. He kept leading me to understand when you get your heart and mind right, you will be able to see through His eyes. For some reason I keep going back to this verse – "You're blessed when you get your inside world, your mind and heart put right then you can see God in the outside world."

God came to our world, and he walked in our pain and suffering. Through His pain and suffering He has led all of us to the cross, if we are willing to meet Him at the cross.

CHAPTER 27:
BELIEVE

Believe – is Blake's word.

The community made these shirts with the following on the back of the shirt.

Just – **J**eff

Keep – **K**evin

Believing – **B**lake

Legacy – **L**exi

Just **Ke**ep **B**elieving in the **Le**gacy.

In 8th grade, the school trip was to Washington DC. Blake was able to convince all three of the eighth grade Brunswick schools to sing *Don't Stop Believin'*. He was able to get the whole 8th grade to sing that song! At his wake many kids came through the line and shared that memory. They said when people passed him throughout the trip, they would belt out that song, *Don't Stop Believin'*.

On August 28[th,] the day after Blake's 30th Birthday, Trapper Jack from *Touched by Heaven*[52] called me. He heard from Father Michael Denk, that I had a story about my son who passed away and about a near death experience that took place. He asked if he could interview me, I agreed. I love talking about Blake.

Brittany had a tough time with his birthday because Blake died when she was only thirteen. Now, she was going to pass him up in years. When Trapper Jack called, I was choked up a little because this anniversary was a tough one. Usually, I handle the anniversaries pretty well. With Blake turning thirty, this was a very tough reality that he was not with us.

Blake's Candle and a Life-Saving Prayer - TBH 318 YT
youtube.com

You can check this out on YouTube – It's the podcast that I did with Trapper Jack.

A few months later in March, I had a dream of Brunswick High school. It was the school I had attended and where I was a cheerleader. Also, it is the school my own three kids attended, and where Blake played football.

God woke me up and said you need to share your story at Brunswick High School. I questioned, God, "How do you talk about God in the public schools?" He said, "Watch what I can do. It will happen." I reached out to my cousin Bonnie's daughter, Maggie, who was a senior that year at Brunswick High School. I asked her, "Do you have any friends, or know kids that are struggling with faith?" She answered that all my friends are pretty close to Jesus. She asked, "Why?" I said, "I had a dream to share my story about Blake." She replied, "I'm in a group at school called FCA – Fellowship of Christian Athletes I can see if my coach, who helps run this group, can have you as a guest speaker." I told her that would be great. She made that happen.

I shared my story of Blake. I asked, "If anyone here was one of the captains of their team?" Almost everyone raised their hands. I informed them, "You guys are leaders of your group, like Jesus lead His disciples. The true victory that Jesus won was the victory at the cross to save us from our sins. You are all disciples. Your biggest victory is when you lead your classmates and friends to know who Jesus is." I passed out blue flashlights for Brunswick Blue Devils as a reminder of the story I shared about Blake, so they too can shine their light. They can be the "light" for others. I placed a scripture verse on the flashlight – John 8:12 ESV – "I am the Light of the world whoever follows me will not walk in darkness. But will have the light of life." God is the true light, and he is our light in the darkness." So, when you go off to college, bring this flashlight with you. Remember to always shine your light to lead others to know Jesus Christ, because when you have Jesus in your life, you have everything that you need.

Also, I wanted to pass out a picture of Jesus, the fun Jesus, but they weren't delivered in time. I went in my prayer room, and I found forty pictures of the resurrected Jesus dying on the cross. I passed that out to the kids. I said when you focus on Christ, He will help you through your toughest days. If you sin or do something wrong, remember the gift that Jesus has given you. God the Father sacrificed His one and only son for you, to save your life. Don't walk away from your sin, walk to Jesus, and He will set you free. So, hold onto this picture, and remember the price He paid for you because He loved you so much.

When I looked at all the kids it brought me back to when I was in high school. I had my 9th grade Earth Science class in that same room, and it brought back so many memories. The football team said that Blake and Jeff's picture is still hanging up in the locker room. Before every game starts, the team members all jump up and hit the picture as they run out of the locker room. My heart was so full that early morning, before school. I returned a few weeks later, and I gave them a cross coin that they could keep and place in their pocket or purse.

When I came home, I couldn't wait to tell Brittany about my experience at the high school. She explained, "Mom that is why you have to write your book. You have been writing it for almost thirteen years when you started journaling. It's time for you to share your story. Mom, people need to hear this than just the small town of Brunswick and the surrounding cities."

I listened to Brittany, and I made a bunch of calls. I called approximately twenty book publishing companies. When I told them, it was a very rough draft, and I just typed at night, they all said that my manuscript had to be in better shape. They suggested, "Maybe call a ghost writer to help you, before you reach out to us." I almost gave up, and I was crying pretty hard. I picked up my phone and on my phone was Facebook. There was a company called

Audiobook Publishing Services that popped up. I thought Trapper Jack was able to get my story out, maybe this too would work.

I talked to this one gentleman for about forty-five minutes, and we truly connected. I shared my story. When he asked me when did my son died? I stated, "On June 3rd." He commented that was his birthday; the head of Customer Support & Marketing Departments, his dad, died on that same date. Long story short, he believed in my story, and so did others. They helped me to bring my story alive. I was so afraid to let go of my manuscript, and it took me forever to say, yes, and take a chance. When I was on my e-mail page, it said "Inbox 36 – Today – 36 – Unread – 36" three number 36's in a row. Just like the three of us who had a connection to June 3rd. So, I took a leap of faith and sent over my manuscript.

It was difficult to let go of the story that I have been writing for thirteen years with God and Blake by His side.

This week has been challenging, as Audiobooks are moving so fast, I cannot even keep up. I was so nervous. I almost gave up, and I wanted to throw in the towel because this was becoming too much for me. That night I had a dream. God said, "Trust me, this will be a journey, but I need you to keep moving forward. It's going to be tough, and you are going to have to make big decisions. Listen to my voice, and not the voice of the devil. You must *believe* in yourself; I am equipping you for this journey."

When I woke up, and reached for my phone, this Bible verse was the message for the day.

Jesus the Bread of Life

John 6:25-40 NABRE - "And when they found him across the sea they said to him, 'Rabbi, when did you get here?'

Jesus answered them and said, 'Amen, amen, I say to you, you are looking for me not because you saw signs but because you ate the loaves and were filled. Do not work for food that perishes but for the food that endures to eternal life, which the Son of Man will give you. For on him the Father, God, has set his seal.'

So they said to him, 'What can we do to accomplish the works of God?'

Jesus answered and said to them, 'This is the work of God, that you believe in the one he sent.'

So they said to him, 'What sign can you do, that we may see and believe in you? What can you do?' Our ancestors ate manna in the desert, as it is written: 'He gave them bread from heaven to eat.'

Jesus said to them, 'Amen, amen, I say to you, it was not Moses who gave the bread from heaven; my Father gives you the true bread from heaven. For the bread of God is that which comes down from heaven and gives life to the world.'

So they said to him, 'Sir, give us this bread always.'

Jesus said to them, 'I am the bread of life; whoever comes to me will never hunger, and whoever believes in me will never thirst. But I told you that although you have seen [me], you do not believe. Everything that the Father gives me will come to me, and I will not reject anyone who comes to me, because I came down from heaven not to do my own will but the will of the one who sent me. And this is the will of the one who sent me, that I should not lose anything of what he gave me, but that I should raise it (on) the last day. For this is the will of my Father, that everyone who sees the Son and believes in him may have eternal life, and I shall raise him [on] the last day.'"

After reading the verse, I prayed, "I believe Jesus that you are real. You are the Way, the Truth and the Life."

When I finished reading this passage the word **believe** jumped out at me. Then when I noticed that **believe** was the last word in the verse John 6:36 - God is truly giving me a message! The message is that this is my body, this is my blood – He gave them bread from heaven to eat. His true *Body* and *Blood* was given up for you, and for me. Jesus sacrificed Himself. He is the LAMB of God! He gave His life for you, and for me. He did not say this is a symbol; He said do you **believe?** – Do you believe He is the LAMB of God – It is not a symbol, but do you believe?

Many of the people left and thought he was crazy, but He asked Peter, "**Do you believe?**" Peter, answered, "I believe Jesus you are the son of God."

John 6:40 NABRE - "For this is the will of my Father, that everyone who sees the Son and believes in him may have eternal life, and I shall raise him [on] the last day."

I read the following verse over and over and realized that God is truly giving a message to me. He said, "He is the Lamb of God; the true, sacrificial Lamb of God that was given to all of us." I decided to read further, to try and understand what God was telling me. These were God's words coming directly from the Bible.

John 6:53-59 NIV – "Jesus said to them, 'Very truly I tell you, unless you eat the flesh of the Son of Man and drink his blood, you have no life in you. Whoever eats my flesh and drinks my blood has eternal life, and I will raise them up at the last day. For my flesh is real food and my blood is real drink. Whoever eats my flesh and drinks my blood remains in me, and I in them. Just as the living Father sent me and I live because of the Father, so the one who feeds on me will live because of me. This is the bread that came down from heaven. Your ancestors ate manna and died, but whoever feeds on this bread will live forever.' He said this while teaching in the synagogue in Capernaum."

So, I want to ask you – Do you *Believe?*

When Blake died, I wanted to know everything about God, and His character. I wanted to know that Blake was safe and in God's loving arms. I have a Father that would die for me and would sacrifice His only son for me. Jesus made that sacrifice; He is the Lamb of God.

Luke 22:19 NIV – "And he took bread, gave thanks and broke it, and gave it to them, saying, 'This is my body given for you; do this in remembrance of me.'"

God loves us very much. He wants us to remember His sacrifice and the love He has for you. You are His precious child. "Eat my flesh and drink my blood, and you will live forever." God will give you His heart and everlasting life. When I let this sink into my heart and soul; I believe Jesus, My God, my Father You are the Lamb of God. "Thank you for your eternal love and sacrifice."

The closer I get to God, the closer He becomes more real to me.

Three days later, I am on the phone with my friend. Her husband is going through treatment for his cancer. She hung up with me and went on with her day. I really wanted to go swimming and get some exercise. In my soul I heard a voice telling me to go to Saturday service in the chapel. Before I knew it, I was right in front of the tabernacle. The gospel reading was about how many disciples deserted Jesus. I began thinking and wondering if this is more of the verse of John 6 that I woke up to three days ago. As I was sitting there, I kept hearing the word *believe*. That word just echoed in my mind and soul. I listened closely to the reading, that many people will hear this, not believe, and will walk away because it is very difficult to understand. I looked down and the verse of the day was John 6: 60-69. It was a continuation of the chapter I had woken up to.

Many Disciples Desert Jesus

John 6:60-69 NIV - "On hearing it, many of his disciples said, this is a hard teaching. Who can accept it?

Aware that his disciples were grumbling about this, Jesus said to them, does this offend you? Then what if you see the Son of Man ascend to where he was before! Spirit gives life; the flesh counts for nothing. The words I have spoken to you—they are full of the Spirit and life. Yet there are some of you who do not believe. For Jesus had known from the beginning which of them did not believe and who would betray him. He went on to say, 'This is why I told you that no one can come to me unless the Father has enabled them.' **From this time many of his disciples turned back and no longer followed him**. '**You do not want to leave too, do you**?' Jesus asked the twelve. Simon Peter answered him, 'Lord, to whom shall we go? You have the words of **eternal life. We have come to believe and to know that you are the Holy One of God.'**"

When I arrived back home, I reread this verse about three or four more times. I realized that sometimes Jesus was very radical, and He was trying so hard to get the message across to His disciples, however, many left, and they stopped following Him.

I went back to reread the part that Jesus fed 5,000; they ate the loaves and had their fill. The next day he was trying to tell His people and His disciples, "That there's going to come a day when I am not going to be here. I'm going to sacrifice my body for all of you. I am the Lamb." Jesus is telling us, "I am the Lamb, I am going to die. I am giving it up for you. This Lamb is the Lamb to be given up for you, and for you to eat the Lamb that this is my body." They were struggling and having a very difficult time believing in what Jesus was telling them. Many started walking away. That is the turning point because Jesus fed all those people, and they were full. When Jesus told them this very difficult message of eating His body, and drinking His blood, they started turning away. Judas was upset and didn't want Jesus to proclaim that difficult message. He wanted Jesus to take back what He was saying, so the people would continue to follow Him. After hearing this Bible verse, it really made me ponder and think of what Jesus was asking of His disciples.

Sometimes we hear only what we want to hear, and we walk away from situations when it's uncomfortable.

A few days ago, I heard, in my inner soul, name a chapter *Believe*. I love that idea. When I think of Blake the word *Believe* comes into my thoughts because of the t-shirts. I also remember the song Blake got his whole class to sing, *Don't Stop Believin'*. As I sat down writing this chapter, listening to God, it took on a whole new spin. I had no idea that it would take me to understand when the disciples had a very difficult time hearing what Jesus wanted them to learn and to know.

I realized, "Not my will, but your will be done." The closer I get to God; I see that I want to do His will over my own will. I love sitting still and listening. When I hear His voice, I start typing. This is what God is laying on my heart.

I know that life can be difficult because I myself lost my son. I'm trying to figure out who God is and learn God's true character. After Bob had his stroke, I had to learn how to survive and take control. My husband handled all the finances. He did all the cooking while I worked for many hours. I had to learn how to take care of him after his stroke, and the whole household. I feel very blessed because my children have helped me so much around the home.

This Bible verse reminds me of life and the choices that we make for ourselves. When my uncle passed away. I didn't want to accept that my uncle was no longer here with me. He was called home. I decided to walk away and draw as far away from Christ as I could. I could not accept that God would allow this to happen or that my uncle was no long part of my life. I chose to turn to self and be angry for a very long time.

When Blake died, I wanted answers. I wanted to learn about heaven, and everything about God. Blake was no longer in my care, as he was in the kingdom of God. I had to learn to trust and find God.

When Bob had his stroke, I learned to surrender. Not my will, but your will be done. All three situations were very difficult situations that I had to face. As I have grown closer to God through scripture, I believe, through these messages, that God is teaching us. He was trying to guide His followers to the truth. The truth and the message were difficult messages to comprehend. Some chose to walk with Him and others decided to leave.

I believe – That God is getting a message to me loud and clear through His love story. I had the courage to get up and listen to His voice, and for Him to send me this prayer for the day. I can see as plain as day the word *Believe*.

I *Believe* in God and that the Eucharist is real, the true body and blood of Jesus.

I admit, before Blake died, I thought the Eucharist was a symbol. I didn't understand how this piece of bread could have the real flesh, and the real blood of Jesus.

At Blake's funeral mass, when Father Bob lifted the Host and was praying for the consecration of the bread and wine, the whole altar lit up in this glorious bright light. It was so illuminating that I couldn't even see the altar. All I saw was light shining from the Eucharist, and then I saw angels. God our Father let me see this incredible miracle. The Eucharist became real for me on the day of Blake's funeral mass. I believe that heaven and earth came together as one that day. God gave me a very special gift to see the Eucharist, as His body and blood came alive. I believe that the Eucharist is real, and that I will see my son Blake again in the kingdom of heaven. God is always with us. His ways are always bigger than our ways. When you live for something bigger than yourself, you are living for the one that created you.

God has been taking me on this amazing path. A path that in my wildest dreams, I never thought was possible for me. But when I look at Moses in Exodus 4:19-12, God reassures Moses that he is capable of speaking for Him. Even though Moses expresses his own lack of eloquence. God emphasizes that He is the one who creates the mouth. He assures Moses that He will guide him in what to say. This passage is about God's power and sovereignty, and His ability to equip even those who feel inadequate.

I have always felt very insecure. God equips us and He sees it through.

This season probably is one of the hardest seasons that I've had to face in a very long time. Letting go and accepting that my son passed away is such a difficult thing to do.

When you feel alone and empty inside, your heart is longing for more. We are all called for so much more. When you reach out to God, He fills you with so much love and compassion. Your heart overflows with so much love. Everyone is looking for a purpose, we were born to have a purpose. When you can't find your purpose, you feel lost, alone, and scared. But when you find your purpose, God fills your heart with so much happiness and joy. Joy is when you find the true love, God, the one who created you. He is the one that completes you and makes your heart full. Love comes from God who pours out His love over you because you are His precious child. The closer you grow to God, listen to His voice, and obey His voice, the more you change your desires. You want to grow closer to His desires for your life.

Not my will but your will be done. You start living for God, and not for your own ways. You begin to trust His ways. Even though you yourself never imagined yourself or even thought of yourself doing certain things. Somehow, He leads you in areas that you never thought were possible.

The closer you are to Him, the closer the devil wants to bring you down and devour you. As the devil does not want God's plan to carry through. However, if you stay close to God, be still and listen for His voice, you will stay on His path. God will carry you through and He will be with you; God will carry out his plan through you.

The Blessed Mother is also very special to me. Can you imagine when the angel came to Mary, asked if she would deliver a baby, and that baby would be God – Jesus, the son of God? Mary said, "Yes." Can you imagine if Mary did not say yes - where would we be? Jesus would have never been born. Mary carried that baby in her womb the whole time. When Mary visited her cousin Elizabeth, Elizabeth's baby, John, leapt in her womb. That was the Holy Spirit leaping in her womb, because Jesus was present to baby John.

Can you imagine Mary carrying God in her womb? Jesus is actually the "new covenant" in her womb. Mary delivered God into this world. When Jesus was born, He is actually God. Mary holding her precious little child and looking into her baby's eyes; she was looking into the eyes of God. Can you imagine her raising Jesus and the time He was lost for three days? Can you imagine losing God for three days? I cannot even imagine. I can't even imagine losing my son for just ten minutes. But Jesus was lost for three days because He stayed in the temple. So much pain and the sorrow she had to feel.

When I look at Mary, I look at my own self because I am a mother. I can relate to what Mary went through, especially when her son had to die on the cross. Can you imagine, watching your beautiful child getting spat upon, and beaten up the way that Christ did with all those whips? Mary stood and watched her son endure all that pain and suffering. All those people rejected her beautiful son. Mary had the courage to watch.

Can you imagine walking to Calvary, with Mary, Mary Magdalene, another Mary, John and a few others. Walking up that hill to see your son tortured and carrying the cross? Mary again had the courage to watch the soldiers strike the huge iron spikes into His wrists, one big spike into His feet, and then watch Jesus hang on the cross. Can you imagine being a mother and watching your son go through that horror? Then, can you imagine looking in the face of your son? As a mother you would want to take your son's place, but she couldn't. She had to watch Him suffer on the cross. Can you

241

imagine when Jesus said, "John behold your mother, mother, behold your son." Jesus, right there is telling us that He wants John to take care of His beautiful mother, and His mother to take care of all of us. We are all brothers and sisters in Christ.

Some people question, "Why do you honor Mary?" Why do you put her on such a pedestal? I think she should be honored. She is a mother that had the courage to endure her own son's suffering on the cross. I have turned to the Blessed Mother, especially when I was grieving over my own son. She understands my pain, and she understands exactly what it is like to lose a precious child. I know in my lifetime, I always turn to my mom when I was hurting, when I was suffering, when I didn't know what to do, when I knew that I was in trouble. I was afraid to tell my dad. I didn't want to let him down. I would always go to my mother. She would break the news to my dad, that is what life is about. Sometimes we don't have the courage to go to the Father. Mary brings our intentions over to God, and Jesus, the Son of God. She understands us. She comforts us. She loves us. She is with us. She is very humble of heart and brings our prayers to her son.

So many days I would cry and sigh to God; sometimes no one understands me. God would whisper to me, "Turn to our mother as she understands you because she lost her precious son." Mary helped me so much through my pain and suffering, as she was a mother that understands me. God comforted me. The whole family of God comforted me. That is what's missing in our world, because in order to have a family you need a mother and a father to have this beautiful child. I know my mother means everything to me, and I'm sure your mother means so much to you. Many people think we put Mary on a pedestal. It's not putting her on a pedestal. We honor the things that she did. When we give our intentions to Mary she intercedes for us, and hands those intentions to Jesus, the Son of God. The whole family of God is with us. I pray for the whole family of God to always look over me.

I'll never forget - God came to me in the middle of the night and said, "During your pain and suffering over these past years, you always turned to me. Sometimes I would tell you to turn to our mother because everyone needs a mother." God told me that, "In this time of our life, we need more people to come to our Blessed Mother. I am asking you to start praying the rosary and to get everyone to pray the rosary." God told me that I need to bring others to pray the rosary. I woke up, and I remembered my whole dream. I reached for my phone, and on my phone was an ad for Our Lady of Fatima. I wondered how did this get on my phone. It was a Facebook ad on how to be a team leader for a rally in honor of Our Lady of Fatima. I signed up and I received a big poster of Our Lady of Fatima, as well as a letter that said, "Gather God's children and bring them to a rally in your home city."

I had all good intentions to do this, but with taking care of my husband, working full-time, and just being super busy, time went by, and I actually forgot about it.

After a couple months, God came to me in my dream again. He was stern this time. He said, "Terri wake up, wake up." I'm in my dream and I answered God. He stated, "Terri you haven't brought anyone to go to the rally and pray the rosary. You need to get up and look at that letter." I woke up, and I looked at the letter. I had just one week to gather people together to pray the rosary for the rally. How am I going to do this? I asked my church ministry leaders, Gayle Oboy and Diane Heilman if they could put out an e-mail. They said anyone that wants to pray the rosary, go to the chapel. They gave the date and time. I wanted it at noon because they told me that the rally was at noon. The chapel was only open at 10 a.m., so I reserved the chapel for 10 a.m.

My husband wasn't doing very well that morning. His leg was in a lot of pain. I said Bob, you have to get up. We have to go to the chapel and pray the rosary. I don't know who's going to show up, and we have to have at least three people. I know two or three friends will be there, but we have to have as many people as we can to pray the rosary. When we arrived at the chapel there were only a few of us. As the time was getting closer to 10 o'clock the chapel was starting to fill up. My friend, Vicki, looked at me, and noted, look at how many people are here! She said, "Terri there's a total of 33 people here." She relayed, "That is the age that Jesus was when he died on the cross." God brought all these people to honor Our Lady with praying a rosary together. After we prayed the rosary, I informed everyone that we could catch the rally in Strongsville at noon.

I brought Bob back home because his leg was hurting too much. When I arrived in Strongsville it looked like it was going to rain. I stood next to my friends, Liz and Diane. The beautiful statue of Our Lady of Fatima was coming out, led by the Knights of Columbus. The Blessed Mother statue was standing right in front of me, and her face was just so beautiful. We all started praying the rosary. We were on about the third decade of the rosary, and my girlfriend Liz whispered, "Look up at the sky." The sun was shining down on Our Lady of Fatima and also on a few of us in the front, "It looks so bright!" Liz noted, "It also looks like there's an angel looking down on us." I was mesmerized; it does look like an angel.

The sun was also shining so brightly upon my rosary. I noticed that half of my rosary was a little darker on the one side, and really shiny silver on the other. I tapped Diane on the arm. Diane looked at my rosary. She whispered,

"Terri go to the next bead." I went to the next bead. As I was praying and moving to the next bead, the link between the beads changed from silver to gold. It continued to happen to the next link when I held the next bead. It continued with each bead in my hand, the link was changing. When I came to the crucifix it remained silver. I held onto the crucifix. All the links between the beads were all now gold! I heard God say, "**It was because you obeyed**." I don't know about you, but how can the rosary turn that color right in the palm of my hands. **Only God can perform that miracle**.

He wants us to remember His beautiful mother. He is giving a message to me, for all of us. A mother matters, your mother matters, your Blessed Mother matters. Mary accompanied Jesus until the day He died. Some people say we pray to Mary, I think Mary deserves for us to pray, to honor and to love her. She matters because every single person matters; you matter. God loves you, He died for you, and you are His child. Don't you think that the Blessed Mother is important too? God Himself picked Mary, the beautiful Blessed Mother Mary, to carry Him into this world. God had to trust her and adore her for Him to choose her to become the mother of Jesus.

When we pray to Mary, she gives all our intentions over to her son. I think that is a beautiful thing. When people ask individuals to pray, as some people may ask, "Terri, will you pray for me?" Isn't that the same thing? When we pray, people are asking us to pray and what kind of power do we have. Guess what, all of our prayers get lifted to the Holy Family. God hears those prayers. The entire Holy Family, of God the Father, Jesus the Son, and the Blessed Mother hear those prayers. God hears all our prayers, even those prayers that are unspoken and come from our hearts.

CHAPTER 28:
IN THE ARMS OF HIS HEAVENLY FATHER

As I walk past my son's room, I can picture him as a young child playing with his "Thomas the Tank Engine" trains and him singing *That Don't Impress Me Much* [53] by Shania Twain. He kept singing it over and over – *That Don't Impress Me Much* as he was moving his trains around the table and belting out that song in "his high-pitched" little voice. He was singing and laughing as he had no idea I was peaking in on him. As I reminisce on this beautiful memory, I go back to the night that he died. I remember the officers coming to my house and sharing the heartbreaking news, that my son Blake and his friends were in a car accident; that Blake passed away when going fast over the railroad tracks.

I walked into Blake's room and sat on his bed. I looked over and I saw his two football jerseys with the number thirty-six on them. One was white and the other royal blue. I rubbed my hands over the jerseys. I picked them both up and held them in my arms as I couldn't stop crying. My mind was going back to all the wonderful memories, and how fast life just flies by. Oh, how I wish I could just turn back time. I remember him always giving me bear hugs. They were so tight that I couldn't get out, and I would scream, "Blake let me loose, get me out of this!" What I would do to have one of those bear hugs again.

I also remember him playing hide-n-seek when he was little. One time I couldn't find him at all. I kept searching and I heard his little voice, "I'm over here Mom." I went running into the dining room and I couldn't find him. I kept looking and looking; the room was not even that big. Then I saw his little face peak out from under the tablecloth, with his huge smile, and I heard his laughter. "Here I am Mom," giggling so hard that he was crying. He placed his legs across the chairs so I couldn't see him. He was truly a character.

I remember working late one night and coming home exhausted. Once home, I opened the garage and walked through the laundry room. He grabbed my ankles and scared me. He was lying on the floor where I didn't see him. I jumped so high and yelled so loud! He laughed it off, and said, "Mom you could never be mad at me." And he was right. He had a way to make every day spontaneous and fun.

As I gaze up at his picture and see him smiling through his helmet, I wonder what heaven is like. I can't even imagine him in the arms of his heavenly Father. A song pops in my head, *Only the Good Die Young.*[54] He truly died at a very young age. It is so hard to wrap my head around the fact that he is no longer with us. I try not to let myself go there because the pain is so severe, that it cuts like a knife in my heart and soul. So, I look up at the fathead picture that was taken on the last play of his life, when he had a Pick 6, and he ran home for a touchdown. He truly ran home; he ran straight to heaven.

Blake's dream since he was a little child was to play under the lights of Brunswick High School, to see the whole community come out and cheer their team on to victory. As I have this image in my head of Blake running with the football in his hand, straight to heaven and into the arms of God – Jesus our Savior; so much light is pouring out and all I see is light.

The night that Blake died, God came to me. A bright light, brighter than any I had ever seen, was shining in my room. I remember thinking, if I could just walk up that ray of light and peek in on Blake and see that he is okay and with God, I would be okay. Blake's victory is that he was called home. It's so hard for us to understand. Only God understands, and one day when I get to heaven, I will find out the answer. God had a different plan and wanted him to play for the angels up above instead of the Brunswick Blue Devils. I look up at the life-size picture of Blake through the tears in my eyes, and I connect to his eyes, and I feel so blessed that he was my precious son. We shared so many beautiful memories that I will treasure for a lifetime. I held onto his jerseys, laid on his bed and just cried. My heart was in so much pain that I could barely breathe. "God hold on to me, hold me tight, don't let me go, just hold onto me." His arms comforted me, as I rested in his heavenly grace.

As I keep my eyes on Blake's smile, I wonder where I would be if, the night that he died, I turned away from God and just walked away. Where would I be?

I called out again, "God hold on to me, hold me tight don't let me go, just hold onto me." His arms pull me closer, and I feel His embrace. God just hold me and bring me near to you.

I gaze into Blake's eyes again, and I feel so blessed that I have this life-size picture of him. I can see every hair on his legs and every wrinkle by his eyes when he smiles so big. I think of the poem my Grandma Boots gave me when she lost her only son, my Uncle Jimmy. She turned to this poem every time

247

she was missing her son, and here I am running to that same poem after the loss of my son.

I went into my bedroom, and I opened my grandmother's jewelry box. I reach for her endearing poem that was written out for her, by her best friend with my Uncle Jimmy's picture stapled in the right-hand corner. She held onto that paper like it was her life. It had tears on that piece of paper, as she held that so close to her grieving heart. Little did my grandmother know that one afternoon, when she slowly handed me her piece of paper, that her oldest grandchild would also need this beautiful poem to help her through the grief of her son.

I'll Lend You A Child
by Edgar Guest

"I'll lend you for a little time a child of mine," He said.
"For you to love – while he lives
And mourn for when he's dead.

It may be six or seven years
Or twenty-two or three,
But will you, till I call him back,
Take care of him for Me?

He'll bring his smiles to gladden you,
And should this stay be brief
You'll have his lovely memories as solace for your grief.

I cannot promise he will stay,
Since all from earth return,
But there are lessons taught down there
I want this child to learn.

I've looked this world over
In search for teachers true,
And from the throngs that crowd
Life's lanes, I have selected you.

Now will you give him all your love,
Nor count the labor vain,
Nor hate Me when I come to call to
Take him back again?"

I fancied that I heard them say,
"Dear Lord, thy will be done,
For all the joy Thy child shall bring,

The risk of grief we'll run.
We'll shelter him with tenderness,
We'll love him while we may,
And for the happiness we've known
Forever grateful stay.

But should the angels call for him
Much sooner than we've planned,
We'll brave the bitter grief that come
And try to understand."

God, I love you so very much. You have carried me through all my days of grief. When I cried out to you, you drew me close; woke me up in the middle of the night to spend time with you, and to write our beautiful story together.

I remember reading this poem on Facebook, I printed it out, and I kept it at my desk for the days that I couldn't keep it together and I had trouble breathing.

Happiness is letting go of what you assume your life is
supposed to be like right now
and sincerely appreciating it for everything that it is.
At the end of this day, before you close your eyes,
smile and be at peace with where you've been
and grateful for what you have.
Life is good.

By Angel Chernoff

Blake's life was cut short, but Blake would not want me to cry and not move on. He has moved on to a place we will all be at someday. He just beat me to the race and arrived there first. He is already in the arms of the Father, and he is waiting for me someday to join him. Until then, I need to live for both of us. God and Blake are shinning their bright light down on me, assisting with writing this beautiful story for me, and for all of you.

It was very hard to let go. Letting go meant seeing all those memories that I shared with Blake and leaving them behind. But nobody can take those memories away, they are for me to treasure forever. It is letting go of how you think your life should be. Picturing your family complete, and all

249

together. Or getting married to the love of your life and having children. Our family didn't get to experience that with Blake. We would never know, but this was God's plan. His plan was for Blake to watch all of us from above. This was God's plan from the beginning. He knew the day that Blake would be born and the day that he would die.

Blake's number was 36 only in the last year, in his junior year. His number represents him so perfectly. I had three amazing children. He died on June 3rd, and his number is 36 (the third day of June). I bless myself at night in the name of the Father, and of the Son and the Holy Spirit. My favorite number since I was a little girl was "three."

The hardest thing I have ever had to do was to say goodbye to Blake and let him go. But Blake, even when he was waving that last goodbye to me, his last words were, "See you later." So, it is not goodbye, it is see you later. I will see you again, in paradise.

This morning, I was on Facebook, and I saw this message. A mother who could relate to losing a child.

When Your Adult Child Leaves This Earth

They weren't supposed to go first.
Not the one you carried, taught to walk, watched grow, and stood beside as they became their own person.

Losing an adult child is a sorrow few can fully understand. The world often forgets that no matter how old our children get, they are still our babies. We carry every version of them inside us—the toddler with sticky fingers, the teenager with big dreams, the adult still figuring life out. And when they are gone, it's all those versions we mourn.

You lose not just their physical presence, but their voice on the other end of the phone, the text that said, "I made it home," the plans that would have unfolded over years. You lose their future, and a piece of yours.

Grief after losing an adult child is quiet but heavy. You might still go to work, smile in public, cook dinner—but the ache never fully leaves. You find yourself reaching for a phone call that will never come, scrolling through photos, or whispering into the silence, "I miss you."

If you're walking through this pain, please know you are not alone. There is no timeline for grief and no right way to carry it. Be gentle with yourself. Speak their name. Share their story. Let their memory live in your every breath.

Even though they are no longer here, the love remains. It always will.

By Kellie Cunningham Sipos

She truly understands my grieving heart.

Grief is real. It reminds me of the ocean. When the ocean is still and barely moving, I feel numb. I feel alone and afraid. When the waves start moving in, I feel overwhelmed, and full of sorrow as each wave comes crashing in. One wave after another, I cannot breathe. "I need you God, where are you?" Alone and afraid, the water is still. Here comes another, will this one pull me under? I feel alone, here comes another. "God, where are you?" I call out your name, "I need you, Lord." He reaches out for me, and He pulls me in. He looks into my eyes and whispers, "You are never alone, I have always been right here."

The days when I feel alone and afraid, I miss Blake. I have to reach for God through His word. One of my favorite Bible verses is this one.

Matthew 18: 3-5 NIV – "Truly, I say to you, unless you turn and become like children, you will never enter the kingdom of heaven. Whoever humbles himself like this child is the greatest in the kingdom of heaven. Whoever receives one such child in my name receives me."

This is what this verse means to me.

When you are a child, you depend on your parents for everything that you need, and you adore them. When I read this verse, I started to cry when I realized that when Blake passed away, I ran to God, and I needed Him to hold me and take care of me. I was truly dependent on Him. I wanted Him to be with me and to never let me go. God wants us to be like children and to adore Him and to run to Him for everything that we need. He is our father, and he longs to take care of us.

I remember being a facilitator for *GriefShare* and so many people shared their losses. With each loss if it is your child, mother, father, brother or sister, aunt or uncle or a best friend, dog or cat, you have so many beautiful and amazing memories of your loved one. Those memories are your memories to cherish for a lifetime. Some people that lost a parent or grandparent would say my loss can't compare to yours. I would say yes, your loss is your loss, and you have special memories of your loved one.

Each loss is precious to each person. The individual brought so much laughter and joy into our lives.

I know that grief is overwhelming, and it feels so good when you cry. You cry because you loved that person so much, and they meant the world to you.

I will never forget this one gentleman that came through our program. He was hurt so much after the loss of his wonderful wife. He would come in each week and share that nobody "gets him." His daughter doesn't understand, his son that is a priest doesn't understand, and he would cry each week. I would ask him each week, "Did you talk to your daughter and see if she is missing her mother?" He would say she just doesn't understand me, and how much he missed her. One week he came in and he was smiling so big. He came over and hugged me. He said you're never going to guess this, but my daughter is grieving over the loss of her mother. I asked, "She is?" He said, "I comforted her, and I shared everything that I learned from *GriefShare*." The next week he brought her with him.

That is the secret of grief. You have to get out of your own pain and see that others are grieving also. When this happens, the healing starts to begin. You have to be patient with yourself and patient with your loved ones that are grieving. When you can step back, look at others that are grieving, and share your grief story together, you begin to heal.

I have shared various lessons that I learned from the loss of Blake. One of the hardest things that I had to face was when I would go out in public, (to the grocery store, or department store) and see someone I knew or knew about the accident. They would whisper, "That is the mother that lost her son in the Brunswick car accident." If they were by themselves and saw me, they would go to another aisle in the store to avoid talking or having that difficult conversation. Sometimes the grieving person has to be the stronger person.

When you lose a loved one, all you want to do is share your memories and for them to be remembered. When people approached me and asked how I am doing and if they shared a memory of Blake, those are the moments I treasure. We love when others remember and share a treasured moment of them. These are new memories for us, and we love when those moments touched someone else's heart. If you want your loved one to be remembered, we are the ones who have to initiate those conversations and keep them and their legacy alive.

The healing process takes place when you can share your pain and suffering with others.

You also start to heal when you let God into your heart. You share your pain with Him. He loves you so very much that He doesn't want you to suffer alone.

When I came across this verse a few months after Blake passed away, this is what was on my heart.

That we all have crosses that we face, and this was my cross. The loss of my beautiful son, and to get through that suffering, I needed to walk and follow Christ. I trusted God, listened to His voice, and He led me to discipleship and to start a *GriefShare Program*. Now I could help others through grief and the loss of their loved ones, and that is when I felt joy again.

It's through our trials and suffering that lead us to the cross.

God tells us through scripture that He is with us, and He will never let us go. This scripture changed my life. I realized how much God loves me and that I am His beloved child. He is truly my dad/father. I looked at myself as Blake's mom, and after reading this verse, I realized that I am a child. I am God's child, and He wouldn't want me to suffer. God loves me, and I am His beloved daughter.

In Isaiah 41:13 NABRE – "For I am the LORD, your God, / who grasp your right hand; / It is I who say to you, do not fear, / I will help you."

In Isaiah 43:1-3 NABRE – "But now, thus says the LORD, / who created you, Jacob, and formed you, Israel: / Do not fear, for I have redeemed you; / I have called you by name: you are mine. / When you pass through waters, I will be with you; / through rivers, you shall not be swept away. / When you walk through fire, you shall not be burned, / nor will flames consume you. / For I, the LORD, am your God, / the Holy One of Israel, your savior. / I give Egypt as ransom for you, / Ethiopia and Seba in exchange for you."

God calls you by name, and He walks by your side through troubled times. He loves you; He created you for His glory, and you are His precious child.

All God wants is to love you. He wants to hold you in His loving arms and take care of you. He wants to look into your beautiful eyes, and for you to reach out for Him. You are his beautiful child. Someday we will be called home to be with Him again. I can't even imagine that day when I see God face to face. What a day that will be! I can't wait to hug Him in my arms and look into his intense eyes and say, "I love you and I know you love me."

So many times, when I was missing Blake, I would just want to cry out, "God are you real? Do you even exist? I don't feel you right now." I would call out His name because there's so many days when you just want to throw in the towel. There are so many days where you're just hurting so badly, you just don't understand why you have to go through all this pain. But God is with you, God will hold you, and He will see you through.

Allow yourself to just be. **It's okay not to be okay**. I thought if I cried, I didn't have faith or belief. Then I remembered that the shortest verse in the Bible is, "Jesus wept." Even our Savior Jesus cried when His friend Lazarus died. We truly miss our loved ones. God is holding you closer when you call on Him, He feels your pain, and He holds your tears so close to His heart.

A few months after Blake passed away, I would hear the voice of God waking me up. "It's time to wake up let's spend time together." Each time I heard that voice I would wake up instantly, run to my computer, and spend many lingering nights with God, my heavenly Father, with Blake by His side, and I felt like God was comforting me. I always loved those nights when God called me out of my bed. It was our special time together. That is when I started having a relationship with my beautiful Father up above for thirteen years. My relationship with God developed as I was writing my story with Him.

On this journey of life, we have so many ups and downs, and we go through so much suffering. Sometimes we question why God? Why do we have to suffer like this? We will never know those answers until we meet God face-to-face. I wanted to throw in the towel and just give up. I wanted to give up and not write this story. Trust me, that is not the voice of God. That is the voice of the devil, who doesn't want you to feel worthy and doesn't want you to have joy or to have a relationship with your heavenly Father. He will do whatever it takes to push you apart, as he will do whatever it takes not to get this story out. The closer you get to God, the closer the devil is trying to bring you down.

The word I keep hearing in my inner soul is **BELIEVE.** God wants me to believe in myself that I can do this. Listen to His voice, not the voice of others, and not the voice of the devil. Be still and listen closely to the voice of God. God wants you to believe that you are His amazing child. He wants to comfort you, hold you in His arms, and carry you through your pain. So, reach out your hand. God is reaching for you. When you call out His name, He holds you close to His heart. He wants to have the most beautiful relationship with you. You are His precious child, and He loves you.

My story is about three losses. How I have learned from each one and through it all, found joy and a purpose in my life. I am going to rise above instead of letting tragedy knock me down. Just like in football you are going to have wins, but you are also going to have losses. My goal is to keep moving forward and the final win is **THE VICTORY**; when you find Christ in your life. God becomes the center of your world, and He is everything to you. In the end all that God wants from us is for us to know His son, and that God loves you so much that he would sacrifice His one and only son for you. He loves you so much that His victory is for you to have a relationship with Him. You are His precious child.

I believe that the three tragedies in my life led me to know who my Heavenly Father is. It was through the trials and suffering that had led me to search and to find the character of God. I wanted to know all about heaven because my son was no longer with me. I wanted to make sure he was in a safe place. It was in the valleys of my life that God held me close to His heart. It was in the joy and victory of finding Him that I found peace, hope and where I found love.

God is in this story. He wrote this love story with Blake by His side, as He carried me through the pages of this book. He shined His light over me in the darkness of the night. This book is a gift that God gave to me, and He wants me to share it with you. God loves all his children, and we are all His precious children.

This story is not over; it is just the beginning because we all have a story to share.

God, you are our Heavenly Father, and I am letting go and laying my beautiful son in Your arms. My son is home and I know I will see him again. What an incredible day that will be, when You can hug us both in Your loving arms, and we are together again in Your kingdom!

APPENDIX 1
Favorites

I'll Lend You A Child
by Edgar Guest

"I'll lend you for a little time a child of mine," He said.
"For you to love – while he lives
And mourn for when he's dead.

It may be six or seven years
Or twenty-two or three,
But will you, till I call him back,
Take care of him for Me?

He'll bring his smiles to gladden you,
And should this stay be brief
You'll have his lovely memories as solace for your grief.

I cannot promise he will stay,
Since all from earth return,
But there are lessons taught down there
I want this child to learn.

I've looked this world over
In search for teachers true,
And from the throngs that crowd
Life's lanes, I have selected you.

Now will you give him all your love,
Nor count the labor vain,
Nor hate Me when I come to call to
Take him back again?"

I fancied that I heard them say,
"Dear Lord, thy will be done,
For all the joy Thy child shall bring,

The risk of grief we'll run.
We'll shelter him with tenderness,
We'll love him while we may,
And for the happiness we've known

Forever grateful stay.
But should the angels call for him
much sooner than we've planned,
we'll brave the bitter grief that come
and try to understand."

It's in The Valleys I Grow

Sometimes life seems hard to bear,
Full of sorrow, trouble and woe
It's then I have to remember
That it's in the valleys I grow.
If I always stayed on the mountaintop
And never experienced pain,
I would never appreciate God's love
And would be living in vain.
I have so much to learn
And my growth is very slow,
Sometimes I need the mountain tops,
But it's in the valleys I grow.
I do not always understand
Why things happen as they do,
But I am very sure of one thing.
My Lord will see me through.
My little valleys are nothing
When I picture Christ on the cross
He went through the valley of death;
His victory was Satan's loss.
Forgive me Lord, for complaining
When I'm feeling so very low.
Just give me a gentle reminder
That it's in the valleys I grow.
Continue to strengthen me, Lord
And use my life each day
To share your love with others
And help them find their way.
Thank you for valleys, Lord
For this one thing I know
The mountain tops are glorious
But it's in the valleys I grow!

Jane Eggleston

APPENDIX 3

The Weaver

by Grant Colfax Tullar (1869-1950)

My life is but a weaving
Between my God and me.
I cannot choose the colors
He weaveth steadily.
Oft' times He weaveth sorrow;
And I in foolish pride
Forget He sees the upper,
And the underside.
Not 'til the loom is silent
And the shuttles cease to fly,
Will God unroll the canvas
And reveal the reason why.
The dark threads are as needful
In the weaver's skillful hand,
As the threads of gold and silver
In the pattern He has planned.
He knows, He loves, He cares;
Nothing this truth can dim.
He gives the very best to those
Who leaves the choice to Him.

APPENDIX 4

Favorites

Letting Go

Happiness is letting go of what you assume your life
is supposed to be like right now
and sincerely appreciating it for
everything that it is.

At the end of this day,
before you close your eyes, smile and be at peace
with where you've been and grateful for what you have
Life is good.

By Angel Chernofff

APPENDIX 5

Favorites

Our Father

(The Lord's Prayer)

Our Father, who art in heaven,
hallowed be thy name;
thy kingdom come,
thy will be done
on earth as it is in heaven.

Give us this day our daily bread,
and forgive us our trespasses,
as we forgive those who trespass against
us;
and lead us not into temptation,
but deliver us from evil.

Amen

••

Hail Mary

Hail, Mary, full of grace,
the Lord is with thee.
Blessed art thou among women
and blessed is the fruit of thy womb, Jesus.

Holy Mary, Mother of God,
pray for us sinners,
now and at the hour of our death.
Amen

(United States Conference of Catholic Bishops)

APPENDIX 6
Favorites

Glory Be (Doxology)

Glory be to the Father
and to the Son
and to the Holy Spirit,
as it was in the beginning
is now, and every shall be
world without end.

Amen

••

SIGN OF THE CROSS

In the name of the Father
and of the Son
and of the Holy Spirit.

Amen

(United States Conference of Catholic Bishops)

REFERENCES

1 *Saving Private Ryan* – war/action film, directed by Steven Spielberg, released in 1998

2 *Mothers' Manual* – written by Fr. A. Francis Coomes, S.J., publisher unknown, 1957

3 *Heaven is for Real* – written by Todd Burpo and Lynn Vincent, published Thomas Nelson, 2012

4 *This Little Light of Mine* – composed by Harry Dixon Loes around 1920s, as children's song

5 *Be Not Afraid* – composed by Bob Dufford a Jesuit priest and composer, 1972

6 *Don't Stop Believin'* – composed by Steve Perry, Neal Schon & Jonathan Cain, *Journey,* Columbia Records, 1981

7 *I Can Only Imagine* – composed by Bart Millard, *MercyMe*, 1999

8 *Sweet Caroline* - composed by Neil Diamond, 1969

9 *Animal House* – comedy/drama film, directed by John Landis, released in 1978

10 *Stripes* – comedy/war film, directed by Ivan Reitman, released in 1981

11 *Caddyshack* – comedy/sport film, directed by Harold Ramis, released in 1980

12 *Blazing Saddles* – comedy/western film, directed by Mel Brooks, released in 1974

13 *Wizard of Oz* – family/musical film, directed by Victor Fleming, released in 1939

14 *When It's All Been Said and Done* – composed by Jim Cowan, released in 2011

15 *How Great Thou Art – composed by Carl Boberg, 1885*

16 *Good Riddance* – composed by Billie Joe Armstrong, *Green Day,* 1993, released 1997

17 *Ave Maria* – composed by Franz Schubert, 1825

18 *Charlie St. Cloud* – romance/fantasy film, directed by Burr Steers, released 2010

19 *Mary Did You Know* – composed by Buddy Greene, 1991

20 *Silent Night* – lyrics written by Joseph Mohr in 1816, melody composed by Franz Xaver Gruber in 1818

21 *The Little Drummer Boy* – composed by Katherine Kennicott Davis, 1941

22 *Jesus Calling* – written by Sarah Young, publisher Thomas Nelson, 2004

23 *Man Says He Saw Brunswick Teen in Near-Death Experience* – YouTube, 2014, Fox 8 News Cleveland, https://youtu.be/bVPnWGogL30 (Approved by Fox 8 News Ceveland)

24 *Hollywood Vibe It's Called Memories* – Brittany Bartchack 2013, youtube.com, https://youtu.be/EsxyWfeHwuU

25 *The Brunswick Post*, Trogdon Media, Inc., founded in 1975, brunswickpost.com

26 *Sun News – Cleveland.com*, Sam Boyer, Project Blue Line

27 *Medina Gazette* – newspaper for Medina County, OH, Nick Glunt, https://medina-gazette.com

28 *Black Betty* – Lead Belly or Huddle Ledbetter credited as writer, *James "Iron Head" Baker sang, 1933*

29 *Little House on the Prairie* – book series by Laura Ingalls Wilder, published by Harper & Brother, 1932 -1943, 1971 adopted for stage or screen, American television series 1974-1983

30 *The Bible in Contemporary Language* – written by Eugene H. Peterson, The Message, 2007

31 *GriefShare* – Grief Support Group, https://www.griefshare.org

32 *Alpha* – Course to create space for open conversations about life, alphausa.org

33 *The Fest* – one-day annual family Christian festival in August, https://thefest.us

34 *Peter's Shadow Ministry* – healing prayer ministry, 1905 Portage Trail, Cuyahoga Falls, OH, HealingPrayer@PetersShadow.org

35 *God Calling* – written by Arthur Joseph Russell, Bibliolife DBA of Biblio Bazar II LLC, 2015

36 *Pray 40 Days (The Personal Relationship with God You Have Always Wanted)* – written by Fr. Michael J. Denk, published by Prodigal Father Production, https://www.theprodigalfather.org

37 *PrayAdvent* - written by Fr. Michael J. Denk, published by Prodigal Father Production, 2021

38 *Catechism of the Catholic Church – (CCC),* promulgated by Pope John Paul II in 1992, referred to as Catechism of the Second Vatican Council, English translation published in 1994, translated & published in more than twenty languages worldwide

39 *The Rhythm of Life* – written by Matthew Kelly, Blue Sparrow, Touchstone and Wheeler Publishing, 2004

40 *13 Powerful Ways to Pray* – written by Eamon Tobin, published by Wellspring, 2017

41 *Miracle Hour: A Method of Prayer that Will Change Your Life* – written by Linda Schubert, St Paul's Publication, 1991

42 *Breathe* – composed by Marie Barnett, performed by Michael W. Smith, released 2001

43 *Day by Day* – written by Lina Sandall-Berg (1920's), *Godspell* sung by Robin Lamont, released 1971

44 *Leave It To Beaver* – American Sitcom television show, *American Broadcasting co.,* 1957-1963

45 *Brady Bunch* – American Sitcom television show, *TV Land/American Broadcasting Co.,* 1969-1974

46 *Charlie's Angels* – American Drama television show, *American Broadcasting Co.,* 1976 – 1981

47 *Amen App* – free Catholic App, https://amenapp.org

48 *On Eagles Wings* – composed by Fr. Michael Joncas (Jesuit Priest), written in 1976, published in 1979

49 *Stephen Ministry* – Ecumenical program that trains lay people for pastoral care, https://www.stephenministries.org

50 *Chris Stefanick* – speaker, author television host, President of Real Life Catholic, https://reallifecatholic.com

51 *The Search* – written by Chris Stefanik and Paul McCusker, published by Augustine Institute, 2020

52 *Blake's Candle and a Lifesaving Prayer* – YouTube, *Touched by Heaven* June 9, 2024, TBH 318, https://touchedbyheaven.net

53 *That Don't Impress Me Much* – composed by Robert John "Mutt" Lange and Shania Twain, *Shania Twain,* 1998

54 *Only the Good Die Young* - composed and recorded by Billy Joel, 1978

REFERENCES

Scripture References

NABRE - the *New American Bible, Revised Edition*, World Catholic Press a Division of Catholic Book Publishing Corp. Copyright dates 2010, 1991, 1986, 1970 Confraternity of Christian Doctrine, Inc., Washington, D.C. and are used by permission of the copyright owner. All Rights Reserved. No part of the New American Bible may be reproduced in any form without permission in writing from the copyright owner.

ESV – *English Standard Version* Bible is a translation of the Bible in contemporary English. Published in 2001 by Crossway, the ESV was "created by a team of more than 100 leading evangelical scholars and pastors."

NIV – *New International Version* Bible is a study Bible originally published by Zondervan in 1985 that uses the New International Version. Doctrinally, the NIV reflects traditional evangelical Christian theology.

NLT – *New Living Translation* Bible is a translation of the Bible in contemporary English. Published in 1996 by Tyndale House Foundation. It was created by 90 leading Bible scholars.

Word Definitions

Oxford Languages – Google's English Dictionary provided by *Oxford Languages*. It is the world's leading dictionary publisher, with over 150 years of experience creating and delivering authoritative dictionaries globally.

REVIEWS

My Bue Devil Has Wings is Terri's story from an energetic high school athlete and cheerleader to a loving wife, devoted mother to an amazing witness for Jesus. Her journey takes her through three tragedies: all building her faith in God and her love for Jesus. You will weep and be inspired to grow in our love for God and the potential He has given you.

Curtis Moll

Such an incredible story about a woman who finds peace and comfort amidst the tragic death of her son. Terri not only shares her story of finding and journeying with God, but models how we too can experience God in our own lives. This book will help people to find peace and comfort in tragic and seemingly insurmountable, heart-wrenching circumstances. The book gives hope, guidance, and encouragement to those that are struggling in life or dealing with loss. It brings new meaning to Bible passages. It teaches us how our choices can lead us out of the darkness and despair of tragedy and death, to lives of acceptance, peace, and hope. Not many books show us how to convert our energy into positive outlets, this one does. This book is a treasured gift with a very strong message of hope and love.

~K.M. Howell

My Blue Devil Has Wings is a raw journey through the unexpected devastating loss of a son, compounded years earlier, by an unforeseen loss of a cherished uncle. Terri made a choice to turn to God to overcome her devastation. God responded wholeheartedly to Terri as a loving Father and drew her closer to Him. This journey in spite of its twists and turns became an inspirational adventure. It is a quest of profound hope that will remain in your heart.

Barbara Ortiz

My Blue Devil Has Wings is an interesting read about struggles, loss and faith. It is a story of triumphs after devastations in life. Terri shares about keeping God close after shattering events in life. She is an inspiration! It is inspiring to see her faith continue as her life journey continues.

Judy Arena

My Blue Devil Has Wings is a beautiful tribute for a son full of light, love and life. Terri writes with such authenticity and raw emotion that she pulls the reader in immediately. Terri's warmth and human truth of her written words displays her deep love of family and God, even though tragedy. The story tells us of a mother's love, grief and triumph after devastating loss. It is her journey of self-discovery and resilience, and an intimate look into all that she has endured and coming out on the other side. A poignant story, but most importantly through it all she never stops believing!!

Carolyn Gaylord

Made in the USA
Las Vegas, NV
05 December 2025

8a913a91-8c40-4cfc-9b54-1cae662e0bacR01